Dedication

This book is dedicated to my Mother,
who can succeed at an age when
most other people have stopped trying.

Commonsense
Direct
Marketing

COMMONSENSE DIRECT MARKETING

SECOND EDITION

DRAYTON BIRD

**KOGAN
PAGE**

Acknowledgements

Although I am indebted to many people, I would like to thank in particular for their help, encouragement and ideas:

Tony Arau, Michael Carpenter, John Epstein, Iain Goodman, Gary Halbert, Brian Halsey, Melanie Howard, Bill Jayme, Daphne Kelsey, Robert Leiderman, Graeme McCorkell, Stewart Pearson, Brian Thomas, John Francis Tighe, Glenmore Trenear-Harvey, Carol Trickey, John Watson, Rod Wright.

First published in 1982 by The Printed Shop, London. This edition published in 1989 by Kogan Page, 120 Pentonville Road, London N1 9JN.

Reprinted 1989, 1990 (twice)
Typeset by J&L Composition Ltd
Printed in England by Clays Ltd, St Ives plc

British Library Cataloguing in Publication Data

Bird, Drayton
    Commonsense direct marketing.—2nd ed.
    1. Great Britain. Direct-mail marketing
    I. Title
    658.8'.72'0941

ISBN 1–85091–544–X

Table of contents

1

Beginnings

'Learning teacheth more in one year than experience in twenty.'

Roger of Ascham

'The only purpose of advertising is to sell;
it has no other justification worth mentioning.'

Raymond Rubicam
Founder, Young & Rubicam Advertising

'When a man knows he is to be hanged in a
fortnight, it concentrates his mind wonderfully.'

Dr. Johnson

In 1957 my situation was bleak. I was making £7.00 a week editing a small trade journal. Even in those dear, dead days when cigarettes cost 10d a packet this would not support a wife and child – even in the two-up two-down cottage with outside lavatory we lived in. I had to do something.

At the time, I was much taken by a smooth aristocratic friend who worked in advertising. He seemed to be making pots of money without too much effort and advised me to become a copywriter. It took six months using all my reserves of servile flattery to find a willing employer.

I had three qualities to offer, apart from desperation.

First, I was brought up in a northern pub with a widely varied clientele. Encountering very different kinds of people after they have had a few drinks is splendid education for life. One minute I might be serving a pint of best mild in the vaults to Alec, whose party turn was describing how his wife had gone out one day for a loaf of bread and never returned. The next I would be listening to a mottle-faced cotton magnate in the American Bar lamenting the Socialist Government's determination to part him from all he possessed.

Second, I could write. You may consider this essential for the job I sought, but this is not apparent to many would-be copywriters. An alarming number cannot spell, punctuate or write long sentences – let alone tangle with such niceties as 'it's' and 'its', 'compliment' versus 'complement' and so on.

Third, I had read every book on advertising in Manchester Public Library and enrolled in an evening course on the subject. You may also see these preparations as obvious, but not all agree: when I finally entered the industry, I discovered few of my colleagues had taken the trouble to study the subject, or were even clear about the *purpose* of advertising.

This ancient ignorance has yet to be entirely dispelled. Over 80 years ago the first and best definition of advertising – 'Salesmanship in print' (still valid if you allow for broadcast media) – was formulated. However, this fairly simple thought has not penetrated the skulls of many practitioners or their clients to this day. You find this hard to believe? A 1980 survey of senior British marketing people revealed that 80 per cent thought advertising had some primary purpose *other* than selling.

Many see this as a comfortable state of affairs. If nobody knows what advertising should do, how can the content (or results) be evaluated? Under such circumstances it is relatively easy to make a fair living in the industry if you have a quick mind and an ingratiating manner.

The amateur approach

This amateur – and in some ways peculiarly British – attitude is deep rooted. Over the years I have interviewed hundreds of prospective employees. I almost invariably ask: 'What books have you read on direct marketing or advertising?' A significant percentage have read none; few have read more than one or two. The following account gives you an idea of the problem.

Bird: 'What books . . .?'
Young (but not inexperienced) art director: 'Well none, really. I don't believe in theory. It kind of, well ... I don't like to restrict my imagination.'
Bird: 'Really. Then how do you learn about the business?'
AD: 'Well, you know, you kind of pick it up by being around. You know, reading *Campaign* and that sort of thing.'
Bird (getting agitated): 'What sort of thing?'
AD: 'Well, working in a good agency, and watching what happens.'
Bird (restraining certain violent tendencies): 'Would you expect to pick up brain surgery by standing around the casualty department at University College Hospital?'
AD: 'Well, no. That's different, isn't it?'
Bird: 'Yes. *Everything* is different. But that doesn't mean you don't have to learn it properly.'
(Interview breaks up in disorder.)

Depressing, isn't it? Especially if you're trying to build up a business. You have to *educate* your staff before they become worthwhile to you – by which time, I might add, they have become rare and coveted commodities on the employment market.

The difficult approach

Returning to my early experiences, I soon discovered that some clients had very clear views on advertising. That was because their businesses depended on it. Either they were mail order companies seeking agents and customers or they were selling products door to door, soliciting inquiries from potential purchasers.

They were often difficult people. They wanted *replies* – and lots of them. Their advertisements tended to be bloody, bold and resolute; intent on results at the right cost. They would tell you very quickly (and sometimes quite offensively) whether their advertising was working.

Few of my colleagues were keen on working for them. They preferred clients with vaguer objectives like 'spreading our good name'. Even better were those who simply spent the agreed advertising appropriation every year in the way they always had. Such clients assessed their advertising quite simply: did they like it?

To this day many advertisers spend enormous sums in the same slapdash way. They and their agencies may claim their efforts increase sales, but it's not always easy to discover by what alchemy that happy result occurs. So many other factors intervene – like what your competitors are doing in terms of advertising, price and distribution – that establishing how sales are affected by advertising is very tricky. This fact gives occasion for many fanciful alibis on the part of agencies and marketers when the sales curve goes down instead of up.

A senior marketing man with one of the world's largest companies recently told me they advertise simply to create *awareness*. Sales were somebody else's problem, I gathered. Many regard their advertising in isolation in this way; they 'uncouple' it from the rest of the marketing process.

If you ignore the matter of sales, you can discover many valuable things about your advertising. Did people notice it? Did they read it? Did they understand it? Did they remember it? Did they like it? This last question in particular can mislead. Some advertising is *so* likeable it obscures the merits of the product. A New York beer company called Piels discovered 30 years ago that their commercials (which were so popular the public demanded they be recalled when they were taken off) did nothing at all for sales.

A puzzle

Why then, you may wonder, are so many still unwilling to use the only foolproof way of measuring whether a message makes people act? Namely a reply device, a coupon.

It is a bit of a puzzle, isn't it? It's a shame, too, because the only research I am aware of – conducted by Daniel Starch & Staff in the USA – indicates that putting a coupon in your advertisements can *double* readership. All advertisers, no matter what their views, agree this is desirable.

To be honest, I think both agencies and advertisers are insecure. They are frightened of discovering that what they do does not work. Yet how can asking people to reply be anything but a good idea?

I formed that view in my early years as a copywriter. I hated being judged on the basis of someone's opinion – be it the client, the client's wife (the case with one famous soap company I worked for), or even the client's customers. I was dying to know if I was making people *buy*. In this way, every time I learned something was working (or not) I could improve my efforts. This simple approach helped me become creative director of a well known London advertising agency at the age of 26, within five years of entering the business.

I became conceited. Soon I was sure I knew more than any of my clients, even the ones who counted their results. After all, it was my copy, was it not, that ensured their business success? Mere trivia like understanding management, or how much you should pay for a product – let alone the boring business of distribution – were far beneath my notice. I decided I would quickly make my fortune in the mail order business.

Some valuable discoveries

Over 200 years ago Daniel Defoe observed: 'The mariner to sail with is he who has been shipwrecked, for he knows where the reefs are.' I discovered several reefs when I set out on my first venture.

A friend of mine and I ran a £560 ad for ladies' hairpieces in the *Daily Mirror*. The ad ran on a Saturday. The following Monday we rushed round to our borrowed office, a little room at the top of a flight of narrow stairs. It was almost impossible to open the door. A huge pile of envelopes had jammed it shut from the other side – envelopes full of money.

We gutted them swiftly and worked out our likely results. It was jackpot first time! We calculated we should make £5,000 profit at least. Our fortunes were clearly made, since the fashion for hairpieces was just beginning. I knew this was the business for me: all the thrill of gambling, only you control the odds.

Having discovered how quickly we could make money by selling direct, we soon learned an important lesson: don't rely too much on other people. Our supplier left all the hair samples our customers sent in next to an open window. When the wind blew them all over the place, we had a fearful refund problem.

The supplier was not put off by this mishap. He could see what a good business it was and decided to cut us out and do it himself. Happily, he lost his shirt. This was because he didn't realise that unless the advertisement was correctly prepared, it would not get replies. Accordingly, he produced one himself which flopped totally. This was probably the only good thing to emerge from this exercise. My partner and I were lucky to escape without losing money.

You might imagine this discouraging experience would quench my enthusiasm. Not at all: I couldn't wait to walk out of my safe job and try again. I went to work with a friend who had the rights to a bodybuilding device called the 'Bullworker'. I used it for 30 days and gained 14 lbs in solid muscle. If it could work for somebody like me – the perfect 'Mr Before' – I was sure I could sell it. I was offered a share of the profits if I succeeded.

I worked like stink and within six months we were selling 1,000 of these gleaming instruments every week. Unfortunately (my second lesson), my friend was not good at arithmetic. We had sold every single one at a loss. The business had to be sold off.

I retreated to the safety of another well paid job in advertising, but remained in love with mail order. It appealed to someone like me who spends every penny he makes. You didn't need much money to set up. No costly premises were necessary to entice passers-by. You could run advertisements even if you didn't have any goods – buying them from the suppliers as you sold them. You could even get credit from advertising agents, who were usually so eager to get new clients they rarely checked your financial status.

I continued to try – and fail – until through force of sheer repetition my enterprises started to do well. One in particular demonstrated the unwarranted self-confidence and extraordinary gall I must have possessed. It was a newsletter advising people presumably even more ignorant than myself on how to make money. It did well – and still does.

Over the years since then, I have engaged in a range of activities so wide that simply contemplating them makes me feel tired. I have written scripts, advised companies on marketing, run a franchise company, organised exhibitions, run a sales force (never again!), helped launch a research company: you name it. In the course of all this I have also been fortunate enough to learn from some very talented people.

I have worked with some of the world's largest (and smallest) companies. Most of my clients have had the sense to ignore my more foolish suggestions and accept my more intelligent ones. I have planned and written hundreds of advertising campaigns and individual pieces. Almost every experience has taught me something valuable.

The mysterious rise of Direct Marketing

In the early days, mail order – direct marketing's most obvious manifestation – was unfashionable, verging on squalid. It attracted the wrong people: those who liked selling something sight unseen which could therefore be described with licence and a disregard for truth only estate agents, motor dealers and holiday companies can match.

In turn this attracted the wrong products; the kind even a street corner tout would disdain to touch. I well recall asking a Belgian mail order operator in 1962 if a product which promised to expand the size of your bust worked. He looked at me with contempt: 'If you ask me silly questions like that, I am going straight home.'

Despite this sort of thing (which still persists), perceptive observers had always found the logic behind direct communications inescapable. In the 1960s David Ogilvy commented: 'Direct mail was my first love – and secret weapon – in the avalanche of new business acquisitions which made Ogilvy & Mather an instant success.' A few years later, Ed Ney, chief executive of Young & Rubicam, the world's largest advertising agency, predicted: 'When you wake up in ten years from now, you will find direct marketing is beginning to take over. If you choose direct marketing, you will be entering the most vital segment of the economy for the next 50 years.'

As time passed, the mail order and direct mail businesses crawled out of the gutter and became mysteriously transmuted into direct marketing. By the end of the 1970s over half the *Fortune* Top 100 Companies were either dabbling with direct marketing or were direct marketers, like *Reader's Digest* or Time-Life. Why this occurred is a principal theme of this book. Until you understand the reasons, you will never know how to make the most of direct marketing.

The potential of direct marketing is certainly appreciated by most senior marketing executives today. A 1987 survey revealed that 60 per cent of the top 250 advertisers in the United Kingdom thought that direct marketing would be of more importance than general advertising by the end of the century. This is rather surprising when you realise that according to another survey recently conducted by my own agency the average marketing executive tends to see direct marketing practitioners as a bunch of unprofessional cowboys. (Hearteningly, those who have actually dealt with direct marketing agencies have a more favourable view.)

To those of us who have been involved in this business for a long time, this new interest in our activities is quite astonishing. Where once we muttered at smart parties, 'Er, mail order', when asked what we did for a living, we can now say with confidence: 'Direct Marketing'.

Ignorance of direct marketing

In 1976 a farsighted friend of mine, John Watson, suggested to me that it would be a good idea to start an advertising consultancy or agency specialising in direct marketing – especially since I knew more about it than most.

I mentioned this to another old friend, Glenmore Trenear-Harvey, and the three of us set up in business. We had no clients and no money (we couldn't even afford an office) but within three or four years Trenear-Harvey, Bird and Watson was the largest direct marketing agency in the UK. This sounds quite grand until you realise that compared to the big general advertising agencies, our 22-man business was the tiniest of minnows.

Despite its growth, few people had a clear idea of what direct marketing was (and this is still true today). Of course, to survive, you had to discover what worked and what didn't. But most of the books purporting to explain the subject were either out of date or long and tedious, however informative; none was British.

In 1980 my partners suggested I write the first book on the subject in the UK. Thus emerged *Commonsense Direct Marketing*, in 1982. I was surprised at how well received it was, and thought I could relax, having made my contribution to the literature of the subject.

However, although the principles which govern direct marketing have not really changed in the past six years, the discipline is being employed by organisations which were barely aware of it until recently. Moreover, it's being used for a much wider range of purposes than merely selling – for instance, to affect voters' decisions. As far back as the Eisenhower presidential campaign, direct mail was being used on a very large scale.

Since 1982 I have had the opportunity to travel round the world several times, meeting and talking with direct marketers. I have learned a great deal about how it is being used in almost every sort of society. I believe that its impact, not merely on business, but even on our world, could be considerable. (A sweeping observation, you may consider; but as you read these pages, you may come to agree.)

For these reasons I was persuaded I ought to revise my original book. In the process of doing so, the task become more than a revision – it became almost a complete rewrite. However, I have incorporated most of the original book and my intention remains the same: to give you the *essentials* of direct marketing briefly, entertainingly and memorably so as to inspire you to make correct and profitable decisions.

The idea of the book is simple. First, I want to define direct marketing and show where it should fit into your business; what role it should play. Business methods flourish when they work for you and your customers; therefore I also want to explore the technological and cultural changes in our society which make direct marketing so relevant.

Second, I want to answer some questions. How should you best plan your direct marketing? How does it relate to your other promotional activities like general advertising, sales promotion, packaging and public relations? How should you implement your efforts and, of course, evaluate your results?

Third, I believe one example is worth a ton of theory. It's all very well isolating principles, laying down rules and issuing exhortations, but I have also incorporated a wide range of appropriate case histories culled from many countries and types of business. These, I hope, will bring the subject to life.

Just commonsense

Fortunately, direct marketing is not difficult to understand, despite the efforts of a large number of half-baked theorists with a penchant for quasi-academic jargon. Naturally, we all like to dignify our craft with a little mystery for the benefit of outsiders; this is particularly true of experts talking to potential customers with bags of money. But really direct marketing is little more than commonsense, which is what led to the title of this book.

Nonetheless, success does not come without great attention to detail.

In few businesses can so many things go wrong so quickly if you don't pay attention.

I have already told you about my initiation into the wonderful world of hairpieces, and throughout this book I shall give you a fair selection of examples showing my rare ability to turn triumph into disaster in quite a number of businesses – sometimes even my present one. As a result of these little coups, I have proved to my own satisfaction that I am as likely as not to get things wrong.

But I consider myself fortunate to have made so many mistakes. We learn little from success. We are usually so delighted that all we do is break open another bottle of champagne. We rarely stop to analyse *why* we did so well, assuming instead that it is our uncommon skill and talent. On the other hand, if you make a mistake you are forced to examine what's gone wrong and compare with previous success to ensure you don't repeat the error. Daniel Defoe was right.

I will tell you as much as I can of what I have learned, with the minimum of technical detail. Like me, you may find technicalities difficult to follow. What I am trying to point out are the *principles* rather than the minutiae. By following them, you should be able to avoid some of the nasty surprises I have had. And the important point I would like to make is that they tend to apply in almost every country, with almost every kind of audience and every type of product or service – and they are not new: indeed they date back over a hundred years.

From ant farming to insurance

One of the books which originally inspired me to go into the mail order business was called – with a directness which appealed to the larceny in my soul – *How I made a million dollars in Mail Order*. Here's a quote that really got me humming: **'I know of no business in the world that requires such a small investment to start, yet holds promise of such tremendous financial gains.'**

The writer, Joe Cossman, started his business 40-odd years ago. Having little money, he started by working from his kitchen table. His staff was his wife. He sold some bizarre products, amongst them lifelike shrunken skulls (which *still* sell, by the way), an ant farm, a garden sprinkler, a spud gun and wild animal heads made of plastic to hang on your wall like big game trophies.

Since the 1940s, our business has changed dramatically. Yet if you were to read Joe Cossman's book today, you might find his writing style a bit breathless but you would still be impressed by the sense he makes.

For though we now sell more expensive products and services, in far greater variety; and though we now use lasers and computers to print and distribute our messages; and though we have now reached the point where people can order direct from their TV screens, the *thinking* you need to succeed in direct marketing hasn't changed at all. You can still start from your kitchen table and make your fortune. Indeed, in the USA, Joe Sugarman with his JS & A company has done precisely that in the 1970s and '80s.

Joe Sugarman sells some very sophisticated products, many electronic or in the health field. Most didn't exist when Joe Cossman set out to festoon America with shrunken heads. Sugarman's ads don't even carry coupons, because the vast majority of his orders come through the telephone with his customers paying by credit card. (I've illustrated an example of his work elsewhere in this book – he is a master copywriter.) But the principles Sugarman follows are much the same as those advocated by Cossman. The potential that awaits you by following these principles has by no means yet been realised.

For example, finance is probably the largest single area in our business. Within that field the largest category is probably insurance.

A paradox

In 1970 an American friend of mine suggested we go into business selling insurance direct. I didn't understand how this could be done: I couldn't see how an intangible like insurance could be sold direct. It seemed too *complicated*, for a start. And therein lies one of the central paradoxes of the direct marketing business. For it is precisely *because* they are complex that many products sell so well through this method – as you will see later in this book.

Three years after my 1970 conversation I went to New York and took a ride on a bus. Inside the bus I was surprised to see hundreds of 'take-one' leaflets hanging from little hooks. The leaflets invited you to insure yourself against the cost of hospital expenses. I was quite amazed.

In the first place, I had never heard of the product before. But what particularly surprised me was that the leaflets featured not the worry of hospital costs, but the large sums of money you would be paid if you did end up in hospital. This seemed to make no sense at all to me. Of course, I was wrong. The thinking behind these leaflets was based upon an important truth: people like a benefit (money) more than a negative, scary thought.

I was equally amazed at finding these leaflets on a bus. A strange place, I thought, to sell a financial service. Looking back, once again, the reasoning is simple. *Everybody* is interested in money. *Everybody* thinks they'll probably have to go to hospital one day. So this policy appealed to virtually everyone – and where better to offer it than on a bus?

Since then this type of policy has been sold in most countries around the world. In England, too, it appeals to the mass of people and is sold through door-to-door leaflets.

Oddly enough, in 1984 at a business lunch I was sitting next to two British insurance experts who also expressed doubt that insurance could be sold through the post. At the same table were two Americans, both of whom had become millionaires by doing precisely that.

Your timing is good

Within the advertising agency group I work for, direct marketing is growing three times faster than general advertising. So there is a great and growing lack of people who take the trouble to understand the business. People like you, in fact. There could hardly be a wiser time either to enter direct marketing, or to learn how to exploit it better.

In a recent advertisement in the British publication *Marketing Week* I analysed the jobs being offered. It probably wasn't typical, but it was very revealing. Four out of ten were in direct marketing agencies; a high proportion indeed, since there are very few direct marketing agencies compared to general agencies. More interesting (and to me surprising), the direct marketing jobs were on average paying just over 30 per cent more than similar general agency jobs.

You may be, as I once was, a young copywriter or an art director. Perhaps an account handler in a general agency thinking that direct might offer a better future. You may be an experienced marketer with millions to spend who is facing an intractable problem and wondering whether direct marketing will help. Would direct mail build brand preference as well as television? Is it as memorable? Would it pay to put coupons in your ads? Should you be spending more money on *retaining* customers through a direct loyalty programme than on trying to attract *new* ones? Can direct marketing help you motivate your salesforce?

Perhaps you have money to invest and are considering direct marketing as a way of setting up in business. Or you may already be running a successful direct marketing business and want to improve your results. For that matter, you may be working in charity or politics. Whatever you are trying to achieve that involves persuading other individuals to do what you want, you should find this book helpful. And I assure you that you will have far greater success by following the guidelines you read here than depending on judgement alone, or that most costly of commodities, *flair*.

There's no certainty you'll succeed. But I can assure you that you are likely to minimise the risk of failure. Marketing is as much an art as a science, because human beings are involved. Every principle does not always hold true. Indeed, you will see quite a number of examples throughout the book where the 'rules' which many direct marketers adhere to so slavishly, with such monotonous results, have been successfully ignored.

In fact, just about the only sure thing about direct marketing is that you will be surprised – frequently. No matter how carefully you plan, based upon how people *ought* to behave, or *have* behaved in the past, they keep giving you nasty shocks. That's one reason why direct marketing is never boring.

One thing I do promise: what you will learn here is a bargain. For I learned it with millions of pounds of other people's money – and quite a few thousands of my own.

Finally, in the best direct marketing tradition, let me offer you a guarantee. I have tried to cram into this book as many thoughts and instances as I can summon up. I hope you find them informative, and the book entertaining. But most of all, I hope I stimulate you into fresh thinking, to help you succeed. So if you don't find at least one idea (and many more, I hope) that pays for the book ten times over, return it and we will refund the money.

On the other hand, if you like the book or you have ideas for improvements (and I am sure it could be improved) then write and tell me. This new edition has evolved very much with the help of comments made by readers such as you.

2

The Three Graces of Direct Marketing

'A Chinese sage of the distant past was once asked by his disciples what he would do first if he were given power to set right the affairs of the country. He answered "I should certainly see to it that language is used correctly." "Surely," they said, "this is a trivial matter. Why should you deem it so important?" The Master replied "If language is not used correctly then what is said is not what is meant. If what is said is not what is meant then what ought to be done remains undone. If this remains undone morals and art will be corrupted. If morals and art are corrupted justice will go astray. If justice goes astray the people will stand about in helpless confusion."'

Recounted of Confucius

'We're here, because we're here, because we're here, because we're here' . . . and so on, *ad nauseam*.

Well known British Army song.

When I reached the august age of 51, one of my family sent me a birthday card. The front bore the legend: 'You have now reached the age where you start to ask yourself important questions like: why are we here? . . . where are we going? . . .' I opened the card, to see inside: '. . . and will the pubs be open when we get there?'

This story prompts me to inquire, dear reader, how often you ask yourself why you are here – what you are in business *for*? I have asked audiences all over the world that question. Nine times out of ten the reply is either: 'To make a profit', or 'To make money'. It seems fairly obvious, doesn't it? And it leads on quite naturally to the aim of making *more* money each year.

Yet some businesses appear to have very different aims. For instance, I was most interested a couple of years ago to read that an eminent Japanese businessman, when asked why *he* was in business, replied: 'To ensure the survival of my company.' I suspect this reply would not be unusual in Japan. For many years Japanese industry has tended to invest a higher percentage of its profits in building for the future than we do. It does not feel obliged to squeeze every yen out of the annual turnover and hand it over to the shareholders.

Clearly, if you are intent upon *survival* rather than a fast buck, you are going to plan more for the long term. No doubt this attitude explains why the Japanese have done better than us over the last 40 years. But whatever your aim, it will colour all you do: the way you structure your organisation, manage your staff and set their targets; everything, right down to the smallest marketing decision.

Short-term thinking

If you have dealt with many large, sophisticated marketing departments, you cannot help but be struck by one fact: the tenure of the average person in a position tends to be fairly short. It's quite unusual for anyone to stay in a particular job longer than two or three years. In that period, each person has to make his or her mark. How? Obviously, by producing quick results – and often, by change for the sake of change. That way one can be seen quite clearly to be *doing* something. (One revealing statistic I came across a few years ago was that in 50 per cent of cases when a company changes its marketing director, that marketing director will then change advertising agencies within the next 12 months.)

This kind of management does not lead to long term planning or even consistency within your organisation. The *urgent* is constantly taking precedence over the *important*. When you come to consider implementing direct marketing, you cannot afford to think this way. You must look long term.

I am anxious to emphasise this to you because most people tend to be attracted to direct marketing for the very reason that I was: you can see what you're getting for your money. That is important; but it is by no means the most desirable benefit of direct marketing. To explain why I believe this, I suggest you try a little test. Ask a few of your colleagues to define *marketing*. I do not know you, your colleagues or your organisation, but I would be surprised if most could do so adequately. As a matter of fact, when I have put the same test repeatedly to marketing people recently, only around one in three seems able to give a good definition.

The British Institute of Marketing, which ought to know, states that marketing is '**the management process responsible for identifying, anticipating and satisfying customer requirements profitably**'.

I want to record that definition, in order to place *direct* marketing within the context of marketing itself. In my experience most people think of marketing very much in relation to selling, publicity and promotion. But if you read that definition carefully, it's concerned with just about every aspect of business, from what you pay for your raw materials right through to how you make, price, distribute, advertise and sell your product. (At this point, I feel I should beg your forgiveness: you, of course, know the answers to these simple questions, and I am just refreshing your memory. Bear with me then if, for the benefit of those who don't know what it is, I now discuss the *aim* of marketing.)

To make and keep a customer

You may have read *Management Tasks, Responsibilities and Practices*, by the American business writer Peter Drucker – a title, in my view, calculated to make anyone except the most dedicated masochist give up any idea of managing anything, ever. In this book he suggested that the aim of marketing was really to *eliminate* the need for selling. 'To know and understand the customer so well that the product or service fits him and sells itself.'

Peter Drucker is one of the best thinkers in the world on business. Many years ago he suggested that the purpose of business was not in fact simply to make money, but to create customers. This thought was developed further by Theodore Levitt of The Harvard Business School as 'to make and keep a customer'.

I think you will agree this definition makes sense whatever your objective – short term or long term. Indeed, if we simply change the word 'customer' to 'supporter', 'colleague', or 'employee', you can apply this to just about anything you want to do: run a successful charity, build a political party, or develop a hardworking, committed body of workers. However, for simplicity's sake, I am going to refer in this book mostly to 'customers' and 'business'.

If you agree with me – or rather with the experts I have quoted – on the purposes of business and of marketing, then I think that once I have defined direct marketing to your satisfaction, you will quickly see the reasons for its growth, why its future looks very promising, and how it can play a valuable role within your business.

What is Direct Marketing?

Since even a mature business like advertising is not clearly understood by many of its practitioners you can hardly be surprised that few understand what direct marketing is. Indeed, whilst preparing this book, I saw that in a survey of 133 leading American direct marketers no clear agreement on what the business is emerged.

When the phrase direct marketing comes up, most people, in my experience, immediately think of the *medium* of direct mail. Others think of direct marketing as a *method of selling*, like off-the-page selling. Others confuse it with a *channel of distribution*, like mail order.

Producing a definition as simple in its way as that of 'salesmanship in print' for advertising has proved an insuperable task for the industry's pundits. So much so that (in what I can only assume was a moment of despair) *Direct Marketing Magazine* – the leading American organ of the industry – eventually summoned not one, but *three* experts to do so. The result of their labours may be seen at the beginning of every issue of the magazine. It occupies one-and-a-half pages, and features one of those gloriously complicated flow charts which always throw me into a state of utter confusion.

You may consider the need for a simple definition unimportant – a great many people using direct marketing are not at all concerned to speculate on what it really is. But I consider it crucial. Imagine spending millions of pounds without clearly understanding what you are spending them on. Not an imaginary scenario, I can assure you.

In fact, quite recently, an important decision on the expenditure of millions of dollars by a major multinational company covering many countries and multifarious marketing problems was fudged for precisely this reason. Was direct marketing an advertising activity? In that case the people in charge of advertising should make the decision. Was it 'below the line'? In which case that company's policy meant that a different department, usually concerned with purchasing everything down to stationery, would deal with it.

I will not go into the full details, save to say that the net result was that different decisions were made in different countries for different reasons – most of them to do with these varying views of what exactly direct marketing constitutes. This is quite obviously lunacy. And it is not likely to be made easier if everybody involved has to memorise a one-and-a-half-page definition complete with graphics before any activity begins.

Moreover, the pool of understanding has been muddied considerably by the fact that many practitioners are not even agreed that direct marketing ought to be called direct marketing. As a result of this, combined with the desire to give brand names to particular companies' approaches to the business, all sorts of names have cropped up. Some have actually been copyrighted; terms such as 'curriculum marketing', 'dialogue marketing', 'personal marketing', 'relationship marketing' and – perhaps the most popular alternative – 'database marketing'. But the most common term remains direct marketing. It is certainly the one I propose to stick to.

Nevertheless, these terms do reveal important facts about the nature of the business. It is certainly true that direct marketing revolves around the building of a database in the same way that general advertising revolves around the use of printed and broadcast media, and sales promotion revolves around point of sale. Equally, building a relationship is one of our objectives. The approach *is* personal; in the process of building a relationship, you can guide your prospect through a curriculum whereby you learn more about them and they learn more about you.

But my simple definition of direct marketing is: **'any advertising activity which creates and exploits a direct relationship between you and your prospect or customer as an individual'**.

If we can agree that we ought to call direct marketing direct marketing, and if you accept my simple definition, then you will immediately appreciate that a very wide range of activities is encompassed.

I am sure you have been stopped on occasion by people standing on street corners with questionnaires bearing such inane queries as: 'Are you able to save as much money as you'd like to?' If you are not careful, these will lead to a visit from an insurance salesman. Clearly these people are engaged in direct marketing: they are making a direct contact and trying to initiate a relationship with you as an individual.

In the same way, somebody who offers you a leaflet inviting you to go into your local hamburger joint and win a prize; or the ad for the introduction agency offering love everlasting; the note in the shop window selling a used ghetto blaster; the ad suggesting you apply for shares in British Telecom; the leaflet coming through your door in praise of your local Conservative Party candidate – they're *all* direct marketing. In fact it's interesting that the most popular section in many papers – the classified section – is nothing but direct marketing.

I'm not suggesting to you that in all these cases a continuing relationship is built up. But I am suggesting that in *almost* every case the possibility is there, if you wish to take advantage of it. And I am certainly going to propose to you that long-term business success based upon making and keeping a customer depends upon building this relationship.

Perhaps it is worth stating here what I believe to be the differences between direct marketing and some of the other communications tools you use. (This is not made any easier by the fact that in the case of sales promotion, the people in that industry are no more agreed about what they do than are direct marketers.)

How does Direct Marketing differ from your other activities?

- *General advertising* speaks to people *en masse*, not as individuals. Also, it normally does not demand an immediate action. It is designed to make people have feelings and inclinations so that they will make a decision in your favour at the point of purchase, wherever or whenever that may be.
- *Sales promotion* is designed to achieve an immediate effect on sales. It often uses the same means as direct marketers – for instance, direct mail and special offers. It frequently generates lists of respondents to promotions. But because it is normally conducted on a short term basis, it does not then proceed to build a relationship with those respondents as individuals by placing them on a database.
- *Public relations* employs media controlled by others to create a favourable climate of opinion. It, too, can create a database, eg replies to editorials.

Are you a secret direct marketer?

You will have realised already that just about every company engages in direct marketing of one sort or another. There can be hardly anyone who at some time or another doesn't make a phone call or send out a letter with the hope of making a sale. These may be individual initiatives which employ a direct approach. A typical example would be the salesman making telephone calls to try and isolate good prospects. If you have you ever tried to control salesmen as I have then you will soon realise that this sort of thing is best done in an organised way. This means you should start looking at it in an organised fashion, I think you will agree. Looking at it as marketing – direct marketing.

For instance, if you have a restaurant and you make the wise decision to collect the names of your customers in order to write to them with news of special gourmet evenings or you are a manufacturer of earth-moving equipment and you decide to send out a regular newsletter, then you have entered the direct marketing business whether you know it or not.

Some businesses are quite clearly based upon direct marketing – *Reader's Digest*, Time-Life Books, or one of the big catalogue companies are obvious examples. Other businesses largely depend upon direct marketing. And yet others, I believe, ought to be thinking about it a great deal more than they do. Let's take some obvious examples.

Credit and charge card companies.

When you think about it, almost every transaction, starting with the way in which these cards are applied for, is effectively direct marketing. Take American Express. Almost every single cardmember recruited comes in through direct marketing. Either the prospect picks up a take-one – a little leaflet in a restaurant or retail store – and sends it in to apply, or responds to a direct mail shot, or uses the telephone to apply after watching a TV commercial.

The transaction is then consummated through the mail, and the relationship between cardmember and company is then conducted almost entirely through the mail or on the telephone. Cardmembers are made offers and accept them through the means of direct mail shots and regular communications within their monthly statements. They are then persuaded to renew their membership or to switch from 'Green Card' membership to 'Gold Card' membership, and perhaps to 'Platinum Card' membership. All by means of direct marketing.

Indeed, the only time when a cardmember is likely to transact any business with American Express in any other way than via direct marketing is when perhaps booking travel or getting travellers cheques, cash or advice from a travel office. Yet I wonder to what extent the marketing executives of the credit card companies or charge card companies appreciate just how important effective direct marketing is to them. I have certainly noticed that the top brass in companies like this are usually far more interested in the latest television commercials than in the direct mail which really brings in their business and maintains it.

Banks
A second example from the financial area. There is no question at all in my mind that most of them do not realise what a valuable role direct marketing could play for them. Research we conducted two years ago showed that during a calendar year, the overwhelming majority of customers of UK banks had no *personal* relationship with anybody at their bank (let alone their manager). The entire relationship is conducted largely through the post and cash machines.

But how many banks, I wonder, appreciate to what degree they could benefit from direct marketing? Of course they're all *doing* it; but how well, and with what conviction, and how much intellectual and financial resource are they putting behind it? In my experience, not nearly enough.

Insurance, investment and home loans
Almost any financial business will find direct marketing of value. All the above are businesses where direct marketing either does or can play an important role. In my view, many of the senior managers are still not concentrating sufficiently on the potential.

Other industries which have always depended for their success to a large extent on direct communications do not, I think, always appreciate they are really direct marketers.

Travel
The travel business is typical. In 1962 when I became a creative director, three of my biggest clients were in travel: two countries, Greece and Britain, and one tour operator. Here is another business which revolves

almost entirely around direct marketing, until the awful moment that the customer discovers that the phrase 'overlooking the sea' in the brochure has a degree of credibility varying upon your eyesight.

A longer view

Because people think very much in the short term, and very narrowly, about direct marketing, many consider it only in the context of making an immediate sale. But many direct marketing activities take a longer view.

One of the many characteristics of this business which delights me is that although it is hailed on all sides as something new, so many of the activities conducted are really old as time. For instance, buttering up the customer.

In the United States the Ford Motor Company once calculated that a customer's value to them if they could sell that customer their first car and every other car in their lives, would be $120,000. Accordingly, they are very interested in direct marketing and its possibilities.

A couple of years ago the Lincoln Mercury Division of Ford started spending a significant budget on direct marketing activities. Their objective was to build a direct relationship with potential purchasers over a period of time so that they eventually chose Mercury, then could be 'traded-up' over a period to Lincoln. To achieve this, the first mailing sent to likely prospects simply incorporated a beautiful portfolio featuring pictures by well known photographers of the new Lincoln Mercury range. No request was made to buy anything. The mailing was, so to speak, a courtesy – a sort of commercial love letter.

The next stage was to inquire whether the prospect liked the pictures and would – as a courtesy in return – complete a questionnaire giving details of future requirements, likes and dislikes. This, of course, led to a series of mailings designed ultimately to make a sale.

Quite clearly, if you ask somebody enough about their car-buying intentions you should be able to match their needs pretty precisely. Equally clearly, when you are talking about high-ticket items like this, if you know what the value of a customer is to you, you can afford to invest quite a lot of money in building up a relationship with them (or as I put it – buttering them up) in the intention of making a long-term substantial gain.

And you certainly need to think long term in many cases. You need to be very patient if you are, for instance, trying to sell a mainframe computer, or a new telephone system. Those are not snap decisions for any company. But direct marketing is often critical: research by our American agency in 1986 showed that 20 per cent of businessmen surveyed had bought a mainframe computer in the previous year as a result of a direct marketing approach.

The Three Graces of direct marketing

What is the purpose of direct marketing? In my view, quite simply to isolate your prospects and customers as individuals and build a continuing relationship with them – to their greater benefit and your greater profit.

You can break this purpose down into three parts, which I choose to call the Three Graces of direct marketing.

First of all, when you isolate someone as an *individual* this automatically implies that you discover what differentiates them from other individuals. What are their peculiar characteristics? And by speaking to them as individuals, using the knowledge you acquire about them and their relationship with you, you will be able to make appeals which are far more convincing to them. You can do this by placing that knowledge on a computer database.

The second Grace: you can build a *continuing* relationship with these people by offering them services and products which your knowledge of them tells you are likely to appeal. This will bind them to you for a longer period. And since in most commercial activity your most expensive activity is recruiting the customer, the longer you can keep that customer, the better.

When first I entered the mail order business, as it was then known, I imagined that what one did was to run an advertisement, sell the goods, and retire after a few insertions. Ignorance was bliss. The truth is that hardly any business depends on one transaction. Direct marketing may have its own peculiarities, but the principles are much the same as those that operate in any other business. If you are a shopkeeper or a salesman or a manufacturer it is very rare for profits to be made on one transaction unless yours is a short-term business, like selling London Bridge to tourists.

The first time you encounter the customer, you are learning about him or her. Likes, dislikes, peculiarities – working out what you can sell next: what other service you can render. It is with the subsequent sales that you make the gravy. You begin to know and understand your customer. You establish a relationship. That is good business.

So it is with direct marketing. Your best customer is not your unknown prospect in the street, milling around amongst others. He is the person you know, who knows you. You can target precisely what he needs, and sell to him much more easily.

My first inkling of the fact that it was a continuing relationship that mattered in this business came over 20 years ago when I saw an advertisement in a newspaper. It said: 'Publisher seeks advertising agency to help in losing money.' This publisher knew he had to invest in acquiring names before he could make money.

Obviously if you understand this need for investment, this need to build a continuing relationship, you have an immense advantage over those who don't. What is more, by building this relationship you can study how your customers behave over a period of time: discover which offers which individuals respond to. In this way, you can establish the value of an individual to you over the 'lifetime' of that individual's relationship with your company.

For example, a few years ago one of my clients told me that each new name they recruit from a particular type of offer generates £12 worth of gross profit over the ensuing three years. Another company (one of the largest in Europe) is happy to wait for over two years before making a profit from a name they've recruited. These companies know there are no quick killings in direct marketing, only *suicides* by those who don't understand the vital principles that govern success.

The third Grace is the one which often has the most obvious allure to the virginal entrant to direct marketing. And that's the ability to *test*. To measure the response from particular individuals to particular messages at particular times. You can find out what works and what doesn't. Moreoever, having done so you can conduct further tests and constantly improve the effectiveness of your activities. You can spend your money where it does the most good.

It will not have escaped your notice that these Three Graces fit in extremely well with a couple of the expert views I gave earlier in this chapter. Direct marketing is a splendid way of making and keeping a customer, as prescribed by Theodore Levitt. And, properly conducted, it enables you to get quite close to the aim of marketing as proposed by Peter Drucker. If you have enough knowledge about somebody on your database, you can approach that wonderful situation where the product fits the customer and sells itself.

Those are important reasons why direct marketing is growing. I would now like to explore some others, to do with the nature of our society and with changes in technology.

How your customer is changing

Let us return to those customers you want to make and keep. Obviously, your success revolves around how well you respond to their needs and their desires. Professional marketers tend to look at customers in a way which dehumanises them. You've probably heard this sort of thing: 'The target market is B1/C2 housewives aged 24-45 in the South West, living in owner occupied properties, etc.'

Sometimes they enlist the aid of psychology to analyse their customers: 'The target market is inner-directed, upwardly mobile, tends to fantasize about her need for . . . etc, etc.' These are all attempts to group people into different categories so that you can speak to them more effectively.

Such laudable efforts to group people are one reaction to the way your customers have changed over the last 30-odd years. When I first came into the advertising business, groupings didn't matter nearly as much. If you wanted to get people to come and try your baked beans, it really was rather simple. You ran a commercial on a Friday night and people trooped in obediently to the supermarket and bought the product the next day. It's true.

That's because in those days, the family sat around the television set watching *Coronation Street* as a group and they *all* liked baked beans. What has happened to the humble baked bean in tomato sauce since then is paralleled by what has happened to the family.

You can now get beans in chilli sauce, curry sauce, low-calorie sauce, with pork sausages, etc. And the people who eat those beans no longer sit together round the television set on a Friday night. The power of the mass media is diminishing as people start to act more and more like individuals.

One striking indication of the trend to individuality is this: by the end of this century the largest household category in the UK will be the single person household.

Research four years ago by the Henley Centre for Forecasting revealed that today the family is more likely to be together when it goes *out* to a restaurant than when it stays *in* at home. The Henley Centre gives two reasons for this: first, the rise of central heating, which means the family doesn't have to stay huddled in one room in front of the fire keeping warm. Second, the increase in, and lower cost of, various gadgets and entertainment devices which people can occupy themselves with individually.

Take my own family. I read in my study; one of my children plays a video game on television; a second is out riding; a third is practising the piano; and my wife is putting our household expenses on our home-computer database.

In fact, there are many ways in which you can see people are much more individualistic. Simply study styles of dress. People were far more conformist 40 or 50 years ago than they are now. And the interesting thing to me is that wherever I go in the world – even extremely conservative societies in the East – there seems to be some trend towards individualism. In any case, no matter how conformist a society, I think you will agree your customers are not statistics: they are human beings. Thus, isolating them as individuals and approaching them as individuals is bound to make a lot of sense.

Interestingly enough, you can take the same question of handling people as individuals and look at it in an historical context to arrive at the same conclusions. (And I must admit that here I am shamelessly plagiarising a presentation I saw made by Lester Wunderman a few years ago on this very subject.)

Two hundred years ago almost all relationships between manufacturers and customers were very simple. The manufacturer of the product also sold the product to the customer. The shoemaker made the shoes and sold them to you face to face – as did the tailor, or the carriage maker.

This form of selling enables the manufacturer to have a warm, personal, direct relationship with the buyer, and also to know a lot about the buyer's personal requirements. In some businesses this is still true. And in many parts of the world where industrialisation has not yet penetrated, many relationships remain like this.

However, in the nineteenth century the second stage of marketing was developed. New technology made mass production possible. In 'advanced' countries such as those in Western Europe, the small manufacturer was lucky to survive. And the chain of distribution changed. Manufacturers sold via wholesalers and retailers, indirectly.

Fortunately for the manufacturer, the same technology led to new printing machinery which made mass advertising possible. Millions of identical messages could be addressed by the manufacturer to the ultimate consumer. However, the personal relationship the individual merchant had with his customers was lost.

Direct marketing inaugurates the third stage of marketing. Its rise is due to many factors, but one major reason is the new ability to personalise messages to people – via the telephone, for example, and also through printed material. Now, thanks to the database which tells you all about your customers' needs, you can renew that direct personal link you began to lose 150 years ago. Now you can add the impact of *personal* selling to the power of *mass* communication. You have the best of both worlds. For instance, when you link your 'theme' advertising, which creates an appealing image, to specific direct offers on TV or through the mail, a powerful synergy is created.

In research our agency conducted in 1985, we discovered that where a direct mail shot featured a scene from a television commercial for a particular airline, awareness of that television commercial as long as four months later was nearly 50 per cent higher amongst those who had received the mail shot than amongst a similar panel who had not received it.

The same synergy works in reverse, and I will touch upon it later in this book. But the important point must be made that companies tend to look at their marketing activities very much from an internal point of view. By some curious process they seem to relate it to their own organisation chart. This is below the line; this is above the line; this is sales promotion; this is public relations, and so on. But your customers don't see it that way. To them it is all news or information or offers from a particular company. This in itself is a powerful argument for making sure all these things are planned together: a process we at Ogilvy & Mather call 'orchestration'.

Controllability: an important benefit

In a world where it is increasingly difficult to control anything, direct marketing makes a considerable appeal because when properly con- ducted it is a very controllable way of marketing.

First, the *content* and *timing* of your selling messages can be controlled. Second, the *costs* can be controlled, and the *results* predicted.

You may instantly respond: 'Well this is largely true of advertising, or sales promotion.' And, of course, it is – but I am referring here in particular of ways of talking to individuals and of predicting the results. Whether you have salesmen talking to prospects or clerks talking to customers, you are stuck with one problem: you can't control what they say, the order they say it in, the way they say it, or the way their personalities affect how the message is received. You're not really in control. With direct marketing, you *are* in control. Every message goes out as you want it to:

- using the style of language you think suits your company and your market;
- in the order you've determined is best calculated to sell;
- in the typeface you select, with the design you think reflects your image best;
- at the time you want it to ... when you've learned it will get the maximum response;
- even a 'phone call will be handled by your 'phone communicator just as your script lays down.

Your messages are uniform and go out in predetermined numbers to precisely targeted groups. They produce responses that can be measured. This leads to the second major benefit: that you can predict future responses and thus how much money you need to achieve a given result. This is rarely the case with some other methods of promotion.

Cut down the risk

All human enterprise involves risk. You're at risk from the minute you get up in the morning. The question is, how much risk do you find acceptable?

Some businesses, by their very nature, involve more risk than others. Either your likelihood of success is very remote or your volume of investment is unacceptably high; often both. But in almost all cases you have to commit yourself to a great deal before you are sure what the outcome is likely to be. Look at the retail business.

If you want to open a shop, no matter how small, you have to commit yourself to quite a lot in advance. Obviously you will think very carefully and compare what others are doing before you go ahead. But whatever you decide, you will have to find an appropriate site, rent the premises, fit them out and buy stock. Then, of course, you'll have to find staff. If the shop is at all large, that will involve advertising costs.

All this before you take a penny.

If you've chosen the wrong site, or the wrong merchandise, or given your shop an unappealing name, you could be in trouble. Or suppose you have decided to sell high-priced merchandise at a time or in an area where people are looking for bargains: you could equally fail.

You could find yourself with unsold stock on your hands, stock you know from bitter experience is hard to sell. You'll have a lease to dispose of, staff to pay off, bills to settle which the gross profits haven't covered.

Let's take another area: what if you want to enter manufacturing? Once again, profit margins are low, and investment high. Before you know where you are you will have laid out a great deal of money. You have to rent or buy your factory, buy machinery and raw materials and hire staff, just as the shopkeeper did. But you are, if anything, even less in control of your destiny than that shopkeeper. For between you and your eventual customer there may stand wholesaler, retailers, salesmen, or maybe manufacturer's agents. (A good reason for selling direct, by the way.)

Will all these intermediaries share your enthusiasm for your product? Will they communicate it to the consumer with the zeal you would have? Will they promote, advertise and sell it vigorously? Or will *you* have to?

If you have not chosen the right product you could fail; even supposing you have, if others do not share your belief in it the results could be just as bad. Except that in addition to the shopkeeper's problems you will have machinery to dispose of.

The point is simple. Few businesses offer much guarantee of success before you invest your money. The risk is high largely because you don't *control* the situation enough. But direct marketing allows you to *test* how people feel about your product and offer and price.

Most businessmen get ulcers because the level of risk frightens them; they can't control what's happening. Being a devout coward, I like the idea of limiting risk. And when Peter Drucker observes that 'The first objective of marketing is to avoid making a loss', then I feel confirmed in my judgement.

Although I do not feel that the ability to test is necessarily *the* most important of the Three Graces I cited earlier, I believe that the control and predictability which testing can give your business activities must be one of the main justifications for choosing to use direct marketing. This is true even if you only use it at the inception of a venture to find out what's likely to work and what isn't.

Mythical economies

Do not be misled by the belief that the principal justification for doing business this way is because it allows economies by cutting out middlemen. You may cut out the middleman very often. Your customers may therefore think they are getting better value – which they may be. You may as a result make greater profits.

But there are many circumstances under which you will *not* cut out the middleman. For instance, if you are an insurance company trying to help your agents, or brokers, or salesmen by putting together a direct marketing programme for them. Or if you are a motor car company trying to help your dealers. Under those circumstances, you are not cutting out any middlemen: what you *are* doing (which is just as important) is using a form of marketing which will make your representatives' jobs easier by giving information to your prospects and customers which they will find helpful. Helpful since it will be relevant to them, because you know more about their needs from the data you call up from your computer.

What I am saying is that this way of marketing does not necessarily mean lower costs. It can often simply mean that those costs are distributed differently. What it does usually mean, in my experience, is that you can deliver a better service to your customer.

Giving your customer a better service

One of the most successful direct marketing companies in the world is unquestionably Time Life Books. The founder of this division, Jerome S Hardy, called his staff together at the outset of the business and said something which I think bears repeating quite a few times: 'We are going to give our customers a service better than they have any right to expect.'

This contrasts vividly with the way in which marketing functionaries of well known companies have started announcing – with the air of people who have just discovered the Holy Grail – that they are about to be responsive to their customers' needs. It's extraordinary, isn't it? Some of these fat organisations have become so big that they forget what they are there for. Where did they think their money was coming from in the first place? Their customers, of course.

It's worth examining here some of the reasons why customers find direct marketing makes sense for them.

Perhaps the major one is that it suits them to receive information or to make purchases directly from the vendor. It's often both convenient and pleasant to sit in your own home and choose at leisure from a catalogue. You don't have to get in your car or on the bus and go into town, find the right store, and the right department, and sometimes hunt down an assistant to tell you what you want to know.

Equally, our research tells us that businessmen appreciate receiving information through the post which they can examine at leisure, rather than seeing a salesman. (Too often it is forgotten that the businessman is not a special breed: he is a *consumer* when he is at home – and he doesn't grow a second head on his way to work.)

We discovered when working for IBM Direct that businessmen often preferred not to see a salesman. If they were buying a typewriter, for instance, they were perfectly happy to buy it through the post. It was more convenient than wasting time talking to a salesman. Equally, research we conducted in 1986 revealed that the majority of business-men prefer to receive information about new office products not through advertising or sales people (the most common means) but via direct mail. And they wish to inquire through the most convenient medium: the telephone.

If you have any position of responsibility, I am sure you also resent spending time on things that could be presented to you just as easily in writing. Direct mail in particular is very good at conveying complex information in a structured and easily digestible form. Something people often seem unable to do.

When we were examining possible pension plans for our company, I had to spend endless hours listening to presentations from salesmen. It was time I could spare only with difficulty. And none of these salesmen had clearly written explanatory material which I could have read in order to make the right decision. Probably nobody could have closed the deal without a personal presentation. But a lead could have been solicited and the initial selling done direct.

Even in advertisements, direct marketers can often do a better job than sales people. I recall a few years ago we ran an advertisement for a watch in a double page spread in a colour magazine. The ad was tightly packed with small type and many pictures. If you read through it, you ended up knowing more about that watch than any shop assistant could tell you – from the type of chip that was used to the ways you could use it to time sporting events.

As goods proliferate and become more and more technologically complex it's almost impossible for one relatively untrained shop assistant to understand all about every item he or she sells. But a skilled copywriter, given sufficient time, can write an infinitely detailed description of a product. A photographer can make it look good – maybe even *better* than it is (which may put up the number of people who ask for their money back!).

Other reasons why buying or dealing direct seems to work for the customer include the fact that some products may not easily be available through any other distribution channel. For instance, specialised products such as rare coins, gourmet foods and wines, collectibles, specialised sporting goods like horseriding tackle, do well.

In other instances, people prefer to deal direct quite simply because of embarrassment. This could be because of the nature of the product, or the customer. One of our clients used to sell a beauty course through the post, and we noticed that a significant proportion of the customers appeared to be gay.

People often feel embarrassed, too, about finance: a good reason why loans through the post have done very well. Some people are quite simply shy and don't like to deal with pushy salespeople. I am sure you have sometimes been approached by an aggressive salesperson in a store and walked out.

One reason which induces both marketer and customer to deal directly is *price*. Customers very often think they are going to get a better deal by buying direct; merchants often think they'll be able to cut their selling expenses for the same reason. I am not at all sure this is true. Nevertheless, it seems to be a powerful motivator.

In my view, direct marketing is growing quite simply because it is a wonderful way of serving your customer better. It is quite clear that if you can understand that customer and their motivations better, you'll be able to do a better job. You'll be able to build a really good relationship with that customer.

I have an exceedingly simple view of what business and direct marketing are all about. I believe the object of business is to locate a *prospect*, make that prospect a *customer* and then turn that customer into a *friend*. If you look at it this way, you'll be surprised how many apparently knotty problems can be resolved.

Let me give you two examples, covering questions which I have been asked more often than any others.

The first question is: how often should I communicate with my prospects or customers? This depends entirely upon how *friendly* you are with them. Would you communicate with a good friend, an established customer, just once a year? Or once every six months? I think not. On the other hand, would you communicate with some-body who was virtually a stranger, a prospect, every week? I think not.

I suggest to you that with a friend you would communicate as often as you had something interesting to say. Something you thought they might appreciate. And if the person were a mere stranger, the same would apply. A stranger would be less interested in hearing from you; would be less likely to listen to what you had to say.

So the frequency of communication would depend upon the context. Which leads me to the second question people ask me more often than any other: what should we say when we communicate?

Once again, the answer is: what would you say to a friend? Or to somebody who was just a bare acquaintance – a prospect, perhaps, whom you had only mailed once. The answer, of course, is you would spend your time thinking of things your friends, or your acquaintances, would find interesting. You would spend your time thinking up appealing offers. News you thought they might find interesting. Things you thought would appeal to them as individuals. And that, in my view, is one of the roots of success in direct marketing.

The spiral of prosperity

The central question in direct marketing may well be: how much is a customer worth? Or to put it another way: how much it is worth paying to recruit a new customer, and what will you gain from keeping that customer?

Each season you set a budget to mail or advertise or otherwise spend money to recruit a given number of new customers at a given cost. You are not merely trying to make sales, you are trying to make new customers, who will become friends – but only at a cost you can afford.

As you have seen, by testing you can produce more effective offers and communications. Thus you will either recruit the same number of customers for less money per name; or you can get a greater *number* of customers for the same investment; or, of course, your money could bring in a better quality of customer. You will be communicating regularly with these customers and, once again, testing will lead to better use of the database you have built up. You will be able to make it more profitable in three ways:

1 You will find ways to segment the database and thus exploit it more effectively. You will not communicate so often to those less likely to buy, which will save you money. You will communicate more frequently with those who are your best friends, as it were.
2 You will introduce new offers and new products likely to appeal to the individuals on your database – based on what you have learned about them – thus enabling you to communicate more frequently and make more profit.
3 You will also be testing new, more imaginative communications so as to get better responses to those offers you are making.

The Magic Number

You will see by looking at the little graphic on p 42 that all these activities begin and end with the individuals you recruit, and how much they are worth to you.

If you do all the things I have mentioned above, the answer to the question I posed earlier – how much is a customer worth? – will change. A customer will become more valuable to you the more carefully you consider them and cater to their needs. Thus you will be prepared to invest more money to isolate a new prospect and turn them into a customer. So, in an ideal world, year after year, you would find it pays to spend more money on acquiring new customers, conducting new tests, developing new offers, and so on.

Of course, the world of business is far from ideal. But only by following this logical sequence are you likely to be able to compete effectively with others. It will probably have already occurred to you that if you do so, and your competitor does not, *you* will be able to afford

Figure 2.1. Spiral of prosperity

to put more money against customer recruitment than they will. You will ultimately succeed; they will ultimately fail. You will have a true competitive edge.

The figure you allocate to recruiting a particular customer has been called 'the magic number'. Clearly, it is a number that can change as your marketing improves.

If you wish to be really sophisticated, (why not? The computer is capable of doing this sort of thing if you are willing to spend the money), different types of customer that you wish to recruit could have different magic numbers assigned to them.

This is perhaps getting overly sophisticated, but the important point I am making is that the entire process of direct marketing derives from the purpose of business and the aims of marketing which I outlined at the beginning of this chapter. And it is by an understanding of the Three Graces that I referred to that you are likely to succeed.

You are isolating people as individuals and building the continuing, profitable relationship you seek through the simple sequence represented in the spiral of prosperity.

Allow for the differences

I would like to conclude this chapter with a famous example. A perceptive observer commented that if, many years ago, the American railways had realised what business they were in (transportation, not railways) they would now own the American airlines.

Turning back a couple of centuries, you could say the same thing about the people who used to own the canals; they would have ended up owning the railways which, instead, were the death of them.

I have already suggested that some companies don't appreciate to what degree they are direct marketers or how important direct marketing is to them. (To be honest, I feel this may be because they don't *want* to know this. Direct marketing still retains a poor reputation, to a large extent richly earned; and the standard of practice within the industry is by no means as high as it should be.)

But if, on reviewing your business or the activities you plan, you consider they do or could depend upon direct marketing, then it is important to appreciate the critical differences between the way the general marketer approaches a problem and the way the direct marketer does. These differences will, I hope, become increasingly apparent to you as you go through the book.

Sometimes I think that within companies people are so busy doing things the way they have always been done, or responding to head office, or engaging in the enjoyable minutiae of intramural squabbling, that they don't spend much time considering what they are in business for, or what their business is. Yet their customers seem to be very well aware of what's going on – because they're at the receiving end.

Take one of the examples I cited earlier. You only have to ask an audience about direct marketing, and many will immediately comment on the insert in their monthly credit card statements. Or they will complain about the mountains of irrelevant tripe that come through their letterboxes. So it may be that your customers are more aware than you are of what your business is all about. Certainly, they react in very different ways depending on the degree of care with which these messages have been prepared and targeted.

The moral of this is: for goodness sake try and get some professional direct marketing help if you can. Don't approach your direct marketing activities in the way you have approached your general marketing in the past. How you go about finding such help is the subject of a later chapter.

I hope I have said enough in this chapter to establish first of all what direct marketing is, secondly, why it is growing, and thirdly, why it should be of such interest to you.

Next, let's consider more carefuly where it fits into your business.

3

Direct Marketing Can Do More Than You Think

'A wise man makes more opportunities than he finds.'

Francis Bacon

In the first chapter I told you how infallible I thought myself 25 years ago when I had my first job as a creative director. Let me tell you another story about my unparalleled sagacity as a young man.

One day, an American came into our agency to ask us to place advertisements for what at that time seemed an unusual – indeed unique – mail order product. He wanted to sell plots of land on a more or less deserted Caribbean island called Montserrat. The advertisement he had prepared consisted almost entirely of copy, the only illustration being a small, crude drawing of some palm trees. The copy was densely set in small type.

The proposition was that people should send through the post a substantial down payment in order to secure one of these plots, which he described (rather horribly, I thought) as 'Beachettes'.

He told us that the product had previously sold very well in America. I was called in as the bright young creative director and agency expert on mail order to give my view as to whether his advertisement would work. Americans, in their naivety, might well be persuaded to fall for his approach but I was certain that the British, with their greater sophistication, would not. Particularly because the advertisement in question was being placed in that upper-class newspaper, *The Times*.

However, our new client was adamant. He was sure the ad would succeed. Since he was willing to put up the money for the advertisement in advance, we were quite happy to help him place it. In fact we even allowed him to use our own agency's address for the replies. This was hardly going to strain our resources, since I was certain there would be few.

What can you sell?

My education in direct marketing took yet another leap forward when the advertisement proved wildly successful. However, apart from being cocksure in my early years, I have always been very forgetful. For in the years since, when asked what you could *not* sell through direct marketing I always used to reply confidently that you couldn't sell very expensive products; nor could you sell very cheap products like, for instance, baked beans or Coca Cola.

My reasoning was simple. With an expensive product, where people were being asked to send a large sum of money to someone they had never met, you couldn't possibly be convincing enough in words and pictures about the product to convince respondents that they ought to take the chance. Cheap products did not have enough margin in them to justify the overheads involved in selling direct. (For many years it was universally agreed by mail order experts that you had to have 200 per cent gross profit margin to be able to sell direct – and preferably much more.)

No doubt many people went away impressed by my expert opinion, always delivered with great conviction. I owe them all an apology. For, as the story I have just recounted indicates, right at the beginning of my career I had discovered you *could* use direct marketing to sell very expensive products. More recently I have learned that even cheap packaged goods can also benefit from it.

In 1986 one of our clients – Comp-U-Card – sent out a mailing in conjunction with the Automobile Association offering discounts on motor cars. Two of the respondents purchased £87,000 Bentley Mulsanne Turbos. In the same year, our Italian agency was able to help Pepsi Cola increase distribution and sales, largely by using mailings.

These two successes were due to factors I had not considered. First, it was possible to persuade people to buy Bentley Mulsanne Turbos through the post because they believed they would get what they were going to pay for. In this particular case they were confident of the quality of the Bentley motorcar; they were also sure that the world's oldest motoring organisation would never offer something it could not deliver.

This demonstrates something general advertisers have known for many years, which direct marketers have not always appreciated: the importance of the brand name.

Of course, in this particular mailing some basic direct marketing tenets were adhered to carefully. The mailing was a very full one, covering all the questions the recipient might want to answer. The copy was detailed; there were many convincing testimonials; every question the possible purchaser might ask, we tried to answer in advance. It was a fine example of the combination of powerful brands with effective direct marketing – a combination which is, in my view, likely to become more and more important in the future.

In the case of Pepsi Cola, once again, the brand was an important characteristic. Also critical was an intelligent contact strategy. The trade in the small town involved were mailed twice to stock up, since Pepsi was about to embark upon a major consumer drive. They were offered incentives, including the chance to win a competition offering a video camera. Posters were used to alert the population to the offer, which was of a one-and-a-half-litre bottle of Pepsi, free. And consumers were mailed individually with the offer. The penetration of Pepsi within that particular market surged ahead dramatically.

But these and other cases have shown that in procrastinating about what could and could not be sold through direct marketing, I was consigning myself to the long list of experts who had proved themselves wrong over the years. The truth is that there are very few situations in which direct marketing cannot help you. As I have already suggested, you must first understand what it is. Second, you must understand how and where it can play a role in your business. And third, you must be equipped to recognise the right opportunities and problems as they come up.

The role of direct marketing

An American wag once observed that the world is divided into two types of people: those who believe the world is divided into two types of people and those who don't.

I confidently predict that you, dear reader, are one of two types. Either your company sells entirely by direct marketing: it's a 'pure' direct marketing company; or you have other means of distribution and selling, and view direct marketing as just another way of improving your business.

Having made this prediction, I now realise I may be one of those who do *not* believe the world is divided into two types of people, because I have already ignored something else you could be: not a marketer, but somebody who *advises* marketers – a consultant, or agent. Even in that case, you will undoubtedly find that in addition to whatever direct marketing can do for your clients, it can probably do a great deal for your own business.

Whatever your situation, my first piece of advice is that you carefully consider the two categories I mentioned originally. Are you (or your client) really a direct marketing company or are you not? What *should* you be? Have you looked carefully enough at the kind of company you are? How important is direct marketing to you? How much direct marketing are you already conducting? You can then determine what potential you have to improve your present activities and how much importance you should attach to direct marketing itself within your business, quite apart from being able to find new areas in which it might work for you.

In short, I think you *must* establish where direct marketing does or should fit into your business. For this reason I have prepared the following list of seven points. I believe you will find it well worthwhile thinking about these when either reviewing the potential of direct marketing, or looking at the way you are using it now. Even if yours *is* a 'pure' direct marketing company you should find most of these points relevant.

1. What is your overall business objective?

Where and how can direct marketing contribute to its achievement?

Let's say you've just entered a market in which there are several well established companies doing well. Your immediate objective is not to make money, but to build volume – to recruit as many new customers as possible at an acceptable cost – rather than to make an immediate profit.

If this is the case, your direct marketing activities probably ought to be skewed towards generating new customers (and being quite prepared to lose money in recruiting those new customers) rather than towards profiting as much as possible from the customers you've already got.

On the other hand, suppose you are a leading company in a mature market with very little room for growth. Under those circumstances you might decide your endeavours should be directed to retaining your existing customers and profiting from them as much as possible by making frequent, attractive offers which will tend to make them stay with you longer and keep the competition out. (Incidentally, one of the major sins I often see amongst companies is that of concentrating too much on recruiting new customers often at very high cost when more profit is likely to come from the existing customer base.)

For that matter, your business objective could be that you wish to go public in the next three years. If this is so, you may be wondering whether direct marketing could help you influence people in the City. Or you may feel that your business should be concentrating on quality control, in which case you would be very wise to consider a direct marketing programme aimed at your own employees to motivate them further.

The point is that until you consider the context in which you are planning to use Direct Marketing – or you are already employing it – you cannot deploy it properly.

2 What is your positioning?

How do your customers see you? How do your competitors see you? Who do you think you are competing with?

I am going to talk more about positioning later on, but I think it's very important to understand at the outset that the way you are perceived and your position in your market will determine much of your direct marketing. For instance, the tone of voice you use when communicating with people, the frequency with which you communicate with them, and the types of offer you make to them. Indeed, everything – right down to the emphasis you place on your brand name in your communications.

While I was preparing this chapter, I came across two contrasting statements. One was from the marketing executive of a direct marketing insurance company called Lloyds Life – an excellent name for anyone in a financial business. He revealed that despite repeated testing, he had never found his brand name did anything whatsoever to increase sales. This surprised me, until I looked up some research we had conducted ourselves into the insurance field. Apparently consumers feel (perhaps rightly) that all insurance companies are much the same. There is very low brand awareness in this field.

On the same day, Bob Scott, founder of the Scotcade company (which introduced mail order to the more sophisticated classes in the UK in the 1970s by paying great attention to the look and tone of his advertisements) gave an opposite view. He believed heavy use of his brand name had increased his response rates by around 30 per cent. The respectability he had tried to imbue his company with, in a market where most of his competitors had rather tatty images, had obviously paid off.

The point is simple: if you were the insurance executive, would you not be wondering how your direct marketing could be planned to give your company a good brand image in a market where nobody else has one? Would this not give you a tremendous advantage?

How could you do it? Well, you could do a little bit more than simply sell insurance. Perhaps you could offer your customers a series of added value services. If you're selling life insurance, for instance, booklets on health. If you're selling car insurance, booklets on getting more out of your motoring, and so on. Like most of the things I say in this book these are not startlingly original ideas – unless you compare them with what is being done at the moment.

Incidentally, adding *value* is probably the smartest thing you can do as a marketer today. A series of research studies revelling in the acronym PIMS – Profit Impact of Marketing Strategies – have revealed how important this is. Three thousand companies in Europe and the United States take part in this programme which is designed to find out what effect marketing strategies have on profits.

One dramatic finding is that those companies perceived by customers as giving more value for money tend to be infinitely more profitable. In fact, within the study, the top 20 per cent of companies judged on this parameter are on average almost exactly twice as profitable as the bottom 20 per cent.

What is one of the easiest ways to add value? Quite simply it is to *communicate*.

Communication under many circumstances is itself added value. You only have to recall waiting at an airport wondering when your flight is going to leave, without any information from the airline, to know that communication can indeed add value; it can in fact be critical.

3 What current marketing activities do you conduct?

How can Direct Marketing assist, complement or even replace them?

Direct Marketing can be somewhat opportunistic – later on I will list many occasions where you can see opportunities and profit from them. But just because it is opportunistic, do not necessarily fall into the trap of simply taking advantage of opportunities as they arise. You need a plan. You need priorities. That means you must review what you are doing already.

For instance, here are three widely different opportunities you could take advantage of:

- Send a letter out to your employees offering them a special discount.
- Write to recent customers offering them the opportunity to enter a sweepstake simply by sending for a catalogue (in the knowledge that most of them will think they are more likely to win if they buy something than not, and that in any case they may be enticed by some offer you are making in the catalogue).
- If you are a manufacturer, develop a telephone and direct mail programme to introduce your products to new retail outlets, thus freeing your sales force to develop closer contacts with your existing valuable retail customers.

Each of these ideas has merit. But unless you have looked at these proposals in the light of everything you are doing on the marketing front, you cannot evaluate them properly.

4 What is the relationship between direct marketing and other promotional activities?

As I've already pointed out, you cannot look at the effect of direct marketing in isolation. Your customers don't. *Every* communication from you adds to the picture they have of you. Every message you send out, through whatever discipline or medium, contributes to their perception of your brand or company. Moreover, in many cases they may offer new channels of direct marketing opportunity.

If you sell packaged goods , then what you do on the pack can be of prodigious importance. For a start, it can build lists of names. One of the great neglected areas is the use of on-pack material. When working for Mattel, we helped build up a list of names of little girls who wished to belong to the Barbie Friends Club. The cheapest source of names came from the membership offer made on the pack in which the doll itself came. On another occasion we were able to build up a very useful database for a client by giving away leaflets at motor racing events.

You must consider the relationship between direct marketing and other channels of sales and distribution. For instance, should you list retail outlets, if you have them, on your mailings which sell direct? One client of mine found this was a very bad idea. People may have intended to go into the shops *or* reply directly – in the event many did neither.

If you've a sales force, unquestionably they may feel threatened by your direct marketing activities. The result, many companies have found, of this political problem is *fright* – and they have given up any idea of direct marketing. The solution in most cases is to sell the concept of direct marketing to the sales force.

In short, your concern to make sure all your activities work well together means you should review the possibilities of everything you already do.

5 What is the state of your database?

Who controls it: administration or marketing? How do you see its role?

Your database is the storehouse of knowledge you have about one of your most valuable assets: your customers.

It is therefore essential that it be controlled and run by people who clearly understand the long-term objectives of the business. In the past, company databases have been controlled by administrators or finance people, for invoicing, paying wages and so forth.

When direct marketers attempted to move in, conflict often resulted. Those controlling the database were concerned to protect their territory. More to the point, having administrative backgrounds, they tended very often to have little sympathy with the marketer. Many direct marketers have roundly condemned the computer processing specialists and administrators as people of little imagination and no awareness of the real objectives of the business. They have dismissed them as *bean counters*.

In my view, this actually betrays a lack of imagination amongst direct marketers. Some of the brightest people I have encountered in marketing have actually come up via computers or finance. Here again – just as with the sales force, mentioned in my last point – the answer is *education*.

If you are in the early stages of direct marketing in your company and are encountering problems, then in my view the first thing you have to do is create a direct marketing programme to your own people. It will not reap instant rewards, but it will be a fine long-term investment. In particular, explaining to corporate people how vital their role can be in marketing is time very well spent. This leads on to my next point.

6 Have you sold the concept of direct marketing within your organisation?

Is top management committed to it? If not, why not? If so, why?

When I first became involved with Ogilvy & Mather Direct, the relationship between the Ogilvy & Mather general agency in the UK and the direct agency was poor. The general agency saw the direct folk as a bunch of amateurs. (I must admit, I had a great deal of sympathy with this point of view.) The direct people saw the generalists as people with an inflated sense of their own importance, being paid far too much money and lacking any understanding of what direct was trying to achieve. This, too, had a lot of truth in it.

My solution was to write to senior members of the general agency and ask them to attend a presentation to explain what we were doing. Most of them did, and this was the start of a fruitful relationship. The relationship is not yet perfect but it is infinitely more cordial, though I fear there will always remain those unreconstructable individuals on both sides of the divide who are deaf to blandishments of any kind.

Direct marketing, if it is to be introduced in your business, needs *champions*. Champions with power. Nothing has changed in the world since Columbus wandered round Europe trying to find somebody powerful enough to sponsor him to go and discover the riches of the Indies. He had to find his Queen Isabella. So do you if you are trying to develop a direct marketing programme in an organisation. The people at the top – or at least one person of importance at the top – must believe in what you are trying to do. Otherwise endless frustration will result.

We experienced this when developing proposals for a very large financial institution. One senior manager of that institution was behind us 100 per cent. We prepared a very long report which analysed in great depth how, where and why direct marketing should be used. Just after we delivered the report this executive was promoted to glory elsewhere. The report was never properly presented to his senior colleagues. We might just as well have saved our breath. No attention was paid to what we had said; a good relationship was never built up; a great opportunity was lost.

7 Where exactly should direct marketing fit into your organisation?

To whom should it report?

Once again, people are tempted to see direct marketing in a tactical way. They will perhaps feel that it should report as a function to whichever part of the organisation is likely to use it most. Thus in a large organisation selling to consumers, the direct marketing function may well be required to report to whoever is in charge of consumer marketing.

Yet direct marketing can play a very important role when dealing with employees, shareholders, the trade, opinion formers – just about anyone.

I do not necessarily know what the right answer to this question is; it will depend upon your organisation. One thing is certain: it should be a question which is asked and answered – carefully.

You will notice that throughout this book I am not tempted to suggest I have the answers to every problem you might have to confront. But I do believe you will do better long term by starting with the right questions. The seven points I have just covered will, I hope, start you thinking about the strategic role of direct marketing within your organisation.

Now let us look at the business in terms of objectives. What are direct marketers normally trying to achieve?

Five major objectives of direct marketers...

Although we've looked at many ways in which direct marketing can be applied, you can break down all the activities I know of into five simple categories. You can ask people to:

1 Buy through the post, over the phone, or off the TV set, either for cash or by quoting a credit card or account number. Here I include charity donations.
2 Ask for catalogues, or literature, or information which may come through the post, on the telephone or in the hands of salesmen (with or without the consumer's prior knowledge).
3 Request a demonstration either in the home, at work, or even at the seller's premises.
4 Visit a retail establishment, a film show or exhibition – or even a political or community event.
5 Take part in some action like joining a protest demonstration, or writing to an MP or some foreign power.

To reach your chosen objective, you can choose from a variety of routes. The possibilities and permutations are bewildering, but it is essential that you are aware of them all. A sale you could never attain in one step, for example, could be wildly successful if the product is broken down and sold in stages as a continuity product, or if the sale is made by asking for an enquiry and then following up repeatedly. Equally, a product you could not sell easily for cash might do very well if you offered it on free trial.

So let's look through the possibilities.

... And four ways to achieve them

1. One stage selling

When people use the words 'mail order' they usually think either of the bargain spaces in the weekend papers, glossy colour advertisements in the Sunday magazines, or those hard sell advertisements that promise to change your life – or shape, or looks – overnight.

This kind of selling does not, in fact, represent the largest segment of the direct marketing industry. Indeed, as you've already gathered (if you didn't already know) any company that depends on this activity *alone* to make money is unlikely to prosper long. But the one-stage sell is a way you can establish the *initial* relationship with a customer (or, in the case of a political party or charity, a sympathiser).

Some one-stage selling – the least sophisticated form of direct marketing – is as simple as offering a product for sale in exchange for the full cash price, to be sent in advance of the goods being delivered. However, as you can appreciate, any way in which you can soften or delay the awful moment when the customer actually has to part with money tends to pay off. Nobody likes paying for anything; even less do they like sending money off to someone they have never met for something they have never actually experienced or held in their hands.

Thus one may offer:

- The Free Trial, where goods or services may be enjoyed on approval for a period before the buyer is committed.

  Response leaps when you use this offer. You must, however, have a very efficient credit-checking system since in some cases as many as 50 per cent of replies can be bad debt risks.
- The Sale on Credit where only a down-payment is demanded.

  This is a method worth using if you have the necessary facilities. However, with the growth of charge and credit card usage it is becoming increasingly restricted to less wealthy markets.

  Years ago it was imagined that no item above £10 could be sold *without* offering credit, but with the growing acceptance of direct marketing and the decline in the value of money, this is no longer the case.

  A high percentage – as much as 50 per cent of the revenue from an ad in an up-market medium like the *Sunday Times* – may be through credit card payments.
- The Sale on Credit where no down-payment is demanded.

  This is, of course, the easiest payment option of all for the customer and thus the method which will generate your greatest response.

  Once again, if you have the credit-checking facilities and the financial resources to be able to afford to wait for your money, this can be the most profitable method of selling in the long run.

  Significantly, many of the most successful Direct Marketers often use this method; eg our client, *Reader's Digest*.
- The conditional free trial where you may have to send all or part of the money before getting the goods, but you are not committed to buy until a certain period has elapsed.

  This method was used by Joe Karbo to sell his book *The Lazy Man's Way to Get Rich*. He said he would not cash customers' cheques for 30 days, so they could be absolutely sure they were satisfied before being committed.

  There is, in addition, of course:
- The sale by credit or charge card where any of the above four options may also be offered.

  This is the easiest sale of all, because it's the *least* painful way for your customer to pay.

2 *The continuity relationship*

Since all direct marketing businesses succeed best where there is a continuing relationship between the buyer and the seller, many marketers establish a contract with the respondent which has a continuing arrangement built in from the start. Typical are:

- Insurance offers, where the initial application may lead to a ten or even twenty year contract.
- Loan offers, where people may be repaying for five years or longer.
- Mortgage offers, which also end up in a relationship over a number of years.
- Charity appeals or political appeals, where the group may solicit a covenant (and in the case of many charities, this relationship may last so long that the final payment will be after death, in a bequest).
- Credit Card applications, where the relationship may endure for decades.
- Membership offers – such as those made by the Consumers' Association, or the Automobile Association which may endure until death brings a merciful release.
- Club offers, where the respondent may be offered a very low price for a selection of books or records or even a free gift to start a collection of cookery cards, for example, and have to make a positive effort to extricate himself from the relationship.
- Collector's offers, where one starts with the first of a series of collectible items, and carries on through to the end, unless one wishes to cease.

Of course, exactly the same sort of financial offers you make to encourage a one-stage sale apply to a continuity sale. Thus, insurance companies selling direct often offer what they call in their quaint argot 'a deviated first premium'. For instance, the first month's premium may be free, or call for a payment of only £1. This, obviously, is a soft option for the prospect.

Equally, you can offer your prospect a free trial-period of three months. Generally, I have found that offering the opportunity to fill in a post-dated direct debit form in the advertisement or the order form pays off. By the time it comes to cancel the mandate, the customer doesn't bother. This is really a sophisticated variation of the technique I mentioned previously, used by Joe Karbo to sell his book. It is really a free trial offer with a hidden pitfall.

From your point of view a continuity relationship gives you a much greater margin with which to finance the original sale. Obviously, if you are making a single sale, then the margin to pay for the promotion has to be built into that one item. But when you know that over a period of time you may sell as many as 40 or 50 items, or receive payments over a period of years, you can afford to finance the initial sale to a greater degree.

3 Multi-stage selling

Flexibility of a different sort governs the third category we are going to consider: multi-stage selling. When you make a one-stage sale, then once the prospect has either responded or not responded, that's it. Either you've made money, or you've lost your chance to make money until the next time that reader sees your ad or mailing.

If you are merely going for an *inquiry*, then once that prospect has responded and you have his or her name on your database, you have an infinite number of opportunities to turn that inquiry into a sale. In fact, even if you don't sell the product or service you originally offered, you can try and sell an alternative.

Moreoever, a one-stage sale predetermines the way in which the respondent buys: either they react in the way you suggest at the price you quoted or they don't. But multi-stage selling is much more flexible – and in one form or another is probably the area with the greatest potential for most businesses.

Suppose you generated an inquiry and followed it up with a letter and brochure. If those don't produce a sale, there's nothing to stop you following up with a phone call or a salesman. For that matter, if you followed up the inquiry with a salesman who did not succeed, there is no reason to believe that a letter later on may not achieve the desired effect. It's worth remembering that to get that sale you can vary terms, reduce the price, or make a free trial offer and further follow-ups. Indeed, you can keep contacting that prospect for as long as it is economically worthwhile for you.

Financially, the implications are simple. Once you have paid your entrance fee – ie paid for the inquiry – you can keep on 'milking' it until the cost of doing so exceeds the marginal profits. To take a simple example: when I was handling the marketing for the Bullworker, we used to send out up to *nine* follow-up mailings.

And like so many other simple examples in the consumer market this principle applies to the business-to-business market. If you are trying to sell an expensive piece of office equipment with a great deal of margin built in, once you have that original inquiry put onto your database, you can keep on exploiting it many times, in many different ways. The diagram entitled 'The Mill' which I have shown elsewhere, shows you how this process can take place.

Let us therefore look at some simple multi-stage operations:

- Sales follow-ups, where information about a product is advertised, information is sent out and a salesman follows up. Common examples in the consumer field are double glazing and other home improvements; in business-to-business, computers, copying machines or typewriters would apply.
- Retail combination, where a product may be advertised in the press (or in a catalogue sent out by the store) and the respondent may go into the store rather than buy direct.
- Catalogue offers, which may be divided into those where:

- the prospect sends for a catalogue to buy things from;
- the prospect sends for a catalogue for which he or she may become an agent, deriving commission (savings);
- the prospect buys and is later offered the chance of becoming an agent.
- Agent's offers, other than the ones outlined above, where the agent will represent a given line of products and may or may not have to buy the merchandise in advance, with or without a guarantee of money back if the goods are not sold successfully.
- Recruitment, where the respondent replies to an ad, gets information and then goes for an interview (as with the armed services) or may go directly to an interview.

As in so many other areas of business, some of these categories merge into each other. For instance, Avon recruits ladies who become spare time agents. The company also has a permanent sales force which 'runs' the sales ladies in given areas.

In December 1984, Avon's business in Germany was not doing very well. How could direct marketing revitalise it?

Among the major problems were insufficient new Avon ladies; lack of motivation amongst the new recruits; and not enough time and effort from the area sales force devoted to handling and motivating these ladies. The reason was that the area salespeople were so worried about trying to find new ladies. Each year, for every twelve they hired they would lose two. The solution, quite simply, was to *motivate* the new ladies. They were written letters when they joined and welcomed to the organisation. They were congratulated on their individual achievements, all of which could be monitored through the database.

But how could new ladies be recruited? The answer was to run advertisements in the form of questionnaires. These were based upon what we discovered about the psychological structure of the perfect Avon lady. Depending on the answers to the questionnaires, the respondents were handled in two different ways.

Those who did *not* fit in with the profile of a good Avon lady were simply given a free gift and thanked for their interest, together with news of what had emerged from the quiz they had replied to. Those who *did* sound like perfect Avon ladies were written to and told that they would do extremely well with the company, and that they should go to their local area representative and collect a free gift. At the same time, a computer profile of the lady was sent to the local area representative who was then able to deal more effectively with her new recruit.

This project which was devised by our Frankfurt office was particularly interesting to me. It used original thinking to create and utilise a database containing details of both the potential new recruit and the existing sales representative, leading to an intelligent personalised approach. A few years ago it would have been difficult to have accomplished anything like this. Technology has made the difference.

Finally, two more multi-stage operations:

- Franchise offers, where the respondent sends for details, meets the company or its representative, and may end up going into business with them.
- Sequence selling. There are many cases where you can afford to be quite patient in getting a sale. You can afford to try and mould people's opinions about your product or service before actually going in for the kill.

    Earlier I gave an example where Ford in America send out a long series of mailings of which the earlier ones are not looking for a sale, but designed to build an opinion which will lead to one. This is similar in thinking to the concept of general advertising. You are building a preference over a period of time. If, for example, you know it takes two years on average from the time when somebody buys a new car to the time when they buy another one, then you can stage a series of communications to keep them loyal to your brand.

    The simplest form of sequence probably would be where you send out an advance mailing or make a telephone call to say you are going to make a very generous offer to someone; you then make the offer; and then you may follow up with another call or mailing to remind people to take advantage of the opportunity before it lapses.

    In some cases you may find it worthwhile to send out a series of newsletters or regular mailings which are intended to inform, educate and persuade people of the virtues of your product or service – or, for that matter, your company.

    This sort of approach is particularly appropriate for a profession like accountancy, the law or advertising. People do not wake up every morning and decide they need a new advertising agency or lawyer. You are simply trying to make sure that when they *do* have to make such a decision, they will choose in your favour.

4. *Sales promotion linked opportunities.*

Many companies – perhaps most companies that are reasonably sophisticated – make offers of one kind or another which can with a little ingenuity be turned into direct marketing opportunities.

What they all have in common is that a list of names can be generated. Names can be very valuable, as I indicated when discussing the selling of Avon cosmetics. So if your company is engaged in any of the following activities, you have a direct marketing opportunity:

- Competitions, where the respondent may or may not have to offer proof of purchase.
- Discounts and free offers, where a coupon may have to be redeemed at the store, or by post. These may be offered in advertisements; in the package, as with a cigarette pack; or on the back of the pack, as with sugar cartons.
- Self-liquidating offers, where a product may be offered cheaply as long as you prove you have purchased the brand.
- Direct offers of merchandise bearing the brand name, as with offers of Guinness sweaters, or Coca Cola beachwear, or London Transport T-shirts.

In all these cases, either direct contact is involved, or it can be introduced. Thus, for instance, if you are running an advertisement which bears a redeemable coupon, then if you require that people give the name and address when redeeming that coupon you are able to capture a name and address.

In fact, one of the most powerful weapons at the direct marketer's disposal has come about as a result of this sort of activity. This is the building of large files of consumers with details about their brand preferences, household characteristics and purchasing patterns incorporated. I deal with this in more detail in the chapter on database.

Which names are best?

How can you put a value on the names you generate through sales promotional activities?

The ideal person is somebody who has bought one of your branded products through the post. This is like getting a mail order buyer's name with the additional benefit that they are favourably disposed to your brand. As we shall see, if a person is inclined to buy direct, this is a very valuable characteristic for you.

On the other hand, somebody who is merely a competition respondent is not necessarily a mail order buyer by nature. He or she is merely someone who in exchange for an inducement will buy a particular product or brand. Whether without that inducement the purchase would be made, you don't know. This makes the quality of the name somewhat weaker when you wish to sell to them or communicate with them again.

In all the examples I have given you in this chapter what is important is the establishing of a direct link between you and your prospect or customer, and the opportunity to exploit that link. How best to go about that is what our business is all about.

I hope the examples I have given you in this chapter have opened your minds somewhat to the almost limitless range of possibilities direct marketing offers. You have probably discovered though, as I have, that your mind is more often provoked by the prospect of solving some problem you face right now, or taking advantage of an opportunity you can already see. The next chapter, therefore, will deal in greater detail with particular instances where direct marketing makes good sense.

4

How to Get Started

'You can observe a lot just by watching.'

US Baseball legend, Yogi Berra

As we've already discussed, your customers today are infinitely more demanding than ever before. They expect a much greater variety of product and service to match their individual needs. They are refusing to be categorised. Marketers are having to change to meet the needs of this new, more demanding customer. I covered this earlier in the context of that most exciting of all products, the baked bean.

But let's look at financial services – significantly, one of the areas in which direct marketing has shown its greatest growth. Take life insurance, for example.

First there was straight life insurance, then came life insurance with the option to invest at the same time. Now there is life insurance with special terms for those who are over 50, or who don't smoke. And – bizarre reversal – one English company, Ambassador Life, has even offered a policy to cover funeral expenses. I wonder what our English ancestors who founded the old co-operative societies as burial clubs for working people would make of that. An interesting counterpoint is that in some parts of the world burial still represents a major expense which can often cripple a family's finances.

You will certainly have noticed, also, that just as consumers are refusing to fit neatly into the categories arranged for them by marketers, those marketers are offering services which were traditionally seen as not in their province.

Once, if you wanted banking services, a bank was the place to go. On the other hand, if you wanted a mortgage, you went to a building society (or Savings & Loan as they call it in the US). If you wanted to invest in stocks and shares, then you went to your broker. And if you needed insurance you went to an insurance company.

Now what has happened? Your building society will provide much the same banking services as your bank. On the other hand, you can get a mortgage from your bank, or make investments through an insurance policy. And to add to the confusion, specialists have set up: there are companies that do nothing but offer mortgages. They have moved into the area once reserved for building societies.

It's all getting rather difficult to understand if you're a consumer. And I haven't even considered other complications resulting from the way some financial organisations are gobbling up others. Building societies are buying up chains of estate agents. At the same time, unexpected players are coming onto the field. I saw recently that a legal firm in the UK is selling property. And, of course, the credit card companies will make practically any sort of financial arrangement you care to mention. They'll lend you money, help you invest, arrange insurance for you and so forth. And why not?

This makes it rather difficult for anybody trying to establish a clear position in the financial services field. Where once it may have been sufficient to persuade customers you were the right bank by saying that you were 'The action bank', or 'The listening bank' – two British slogans – this is not all that persuasive when it comes to actually selling products or services. This is particularly true when you realise, as I discovered when looking at one British clearing bank, that they offered over 270 different financial services of one kind or another. How on earth do you match the right service to the right customer? And how on earth do you explain the differences between all these services?

Take a typical instance. What if you are the Birmingham Midshires Building Society, trying to persuade me that I should stop letting my *bank* manage my money and let *you* do it? That is going to take a great deal more than a slogan. You will have to explain to me how your new Mastercharge Account not only gives me all the benefits of a bank account, but a great deal more. That requires a long, detailed communication directed to me personally – preferably based upon knowledge you have about me. I choose this example because this organisation did write to me personally. But they knew hardly anything about me, and consequently weren't very successful.

There is a converse side. I may see no good reason to switch my banking to a building society. But when the Midland Bank suggests to me that I should invest through it as opposed to a stockbroker, this seems to me to be a splendid idea. Stockbrokers aren't really interested in private individuals unless they have more than £100,000 to invest. And no stockbroker has taken the trouble to find out that I am in that happy position – which, of course, brings us back to building a database.

This lengthy preamble is quite simply to make the point that changes in the way we buy and sell are making direct marketing a natural choice for buyers and for sellers. It doesn't just apply in the consumer field, it applies to businessmen with equal force.

It may have been quite easy a hundred years ago to explain to the average office manager why Watermans ink was better than Stephens ink. It was even quite easy 50 years ago to explain the difference between a Remington typewriter and an Underwood typewriter. But just you try and explain in a 30-second television commercial why an Apple computer is better than an IBM PC. It's exceedingly difficult, and this is one reason why such companies are turning to direct marketing to help them.

In this chapter, I am going to examine in greater detail how direct marketing can play an effective role for you – or play a more effective role if you are already employing it. To do so, I am going to take some typical marketing problems and opportunities. I'll be very surprised if at least one is not relevant to your own business.

Does your business have a continuing relationship built in?

A while ago I went to see a client in the hope that I could persuade them to appoint us as their direct marketing agency. I had a slight problem which was that firstly, they were not in the direct marketing business. Secondly, they had no desire to get into it. Thirdly, this was not surprising, because they didn't even know what direct marketing was.

However, they did have an excellent catalogue, offered to customers who came to their stores. Thinking about the possibilities this catalogue offered led to a sequence of activities which will give you some insight into the possibilities open to you once you start thinking seriously about direct marketing.

- Instead of waiting for people to come to the stores so that we could give them a catalogue, we started offfering the catalogue in all their advertisements. The replies to these offers from the various media enabled us to discover which media were doing well for us. This confirmed what research had already suggested: their customers are more upmarket than the average. This in turn enables us to improve the tone of our communications and the targeting of our direct mail.
- We run advertisements which invite people to come in directly to their nearest store and take advantage of a bargain offer. At the store we collect their names and communicate with them later.
- Mailings to existing customers go out when we are launching a new product. As many as 10 per cent of all customers come into a store in response to one of these mailings – and many more over a period of time.
- By studying the locations in which the majority of our customers live around a particular store, we can target door drops in the areas around which new stores are about to be opened to encourage people to come in.
- Letters go out to the company's shareholders offering them special discounts on the company's products, thus strengthening the link between the company and that important group.
- Regular letters go out to employees telling them of the progress of the company, thanking them for their efforts and asking them to make greater efforts still.
- Recruitment advertising – the success of which, in my view, determines the success of *any* business, because good people are the lifeblood of your company – calls for direct responses, obviously.
- A monthly direct mail shot goes out to all the trade customers making special offers not available to the general public. A special trade card has been produced which offers these customers credit and strengthens the relationship between them and the company.
- A list of people moving into new homes has been acquired, and

mailings go out regularly to them, encouraging them to come in and see the client's products.

Obviously, with the intelligent use of the database all these various activities can be further subdivided to make them more accurate. Thus, it is wasteful to mail *all* the existing customers with every offer you make. You will find that for some offers you are best off mailing people who have recently bought a certain type of product. For instance, if they've bought a kitchen from you, there is little point in mailing them with a kitchen offer. It may, however, make a lot of sense to offer them built-in bedroom furniture made from the same wood and with a similar design to the kitchen they have bought. Clearly the more you eliminate the wrong kind of customer and make the right offer to the right kind of customer, the better your results – as we discussed in the last chapter.

Just by looking at the examples I have given of this one company, I think you'll agree with me that the problem today is not discovering where you should apply direct marketing. It is more deciding where you should apply it *first*. Because everywhere you look, if you look thoughtfully, you will see opportunities.

Sales-force help

One place where many companies immediately see they could apply direct marketing is in helping deploy the limited and expensive time of a sales force.

I have derived some pleasure over the years from keeping track of the astronomical costs of making a sales visit – costs which go up, as far as I can make out, faster than inflation. These figures are regularly collected by McGraw-Hill. The most recent figure they quote for the US was $230 a visit. That's a *visit*, let me emphasise – not a sale. If that visit is unsuccessful, you've just lost $230. In Europe, costs can be even higher. The lowest: $128.18 in Ireland. The highest: $1,439.62 in Denmark. In England, the figure is $303.82.

To put this expense in context, on average, European salespeople complete one sale every six calls. This makes you wonder how any company in Denmark employing salesmen can *ever* make money. But it also underlines the importance of using direct marketing to make the most of that valuable asset, the salesperson.

Much thinking on this subject goes back to the very old observation that most of your business tends to come from very few customers. It was in fact the Roman philosopher, Prato, who first observed that 10 per cent of the people spent 80 per cent of the money.

In the United States a major drug company had the problem that their salespeople simply could not visit all the thousands of outlets they dealt with, except on a very rare basis. By segmenting the outlets down, they were able to reallocate the salesmen so that they devoted most of their visits to that important top 10 per cent. Less profitable outlets received only occasional visits from the salespeople, but were dealt with very effectively on the telephone and through direct mail. The overwhelming majority of outlets, which were barely profitable at all, were dealt with entirely through direct mail supplemented by telephone.

In the UK our agency launched IBM Direct. The company realised that some products – typewriters in particular – might not need personal selling at all. Their customers understood perfectly well what a typewriter was, and particularly what an IBM typewriter was. They just wanted to buy them conveniently. We introduced direct mail to sell typewriters. It worked. Thus, the salesmen were free to sell more expensive products. Eventually, a complete catalogue was put together. Today we do much the same sort of thing for Xerox.

Launching new products has always been particularly expensive. Quite a few years ago in the UK we had the challenge of helping the sales force to introduce a new catering product to many thousands of outlets. We found that a simple mailing offering a free sample could get 25 per cent of the recipients to try the product. At the same time, we collected information about the outlet, numbers of meals served, what type of food sold, and so forth in order to enable us to build a better relationship with them.

In France, the Compagnie Coloniale, who supply top quality tea with 25 different flavours, wanted 3,000 owners of quality delicatessens and caterers. Their problem was they only had a sales force of two. Our French agency suggested direct mail, followed up by telephone. The result? Seventy-six per cent of the prospects favourably considered the proposition on the phone. Forty-four per cent requested a salesman's visit. All the salesmen then had to do was to go around signing people up. The proposition had been pre-sold. In the event it cost them no more to sign up a pre-sold prospect than it did originally to go in and merely visit a prospect.

Some pertinent questions

I would frankly be astonished if somewhere in your business there were not obvious direct marketing potential. You can often find out where it exists by asking the right questions.

- Do you offer after-sales service?
- Do you offer a guarantee that people have to fill in?
- Do you have a *family* of related products?
- Do you offer account facilities?
- Do you sell on credit, and have to invoice people regularly?
- Do you have accessories or software to sell?
- Do you have (or need) repeat purchases?

In all these cases you either already have a situation ideal for creating a continuing relationship, or you could easily create one. For instance, if you offer after-sales service, or have to bill people regularly, either because you sell on credit or have account customers, you have a reason to talk to them about other things they can buy. And if you haven't got a reason, it's often a good idea to create one.

I was talking to a friend about a company we were working for. I asked him how much discount they offered if, instead of paying over a period, you paid cash. 'None,' was his reply. 'They don't *want* you to pay cash. They want as many opportunities as possible to communicate with you, and sell you something more.'

The retail trade furnishes many examples of the power of the relationship with the account customer. Indeed, figures I have seen suggest that one account customer can produce more profit than *five* non-account customers.

Offering previews of sales to account customers is now very common. When it was first initiated, a few years ago, I was told that Harvey Nichols, the elegant London 'flagship' department store of the Debenhams Group, used to make more money from the one-day preview reserved for their account customers than during the entire two-week sale that followed.

Another spectacular example comes from Murray Raphel, the American direct marketer who also owns a retail store in Atlantic City. His five-hour sale at New Year which he promotes heavily, largely through direct mail, also produces more than the regular sale that follows.

The most extreme example I have seen of the power of a company/customer relationship was the case of a US mail order company which sent its customers a letter apologising for the delay in shipping their order . . . with, on the back, an invitation to buy six more items in the meantime. It worked.

Barnardo Publications – the arm of Dr. Barnardo's that sells merchandise – ran an ad to sell a machine that plays chess with you. The ad did quite well, but the returns, instead of being the usual 5 per cent, were more like 20 per cent. Jeremy Shaw, the executive at Barnardo's responsible, couldn't understand. He conducted a little telephone research and soon found out the problem. The machines were perfectly all right. They just weren't *advanced* enough. So he wrote to all those who had asked for their money back, saying: 'Here's your refund. But would you like a machine that's much more advanced, but costs three times as much?' The mailing was a simple five-page letter – no illustration – and an order form.

Twenty-five per cent bought the more expensive machine, because a relationship had been established and the company was clearly planning to behave honourably by refunding. I understand the company may have made more money from the returns than they did from the original advertisement.

Use your names

One of the most obvious, yet frequently neglected, opportunities is that of the guarantee form. When people have bought something from you, they are usually in a pretty good mood. There will *never* be a better moment to create a strong relationship with them. Indeed, a few years ago I conducted some tests which proved this to be the case. The quicker you sell an extra product to somebody who has just become a customer, the better you will do long term. Yet most companies never do anything with their guarantee form, though there are usually obvious opportunities for cross-selling.

Another area frequently neglected is that of the names generated through sales promotion. These names, whilst not nearly as valuable as the names of people who bought from you by mail, can be highly responsive. In one instance, we managed to generate a 51 per cent response from a list of such names.

The seventh question on my list, 'Are repeat purchases important to you?', is obviously one to which everybody ought to answer 'Yes'. Indeed, as you've already gathered, it is one of the three reasons why every business should be interested in direct marketing. That is why it is so important when making a sale to record the name and address of your customer – and do it accurately. After that it hardly requires genius to keep in touch. Yet how many people bother?

A few years ago, I took my young children to Lord Newport's restaurant, Porters, in Covent Garden. The waitress asked them the dates of their birthdays and where they lived. The next year they all got a birthday card, with an invitation to a free meal. How do you think that made me feel about Lord Newport? I was amused at the commercial shrewdness, as well as being impressed.

How many companies do you know that take this kind of trouble?

Retail problems

Earlier in this chapter I quoted examples from one of our clients in the retail business. There are many obvious ways that tactical offers of discounts, special gifts, or staging events, can bring people into your stores.

You can help overcome such common problems as outlets that are empty on some days of the week; badly situated stores which won't attract passing trade; and, of course, stores with high rentals. Also, if a store is selling products that people buy at particular points in their lives, or consider for long periods of time before making a final decision, direct marketing techniques are often ideal for keeping in touch.

For instance, when I moved into a new house a few years ago, I was struck by the fact that one retailer – Wickes – used to mail me a booklet every month with do-it-yourself offers. In fact I was a peculiarly poor target for such offers: I can't change a plug without a map. But if I were interested in DIY, I probably would have responded.

Yet what they do is not particularly remarkable. They just communicate *directly* with likely prospects. At the time I am speaking of, not one of their competitors did.

I have already talked about the way the car industry is beginning to get into direct marketing. However, at a *retail* level, the small entrepreneur is doing very little indeed. Few retail showrooms take the trouble to get your name and address, inquire about your requirements and future plans, then follow up regularly. I believe they are going to have to do so vigorously in future because the car trade, which used to provide a cushy living to all sorts of fast talking ne'er-do-wells, is becoming a buyers' market, not a sellers'.

The key to profit

Here are some other obvious marketing situations where the direct link could well be the key to profit.

Do your retailers or wholesalers dictate to you?

Why not go round them, direct to your customers? Or build an alliance with them by creating a direct marketing programme they can use? They will come to look on you as a more desirable partner than your competitors. This is something I would particularly recommend to anybody in the insurance business who deals with brokers or other intermediaries.

Does your brand suffer from regular attempts by others to steal part of your market?

Then create a list of your customers by making attractive offers, and *keep* making them good offers so that they stay with you. Such a list can be particularly valuable at a moment when you realise one of your competitors is about to launch a new product. You can pre-empt their activity by making attractive offers that will diminish the likelihood of your existing customer switching.

Would you like to steal other people's customers?

Following the previous point, I am talking here about taking the battle to the enemy, as it were. It's perfectly possible to do so.

Recently, Imperial Tobacco decided to cut the number of their pipe tobacco brands by 60 per cent. Rothmans then ran an ad informing pipe smokers that if they thought they might be missing their favourite brand, all they had to do was write in to receive details of the Rothmans brand closest to it. A neat approach to database building.

This kind of thinking also worked extremely effectively in a programme devised by our Atlanta agency, acting for a computer company. They asked potential customers to give details of the computer they were currently considering. They then mailed them a detailed comparison between that computer and the brand we were selling. It was very successful.

When we come to talk about databases, you will see that proprietary databases also enable you to attack competitors' customers extremely effectively.

Do you appeal to a specific group of people?

Any situation where you are not appealing to everybody is one where direct marketing makes sense. For instance, where you have patchy distribution. Why waste a fortune in national press or TV? Try direct mail or the telephone.

This is so obvious, yet so frequently neglected, it is quite remarkable. How many times have you seen enormously expensive national campaigns when what is being said could only be of interest to a limited number of people? This has been most conspicuous in recent years during campaigns aimed at shareholders of particular companies. Surely, direct approaches to these people would be infinitely more cost-effective than general advertising.

However, the fact that you are not trying to sell to the whole world does not mean you do not necessarily wish to speak to people who are not your prime target customers. If that sounds contradictory, let me explain.

One of the direct marketing programmes put together by a car company in the United States, although it seemed to make eminent sense, proved relatively unsuccessful. The reason was that the client decided to do virtually no general advertising at all. Consequently, apart from the people who were being approached directly, nobody knew anything whatsoever about the car. It had no reputation. As a result of this, if anybody bought it they would not benefit from one of the great pleasures of buying cars: having other people admire your choice.

A powerful example to show that however much sense direct marketing may make, it is not necessarily always going to be able to do the job on its own.

Do you recruit people?

Talk to someone who specialises in direct marketing. Amongst the biggest direct marketers are the agents' catalogues. I think direct marketing people often know more about recruiting than most recruitment agencies do.

Do you have a catalogue or brochure?

Direct marketing grew to a large extent out of the mail order catalogue business. The skills required to make a catalogue work more effectively are specialised ones. And they reside for the most part inside direct marketing agencies. In my view, anybody who has a catalogue or a brochure who doesn't at least talk to somebody in a direct marketing agency who understands these things is certainly missing an obvious opportunity.

And, finally, can you afford to advertise as much as you'd like to?

If not, then transform your 'image-building' advertisements and make them *sell* something. You will find new revenue for advertising.

If the examples above don't set you thinking about how something you're considering right now could be approached, your business probably has no connection with the subject of this book. I should put it down right now and go and have a drink.

Employers and politics

Two areas I have touched upon previously are those of employee relationships and politics. Increasingly, direct marketing is being used by political parties to recruit members, raise funds, expound policies and gain support. Sometimes, politics and employee relationships merge so as to become almost indistinguishable.

This was the case a while ago when union leftwingers had more or less gained complete control of the British Leyland Motor Company. The solution adopted by the company was quite simply to use direct mail to the mass of employees and point out how their future was being threatened. In this way, the company was able to get employees to agree to policies which for years they had steadfastly rebuffed.

Unfortunately, on those occasions when companies do resort to communicating directly with their workers, it is all too often because they are in a panic about a particular situation. If they were to bear in mind the importance not just of an occasional communication but of regular ones, they could, I think, mine a rich vein of gold. (I do not mean the sort of anodyne puffery contained in most company newsletters, but personal, thoughtfully constructed communications revolving around the employee's true interests.)

Who complains?

Another area which companies tend to ignore is that of *complaints*. However loud and impressive their protestations of dedication to the customer, few companies like to think about complaints. This is not true of the really outstanding marketers, amongst whom one would have to number Proctor and Gamble.

A while ago, the US P&G started addressing the subject of complaints. They discovered that when customers were unhappy, only around 40 per cent of them could be bothered to write to the company and complain about a particular product. This is not really surprising when you think about it: nobody gets into a lather of excitement over a laundry detergent (forgive the dreadful pun).

Proctor & Gamble, on the other hand, are always excited about detergents and similar products – they are their livelihood. Accordingly, they wondered how they could make it easier for their customers to complain, because they had also discovered that of those who did bother to write, 90 per cent were satisfied with the company's explanation, and continued to be customers.

Accordingly, P&G decided to put an 0800 number on all their packs so that anybody who had a query could ring up free. Result? Ninety per cent of potential complainants did ring up. And 90 per cent, once again, were satisfied.

Apart from retaining customers, P&G also said they learned a great deal of value from this activity. They learned which customers were using which brands. They received lots of helpful suggestions about packaging, advertising and even new product ideas. Quality control was improved and recalls avoided.

Clairol heard about this activity and formed a completely separate division – a profit centre in itself – to deal with complaints. This is a wonderful variation on the old salesman's saying that the sale only starts when the customer says 'No'.

What mail order teaches

I am biased, but I believe mail order is a marvellous education. 'We sell, or else' is the motto David Ogilvy devised for O&M Direct – one which grows directly from mail order. And although today direct marketing is employed by all kinds of company, looking at what mail order companies have learned will teach you valuable lessons.

To start with the basics, if you look today at some of the better mail order catalogues you will see they are very different to their forebears. Twenty years ago the average catalogue did not offer a better quality product, nor a more imaginative selection of products; it flourished because it offered credit and home delivery. The prices were rarely competitive.

No longer so. Catalogues today often offer genuine bargains, and imaginative products. I picked one up at random the other day and saw some excellent buys. Gold-plated watches, well designed, with a saving of £40 off the original price of £70. A cordless infra-red headphone system – no need for jackplugs. And a fully automatic camera outfit with zoom lens at less than half price.

One product that particularly interested me was an ingenious 'desk briefcase ideal for working on the move'. Right up my street. I haven't seen this product offered in retail stores. I am always buying briefcases, and I spend much of my time on the move. This is a product which could change my buying habits. And the reason is – I blush to confess – that I have *never* bought anything from a catalogue. This product might persuade me I should.

What I am saying is that the mail order companies are reacting to meet a more sophisticated market. They're producing good products, selecting them imaginatively, presenting them well, and making good offers.

Pretty basic stuff, you will probably say. How can you succeed in marketing without offering something good? Well, surprisingly enough, many of the companies who enter direct marketing do so because they see it as a way of solving a problem – often that of getting rid of products they hadn't been able to sell any other way. There are few occasions on which this happy result is likely to eventuate, I can assure you.

Three major errors

Getting started successfully in direct marketing requires just as much hard work and application as getting started in anything else. Here are the three major errors I have noted amongst non-direct marketing companies who wish to get started.

1 Failing to espouse direct marketing thinking

General marketers have a disdainful attitude to direct marketing. They see it as a junk mail, hole-in-the-wall business. I have already explained that I have great sympathy with this point of view. But it doesn't mean you ought to approach the business casually.

Good direct marketing, as you have seen already, calls for its own special way of thinking. And those who understand it are few; there's a great shortage of talent. Accordingly, many companies employ people with *general* marketing experience. Often, just as they choose *products* that have failed, they choose *people* who have failed in general marketing. The result: disaster.

If you can't find people who have direct marketing experience, then for God's sake try to make sure that the people you do select are really good. Then make sure they learn as much as possible about the business. There are many training programmes, hosts of seminars and conferences, and a number of excellent books. Make sure they are exposed to all these. I recommend in particular the training of the DMA in America, The Direct Marketing Centre in Britain, and the conferences organised by the national associations in those countries, as well as in France, Switzerland and Australia in particular.

If all else fails, tell them to get a job with Ogilvy & Mather Direct. We are famous for giving more training than any other agency in the business. And I can say in all honesty that this is true: one of our major competitors, Ed Ney, head of Young & Rubicam, commented on the fact some time ago.

2 Trying to do without specialist help

When General Mills in the United States went into direct marketing a few years ago, they conducted a two-year study to establish what you have to do to succeed. They thought it was essential to get direct marketing experts in right at the beginning and 'engage a competent direct marketing agency to help set up the operation, manage and train the people . . . and maybe even run the business in the short term'.

Whether you have to go to that much trouble, I don't know. But one thing is sure: hiring a 'below-the-line' specialist, ie somebody who knows all about sales promotion or merchandising but does not *specialise* in direct marketing will almost certainly prove fatal. Indeed, despite the fact that many sales promotion agencies have set up direct marketing divisions, I have yet to see one of any great competence. And a general agency is almost certainly the kiss of death. I have yet to come across one that understood direct marketing at all.

3 Trying to do it too quickly.

Again, to quote the General Mills study, 'This is not an overnight success formula, but something that will take a major investment in time and funds.'

You will notice that when considering the advantages of direct marketing I have never suggested that it's a way of marketing on the cheap. You may be able to eliminate risk, but you will still have to invest. You must look at it in the same way as you would any other business. When I talk about investment, I do not merely mean investment in money. I mean investment in time. The time needed to install the necessary infrastructure.

Some years ago, a major US company came to us with the bold intention of seizing a major share of the private health insurance market. There were a number of reasons why this was a difficult thing to do. First, in the UK the National Health Service, though badly run, is much liked. Second, this particular market is and has been dominated for nearly 50 years by one company. Third, nobody had ever heard of this particular American company, though it is very famous over there.

It is possible that their long-term objective might have been met, but they certainly made it difficult by trying in a space of six months to put together an organisation to set up this project. This involved not merely marketing personnel, but people to set up a database, a telephone operation and all the considerable logistical minutiae involved in such a business. (Reflect, for instance, on the challenge of recruiting a sufficient number of private hospitals to co-operate in such a venture, and you will get some idea of what I mean.)

Merely from a direct marketing point of view the whole thing was utter chaos. In a period of 12 months, from a standing start, we produced over 700 separate pieces of direct mail and advertisements. Never was time given to stop, consider what was being learned, adapt accordingly. Many valuable lessons *were* learned, but amidst the panic-stricken gallop towards an unattainable target, these were obscured. The company did learn quite enough to realise that over a long term, approaching segments of the market, they could succeed. But it was difficult for them to see this. A great opportunity was wasted when the business, after little more than 18 months was, to all intents and purposes closed down.

What should you sell?

I have just given an example of a service which was a natural for direct marketing. In fact, there are few products or services you can't sell direct as long as you give it a little thought. If you are already in business with a range of products and services, then you will probably have isolated a number of possibilities for yourself by now. However, here is some advice based largely upon my experience in the mail order business. Clearly, not all the points I am going to make will be applicable to you, but I would be surprised if some were not.

Firstly, the right product does not necessarily have to be the cheapest, or the most unusual, or one with some special gimmick. Moreover, it can be something that is also available through other channels. (Some people think it has to be uniquely available direct. This is clearly not the case. For instance IBM, to whom I have referred already, have in some cases offered a range of different prices to the customer for certain products depending on how they buy them: from a salesman, from a retail outlet, or direct.)

Generally, the thing to consider is whether the product represents good value, or is one on which you can make a good offer. Perhaps a little story will illustrate what I mean.

Some years ago, I was called in by Gerald Lipton, the chief executive of Chinacraft, an extremely successful chain of retail stores. He had heard from another of our clients that we were hot stuff at direct marketing, and he summoned us to his rather grand office in north London.

Before talking to us, he said: 'Let me show you round my warehouse.' It was a most educational tour. I have never seen so much beautiful china in my life. Nor so much *expensive* china. There were cups and saucers there selling for nearly £100 each. I was bowled over.

Then, he said: 'Let me show you all my cheap lines'. He took us to see the crockery he sells to the big supermarket chains and catalogue houses. This was impressive in a different way. He had everything there: plates, saucers, service dishes, glasses, cutlery. I'd seen a lot of it before in various stores.

After he had shown us round, he took us back to his office, and said: 'For many years I've wanted to get into mail order. I don't actually know why, but I've got this itch. I've tried a few times. Sometimes I've made a little money, sometimes I've lost a little money. But I've never succeeded as I would like to.' He asked us whether we thought we could help and – eager to get the business – we said we could. He asked what we thought he should sell. With the wisdom of more experience since then, I think we should have kept our mouths shut. The selling of products is tough enough without getting into choosing them. However, we made three suggestions, all of which he tested in the press. Only one did well. It was the *least* original.

At that time, another company was running an offer of complete sets of plates, glasses, serving dishes and cutlery. Gerald Lipton knew how well they were doing; moreover, he knew exactly what they were paying because he supplied the plates. As a matter of fact he even thought they would go broke. He was right about that, too.

Our suggestion was to make the same offer, but improve on it. So he did: he offered an additional piece of crockery, and a free gift of oven gloves to go with the set. He ran that offer for years; for all I know he still is doing so. He was able to outlive the competition because he had more margin, and he made a better offer.

Can you offer a good deal?

The moral is that your offer doesn't have to be original. It just has to be something that you are well placed to offer a good deal on. The deal doesn't have to be an outstanding one: in this case the cost of an additional piece and an oven mitt was minimal. All you have to do is to come up with an offer which is sufficiently appealing to a *very small* section of the public to pay off. If only one person in a thousand amongst the readers of a national paper buys one of those sets of cutlery and crockery, then the ad is extremely profitable.

That leads me to my second piece of advice: remember what business you are in and who your customers are. That's a very old adage, but it's vitally important. If you are in the china business, then you understand it: the customers, what sells and what doesn't, how much you can charge. You are best to stick to what you know.

This cuts both ways. Thus, if you have customers who have always bought china from you, you will be ill-advised to suddenly mail them with offers of garden seeds. They are china buyers; and to them you are a company that knows about china, not gardening. Your offer must fit your position: be compatible. However, considering what is compatible with your present business in an *imaginative* way can pay off splendidly. And perhaps the company which has given one of the best demonstrations of this is The Franklin Mint.

I used to be a consultant to this company, working for a man called Ed Segal. I learned a great deal from him, at a time in my career when (not for the first time) I was sure I knew everything. He taught me a lot about writing direct mail. He also told me a very interesting story about how the Franklin Mint managed to expand its business base successfully.

The Franklin Mint was, by coincidence, founded by another Segel; no relative – as you can see, the name is spelt differently. Joe Segel was originally in the advertising speciality gifts business, where he became something of a legend. But the best idea he ever had came as a result of seeing a picture of a queue of people buying the last of the US silver dollars ever to be minted.

This made him think about how keen people are to collect rare things (or things likely to become so). He conceived the idea of *creating* things for people to collect. Items on which he would confer instant rarity, by limiting the period of the offer. He started with medals. By the age of 42, he retired with millions of dollars. (He must have got bored, because a few years later he came back into business in the broadcast media field).

However, there's a limit to the number of sets of medallions, ingots and coins you can sell. Eventually you start to run out of themes. Or alternatively, you start introducing themes which are difficult to justify.

Thus, when I was working for Franklin, one of my colleagues there spent many months fruitlessly wrestling with a series of medals called 'Heroes of the Mexican Revolution'. The problem was that most of the featured heroes had done extremely unpleasant things to each other, and most other Mexicans, too. It was difficult to bring out their heroic side with any degree of conviction. Franklin, realising that they needed to do something else, decided to find something outside their existing field to sell. But they had the sense to stay in the *collectible* area. They invented the 'Ultimate Private Library'.

This was a limited edition of magnificently produced and bound classic works. As a matter of fact, so precise was their targeting that they deliberately avoided telling buyers *which* books the series contained. They appreciated that their customers were *collectors* not *readers*. *The Times* reported that the programme was so successful it created a world shortage of second-grade goat skin.

Today, the Franklin Mint sells just about anything you want to collect. Porcelain, furniture, decorated thimbles, plates, china dolls, vases –

anything you like, (unless of course, you know what you want to collect already).

Ask your customers

I never cease to be amazed at some of the things people think they can sell. On one occasion someone came to see me and wasted a great deal of my time trying to persuade me that what the world really needed was a little trolley that would carry two dustbins in it. He was absolutely obsessed with this. I asked him why this was so essential. He explained that he had two dustbins at his house, and that it made it easy to put them out for the bin men to collect.

I informed him that in my country home the bin men very kindly came out and collected the dustbins themselves; and my London flat was a penthouse so a trolley would be no use. He still went away convinced that mankind would be saved for evermore if somebody were to offer this product direct.

On another occasion a man came to me who had spent all his savings – and his family's savings, and everything he could borrow – putting the Bible on tape with a cast of actors. Net result: bankruptcy.

If you want to know what to sell, for goodness sake do a bit of research in advance. There are occasional inspired entrepreneurs like Joe Segel. But most of us are just fallible human beings. So don't invest in hunches; ask your customers. I cover this to some degree later on when dealing with research.

I applaud all kinds of research, but I must emphasise that people cannot tell you what they will buy until you ask them to part with money. One company used to get their customers into halls in groups, then show them potential products and get their opinions. They would then rank the possible products in order of appeal. After the session, the products were displayed at the end of the hall, and customers were allowed to take away the sample of their choice.

The first interesting thing the company discovered was that the customers *never* chose the products to take away that they said they preferred in the discussion. And the second interesting thing was that an infallible guide to what would sell (this was a rather downmarket audience being appealed to) was to leave samples out on the table until the company cleaners arrived. The ones which were stolen most generally turned out to be best sellers.

The truth is that people will tell you they like the product they think they *ought* to like. But when they have to buy or even get a free gift, they choose what they really like.

For that reason, the right way to start establishing how products are likely to do is to go through a simple sequence. First, write to people asking them which of a list of products, briefly described, they find most appealing. Then choose the products that come out best, and write sample mailings for each one. Test these mailings on your list, making it clear that customers will be able to buy the product later if and when it comes out, and giving a price, so that the offer is a real one. Then you choose the one or two products that do best, and start selling them seriously to your customers.

That's a very simplified description of a subject that deserves a lot of consideration. But one thing I would like to emphasise – and I make no apologies for saying this more than once, in different ways in the course of this book, because it is a mistake people *persist* in making – don't ask your customers (or anyone else, for that matter) what they 'think' of an ad or mailing. They are not critics. They are buyers. Even experts usually guess wrong. The ads people like are rarely (in fact almost *never*) the ones that do best.

What you really want to know about your messages is: do people understand them? And do they think the product in question would be useful to them, or is worth the price? All useful information to give you some idea (but no certainty) as to what is likely to happen.

How does it compare?

My next point is very obvious but much neglected. Compare your product with the existing competition. In what way is it superior? And if it isn't superior (despite the fact that you may be unwilling to admit it) then for goodness sake apply some objectivity, and see what you can do to improve it.

The ability of marketers to delude themselves about the wonders of their products and services is almost boundless. In practice the consequence of this is quite simple. A client comes along to you with a product and says it's superior to competition in every respect, and it's cheaper, and it's revolutionary. And so on, and so on. After a certain period of time it suddenly emerges that, 'Well, it's not *that* superior. There are in fact one or two areas where competition is better. And it isn't *that* cheap.' And so it goes. It's a process of disillusionment, which almost everybody in our business has experienced. It usually ends up when you find there is virtually no claim you can make for the product. It's just the same as everyone else's. The client had just fallen in love with it.

One point which many people ignore is: can the product or service be copied easily? If so, you may have something with such a short-lived appeal it's not worth bothering with. It's also important to check whether there are alternatives to your product – possibly from other suppliers. Products that may do the same job, even though they're not the same product.

Let me give you an example. The fax machine is a product which is competing with and making obsolete a number of services. Yet I do not think many people realised when it came out that it would represent an appealing alternative in some cases to telephone calls themselves, the mail and – one service which has definitely suffered – the telex.

Having chosen a product, you must also, pay great attention to quality. If you are selling merchandise, get several samples to make sure the product is reliable. Ensure, too, that it conforms to all the relevant authorities. If it has any health connotations, be *very careful indeed*.

If it's a service, then there is a wide range of factors you must consider. Principally, they revolve around whether you are going to be able to deliver what you promise – or at any rate deliver it with the speed and efficiency required. Eg: if you're offering to give people information when they call in, have you got the necessary infrastructure set up? Will your telephone communicators, for example, have the knowledge required or easily available on a database to respond to queries? Will you be able to send out the product quickly, properly packaged? All simple stuff; all very important.

Equally important is: have you got an alternative supplier? My hands tremble as I record this advice because 20 years ago I lost a small fortune (and many nights' sleep) because a supplier let me down when I was selling records in Scandinavia. More recently, we nearly lost a very large account because a supplier of personalised plastic cards let us down. On this occasion, thank goodness, we did have an alternative ready.

Pay the right price

My next piece of advice: negotiate carefully. There is the world of difference between someone who just buys, and somebody who *negotiates* to buy a product.

In 1981, we had occasion to look at the figures of two of our clients. In both cases, their advertising results were well above what we know the market average to be. But neither was doing well. The reason was quite clear when we saw the figures. Neither company had enough margin to make a profit on many lines. This was not through a deliberate policy of low pricing to get names. It was just lousy negotiating. So haggle. It can mean the difference between profit and loss. You may not like talking about money but when you go broke, you'll find yourself talking about it all night. In your sleep. (For advice on negotiating, see chapter seven.)

Linked to this last point is the need to make sure you have enough margin. How much is enough? The answer will come through testing, but as a rule, in lower-priced products (ie up to £20) you need at least 200 per cent gross margin on the cost to you. If you go below the £10 mark the margin should be even higher, assuming of course, that you are hoping to make a profit, and not simply 'buying' names.

In higher-priced products, you need less percentage margin. But don't imagine that simply by halving your price, you'll always increase your orders sufficiently to cover that loss of margin. You rarely will.

My next point is one to be read, marked, and inwardly digested.

Don't over order

When we first started working for one company the general manager showed us some of the products he was planning to sell. We were full of enthusiasm. Two products we all agreed couldn't miss were a new kind of calculator that worked by direct light so that it needed no batteries and a dictating machine which had a calculator on its reverse. Two in one. What's more, it was to be sold at a price lower than Philips were charging for a dictating machine alone!

The client ordered these devices by the container-full to get a keen price. And if anyone wants to know where to get hold of a large number of calculators that work without batteries, I can put them in touch with someone who has lots for sale. We never realised that nobody *wants* a calculator without batteries. Calculator batteries last a very long time indeed. They're no problem.

We did no better with the calculator/dictating machine. First, we didn't think very carefully about the market potential. How many people need a dictating machine? And what kind of people are they? The answers are: not a lot; and only business executives. Yet in order to get rid of the volume we had ordered, we had to go into mass circulation publications of general interest. There simply weren't enough executives reading these media to sell our product at a profit.

This failure may also have had something to do with the fact that a two-sided product like the one in question is almost impossible to illustrate. We had the front of the product on the left hand side of the layout and the back of the product on the right hand side of the layout. At first glance, it looked like two products. And the first glance is the *only* glance you get in selling off the page.

Moral: always order a test quantity. You may have to pay more to start with, but you could end up paying a lot less in the end.

My last suggestion is obvious, yet almost invariably ignored when people choose what they ought to sell. Talk to the people who are going to have to do the selling for you: the copywriters and art directors at your agency. As a matter of fact, even a biased creative chap like me is willing to admit that it's a good idea also to talk to the client service people. They have been known to come up with the odd good idea from time to time.

Remember, in the mail order business particularly, the message *is* the marketing.

You really need to have everybody in the agency convinced that they can create messages which will sell that product. For instance, a good copywriter and art director should be able to tell you whether a product is going to be easy to demonstrate in print or broadcast. – If you can't do that, then your chances of success are low indeed. Notice I said a *good* creative person. Make sure that when you're discussing your product you talk to somebody who is really first class, not an amateur. For that matter, I would suggest you speak to more than one set of creative people, if at all possible. You will get a more rounded view of your likelihood of success.

Where to look

You may wonder *where* people find ideas for what to sell. I am tempted to say either you've got it or you haven't; but that's an easy way out.
Here are some suggestions:

- Copy other people (like Chinacraft did) and improve on what they offer.
- Go to a 'syndicator' – a person who puts together mail order deals for people, in order to supply the product. But be careful that you have enough margin: it is not as easy for two to profit as one.
- Go to trade shows.
- Travel. Look at what is being sold in other countries.
- Read foreign papers and magazines. Look at the ads.
- Put together lots of items into a different combination. Like a set of motoring tools, or kitchen knives – both best sellers recently.
- Try a successful catalogue product. A collection of sewing thread in every colour of the rainbow is one example. Several companies have done very well with exercise bicycles, which did well in catalogues to start with and then moved into space advertising.

    Successful catalogue products don't always do well 'solo', but they often do.
- Try to sell something connected with your own favourite hobby or interest.

    One good friend of mine has lived off a business in rare coins for 30 years. It's much easier to work hard at something if you know and love the subject.
- Look at something presently being sold by salesmen. It could very probably be sold direct through the mail. And it is almost certain that you can use direct marketing one way or another to help you.
- When you've got started, don't worry. People will come to you with products.

Here are some personal views on the best products to sell.
I have always believed that the very best services and products to sell

are those which involve the minimum of administration and the maximum of continuity, preferably with the greatest possible mark-up. Thus, insurance is a wonderful product. There is no warehousing cost and you are merely selling pieces of paper, which you can print as you need them. And, of course, a continuity element is built in (except, perhaps, in the case of the burial expenses policy I mentioned earlier in this chapter).

My favourite example of continuity in insurance came about when I was approached to write a package for a product designed to sell insurance to babies. You may imagine that the average baby is not particularly concerned about insurance – so let me explain.

In this case, the communication was in the form of a letter to be placed in the 'Bounty Pack' given to mothers when they have just had babies in hospital. These packs contain information and samples of various products the mothers will find interesting. The piece I wrote simply suggested that at this wonderful moment in the parents' lives the one thing they would obviously be concerned with would be the future of their baby. It was, I proposed, a most appropriate time to consider the baby's protection and financial future.

This was a very successful pack. Certainly, from the point of view of initiating a continuing relationship with a customer I cannot see any way of starting much earlier. (Having said that, I have no doubt that somewhere, a wily insurance man has already considered sending mailings to ladies who are *expecting* babies.)

For much the same reason that insurance works very well, loans and other financial products are good direct marketing.

Any product which is simply printed paper – like a course on some subject – allows for big mark-ups. This is particularly so if you take a book and break it up into a series of lessons. A £10 book can easily sell for several times as much when broken up in this way.

The most extreme example of taking paper and giving it high value is with the collections of cards on subjects like cookery, which I mention elsewhere. The margin on that particular type of product is colossal.

I also believe that *any* product aimed at the business market has a built-in advantage. The business buyer is usually not the principal of the business so it isn't normally his money. At the same time, many business products nowadays are exceedingly complex and therefore lend themselves particularly well to the detailed explanation direct marketing can bring to bear.

My final thought on this subject of what sells and what doesn't: don't ask me – I'm always getting it wrong.

5

Positioning and Other Mysteries Explained

'This above all: to thine own self
be true.'

> Polonius's advice to his son Laertes.
> *Hamlet.*

'If I have seen further, it is by standing on
the shoulders of giants.'

> Sir Isaac Newton

Put your mind at rest: I have no intention of comparing the joys of positioning with the laws of gravity. But if Isaac Newton could learn from his predecessors, why shouldn't we?

The history of direct marketing is long. Back in the fifteenth century an Italian printer was selling books direct, almost as soon as printing itself had been introduced to Europe. He must have known something, because I believe the company survives to this day.

As early as the eighteenth century the great writer and wit Dr Johnson summed up in two sentences the principles that govern success in advertising – and direct marketing. 'Promise, much promise is the soul of an advertisement', he said. And when auctioning off Mrs Thrale's brewery, he told potential buyers: 'We are not here to sell off a parcel of vats and boilers; but to offer the potentiality of wealth beyond the dreams of avarice.'

Once you study the results of tests you learn very quickly how correct his thinking was. Firstly, advertising works best if you promise people something they want, not – as many imagine – if you are clever, original or shocking. This is not theory: in 1985 the Ogilvy Centre for Research in San Francisco set out to discover whether people buy more goods as a result of television commercials they liked. The answer, not surprisingly, was that they did. But what did they like? 'Emphatically not something original or clever, but something relevant', said the report.

Secondly, of course, people are attracted more by what something can *do* for you than by what it *is*. If every marketing director in the world, whether engaged in direct or general marketing, acted upon these two principles, I believe our industry's effectiveness would dramatically improve overnight.

Here are some other theories and principles you should find helpful, some dating back to the early days of modern advertising.

As I have already explained, today's direct marketing has come about largely as a consequence of social and technological changes which echo those that occurred in the ninteenth century during the Industrial Revolution. At that time, the technology which led to steam printing, for example, made both cheap newspapers and cheap mail order catalogues possible. Educational and economic changes created customers for the new mass-produced products – customers who were able to read the advertising that promoted them.

Sound advice on boasting

Soon, advertising started to produce its own trade organs. One in particular in America was called *Printer's Ink*, published by George R

Rowell, who also ran his own advertising agency. This is what he wrote over a century ago about advertising:

> Come right down with the facts, boldly, firmly, unflinchingly. Say directly what it is, what it has done, what it will do.
>
> Leave out all ifs.
>
> Do not claim too much, but what you do claim must be without the smallest shadow of weakness.
>
> Do not say 'We are convinced that', or 'Surpassed by none'. Say flatly 'the best' or say nothing.
>
> Do not refer to rivals. Ignore every person, place or thing except yourself, your address, and your article.'

Many people could learn a lot from that even today. Much copy ignores the facts and doesn't tell what the product is, what it will do, or how it has performed for others. Much copy overclaims. Much copy boasts. And much copy denigrates rival products – often a waste of time, because the reader ends up believing nobody.

Rowell's fame was eclipsed by that of John E Powers, a man who made a mint selling sewing machines in England (literally by the shipload) before going to America to write copy. Soon he was earning the astonishing sum for the time of $100 a day.

His secret weapon was the *truth*. He would have been a good soulmate for the late American advertising man, Charles E Brower who observed: 'Honesty is not only the best policy. Nowadays it is sufficiently rare to make you pleasantly conspicuous.' (You may wonder what happened to honesty when you look at what some big advertisers say. In Britain, for example, the railways ran a slogan for some time: 'We're getting there'. It had to be withdrawn because it infuriated the average traveller, who was all too well aware that many British trains arrive late. Unfortunately, advertisers squander prodigious sums saying what they would *like* to be the truth.)

But to get back to Mr Powers: his great discovery was that if you give people a *reason* why what you are saying is true, they are more likely to be swayed by your arguments. The fact is, people are suspicious – and the more seductive the offer, the more suspicious they tend to be. (On a TV programme in the UK some years ago a man offered people £5 notes in the street. Nobody would take them although they were perfectly genuine. They believed there must be a catch.)

Powers was *so* honest that one of his employers, John Wanamaker, founder of the great Chicago department store, eventually fired him in exasperation for running copy such as: 'We have a lot of rotten raincoats that we want to get rid of.' Or, '[The neckties] are not as good as they look but they are good enough – 25 cents.'

You may be asking yourself: does this advertising archaeology have any relevance today? The answer is an emphatic 'Yes'. Even to-day, few advertisers appreciate the importance of giving a reason why.

Suppose you are planning a sale. Believe me, you will do much better if you give a reason for it. 'Closing Down Sale' is more convincing than just 'Sale'. People think that if you are closing down you really *do* have to sell off your stock cheaply.

One shop in Soho had a 'Closing Down Sale' for 20 years to my certain knowledge. And four or five years ago the 'Closing Down Sale' of a London department store was so successful they decided to stay open – and did, for a whole year.

Would a salesman do this?

The most valuable single statement ever made about advertising is that it is 'Salesmanship in print' – I mentioned this in Chapter 1. This was said originally by John E Kennedy, the first copywriter with the American advertising agency Lord & Thomas. Because nobody else appreciated this fact at that time, Lord & Thomas quickly became the world's largest advertising agency.

I advise you, every time you plan or review anything, to ask yourself: 'Is this good salesmanship?' Direct marketing is so intimately concerned with salesmanship that you might imagine it is almost impossible to forget this fact. However, I must warn you that there are many alluring sirens lying in wait to seduce you as you make your plans or review your objectives, and they congregate particularly densely during advertising agency presentations. You will be amazed how quickly you can be persuaded you really ought to be 'building prestige' ... or 'letting people know what we are doing' ... or 'developing awareness'. The minute you hear phrases like this, start worrying. Your plans are almost certainly threatened. You should immediately sound the alarm and get back to salesmanship.

I don't mean by that you shouldn't be letting people know what you are doing, or that you shouldn't be building prestige or developing awareness – all these are very desirable. But never forget the *ultimate* objective: one way or another you want to make a sale – to persuade somebody to do what you want.

Good salesmanship has a cumulative effect. If your tone and message are consistent, you build a clear reputation. A reputation is worth a lot of money. If you go into any supermarket you can see this demonstrated quite clearly. Next to each other on the shelves are products which are as near as damn it identical save for the brand name. One, a brand which through consistent advertising has built a fine reputation, commands a higher price than another (often the unadvertised house brand of the supermarket). Research has shown that heavily advertised brands as a whole are substantially more profitable than brands that are lightly or not advertised.

Of course, reputation benefits the supermarket itself. Companies like Sainsbury or Marks & Spencer which have good brand names sell products which themselves can sometimes command a premium. Significantly, in recent years sophisticated financiers have suddenly realised that the value of a company can depend often on something which is not even mentioned in the balance sheet: the value of the brand names it possesses. A value which has been built up by years – sometimes generations of advertising.

Added value

James Webb Young, a famous creative director in the early days of J Walter Thompson, theorised that the purpose of advertising was to build into the product an added value beyond its physical constituents. This added value derives from the constellation of qualities which together make up the brand image.

One of the great names in packaged goods is Heinz. Probably its most famous product is baked beans. Other companies obviously make baked beans, but none is as successful as Heinz. Much of this has to do with the power of the Heinz brand. Indeed, one of my colleagues who advertised for a competitor recounts that they used to conduct regular taste tests to find out how their product compared with Heinz. The taste tests were 'blind', ie the brands were not revealed. Their product used to be preferred by consumers in the ratio of 2:1. The minute the brands were revealed, the very name Heinz changed consumers' perceptions. They preferred the Heinz product.

Jim Kobs, in *Profitable Direct Marketing*, tells the story of Montgomery Ward, the American catalogue company which wished to launch an automobile club. They tested the power of their brand name by doing identical communications to similar target audiences. There was only one difference: one file of prospects were told this was the Montgomery Ward Autoclub; to the others the name Montgomery Ward was not revealed. At that time the company was nearly 100 years old. It had a fine brand image. The name doubled response.

It is because of the importance of the brand that the word 'image' has emerged from the world of advertising and become general currency. Indeed, if one were able to calculate the money squandered as a result of that word, I suspect the sum would be colossal. How many times, for instance, do corporations imagine that the solution to some endemic problem like lousy products or second-rate service will be simply to have a new 'corporate image' created at vast expense by some specialist in this arcane art.

Your brand, and its image – or personality – result from what you are, what you do, far more than what you *say* about what you are and what you do. The way you have dealt with your customers, the products you have sold, the value you have offered, will do more for your brand and its image than anything else.

What is more, the consistency with which you behave and speak is of extreme importance. Wiser heads than mine have commented in the past that one mediocre advertising campaign run consistently for 20 years will do you infinitely more good than 20 brilliant campaigns introduced at yearly intervals. This is often demonstrated in advertising research where people are asked which campaigns they remember. The answer is they tend to remember campaigns which have run for a long time, despite the fact that in some cases they may not have run for many years. The moral is that once a brand image is established in the minds of the public it is very, very difficult to shift the public's perception of that particular brand.

Some advertisers are so obsessed with the importance of the brand that they devote nearly all their efforts to registering the brand name, to the point of not even asking people to try or buy the product or service. But the image is not the name alone.

Every communication you make affects the image your public has of you and your product. I once saw an excellent exposition of this point made by Jeremy Bullmore, a former chairman of J Walter Thompson in England. He showed a picture of a sign on a country road drawn in chalk on a rough piece of board. Scrawled capitals said: 'Fresh eggs'. The style and setting of the communication were perfect for the message and the product. An image of bucolic wholesomeness was projected.

Then he showed the same sign in the same rustic setting. But the message had been changed – though not the style of the lettering – to 'Flying lessons'. The audience roared with laughter. The point was made: who would want to learn to fly from people in such a place, exhibiting such a sign?

Unique selling proposition

Your brand image is primarily an emotional construct. Emotion is probably always more powerful in swaying people than reason, but people like to be able to rationalise their choices. This is where awareness of another advertising theory – the USP – can be helpful to you.

The USP, or unique selling proposition, formula was developed by Rosser Reeves, an ex-copywriter who became head of the Ted Bates agency in New York. He wrote an excellent book, largely dealing with this theory but also covering other aspects of advertising, called *Reality in Advertising*.

To establish your USP, you compare your product or service with your competitors. Then you determine one feature you have which no one else can offer. This is your unique selling proposition. It is this which you must promote singlemindedly.

A 1987 issue of *Marketing Week*, the British trade paper, gave a wonderful example of how little the average marketing executive understands the phrases he deploys with such gay inconsequence. The subject was 'Store credit cards'. A bank executive said: 'The whole point of a Marks & Spencer, Boots, Dixons or even Fortnum & Mason card is to bring people into the store – and to provide *a bit of a USP*' (my italics).

How a credit card can be a *unique* selling proposition when the same facility is offered by any number of retailers is difficult to comprehend. It reminds one of people who refer to things as being 'rather' unique, or 'fairly' unique.

Here are some typical USPs:

'Cleans your breath while it cleans
your teeth.' Colgate toothpaste.
'The too good to hurry mint.' Murraymints.
'There's more for your life at Sears.' Sears Roebuck.
'It ain't fancy but it's good.' Horn & Hardarts.
'The mint with the hole.' Polo Mints.
'It takes a tough man to make a tender chicken.' Perdue Chicken

And, finally, another gentleman in the chicken business:

'It's finger lickin' good.' Colonel Sanders

One of the problems with the USP is that you sometimes have to rely upon some pretty trivial points of difference to arrive at your proposition – as you can see from the list above. And although, for simple products a good USP may often supply a successful selling idea, I think it is difficult to arrive at one for complex services such as American Express or The Consumers Association.

However, comparing yourself against your competition to discover what USP may exist is a great aid to clear thinking. For example, I was able to improve results for Odhams' Kathie Webber Cookery Club by writing a headline which was simply a personal way of expressing a USP: 'My cookery cards mean you control your weight without giving up luscious food you love to eat.' This did well in the UK, and even in France, home of gastronomy. Moreover, subsequent approaches to selling this product revolved around this original thought.

Positioning: today's theory

A client once unkindly observed that advertising men go very deeply into the surface of things. I think there is truth in this. We are fickle and fairly easily impressed by new, fashionable theories.

Some of these theories reach the far shores of the ludicrous; and where better to find a ludicrous theory than an advertising agency whose very name has given pleasure to many over the years? The agency in question is BBDO – Batten, Barton, Durstine and Osborne – once described by somebody as sounding like a man falling downstairs. One of the founders, George Barton, wrote a successful book in the 1920s which put forward the proposition that Jesus Christ was the first great salesman. But I digress (because I enjoy it).

Returning to today, the fashionable theory at the moment is 'positioning'. An ugly word, but the thinking behind it is well worth your attention.

You might describe positioning as a synthesis of the two ideas of brand image and USP. In my view it is better than either. To try and explain what people mean by positioning, let me take you back 60-odd years and tell you a story.

What you do is the most important factor in success; what you say comes next. But sometimes, the way you say it can have great impact. This was demonstrated when, in 1919, a man called Dick Jordan decided to go into the motorcar business. He launched a car called the 'Playboy' with an advertisement which I have illustrated (see page 96).

You will immediately notice two things about this advertisement. First you can't see what the car looks like; second, there are virtually no facts about how it is made, or how it performs. You may think that these considerable shortcomings would prevent the advertisement from working. But they derive from Dick Jordan's problems, and the way he overcame them.

Mr Jordan didn't have much money. In fact he couldn't even afford to make the car himself – he subcontracted the manufacture. So he could hardly afford to produce a car which was technically superior, more rugged, or cheaper than Ford or General Motors. Even the design of the car was copied on the back of an envelope from a Packard custom model and 'bumped out of aluminium' as Mr Jordan elegantly put it.

What he did was to find a unique position in the marketplace: he sold the Playboy as a *fun* car – one which would be likely to appeal in particular to women, who were for the first time beginning to attain some economic power in America. The copy reflects this clearly.

The car may not have been rugged, but in keeping with the positioning, it was lightweight, and he put into it the new Delco starting and lighting system. This enabled him to talk about the fact that: 'Any woman could crank a car without breaking her arm.' And: 'Everything that women want in a car . . . to hell with the old mechanical chatter . . . like a woman likes to look to the man who likes to look at her' (whatever that means).

I actually think this is an appalling advertisement; however, it reflects the positioning of the product perfectly. And this is the reason why, no

This classic ad shows how you can get away with anything (even without telling people anything about the product) if your positioning is clever enough.
It also shows the power of emotion over reason.

Figure 5.1 'Playboy' car ad

matter how abysmal the execution, it succeeded, and the product was a howling success.

The Playboy was only sold for around 10 years; the company was liquidated, with a great sense of timing, in 1928; Dick Jordan and his partners made 1,900 per cent on their investment. In fact, as late as 1958, when Jordan died, everyone was still living happily on the proceeds. I do not know of a better example of the way clever positioning can overcome otherwise impossible obstacles.

Positioning is exactly what your commonsense tells you it is. Your position should reflect where you fit in the market; what differentiates you from your competitors – not merely in fact, but in the minds of your potential buyers. What they think about you is as important, possibly more important, than the truth about you.

The positioning statement

Positioning should be expressed through a short, simple *statement*. It should not be confused with a slogan, though if the positioning and the slogan can be the same, wonderful.

The purpose of the positioning statement is to be borne in mind and conformed to in everything you say and do. And it should not be forgotten that as in everything else in life, it may be a position you aspire to, as opposed to the one you actually have. When you conduct research you may discover that your customers do not see you the way you would like them to. That might be described as position 'A'. Then, based upon what you have learned about your customers, your business, the future of the market, and your own plans there will be a second position, 'B', which is where you would like to arrive.

The way you handle your customers from that point on will affect your position in their minds; as will where you advertise – upmarket media or downmarket media. So will the type of language you use when communicating with them, or the type of layout. Everything contributes in its own way to your positioning and to how effectively you move it from point A to point B.

If you are a new company, you start with a blank sheet, in which case you might like to remember a phrase I once read expressing the principle of positioning very well. I saw it in the most improbable place, written in a dead language. I was travelling through France and stopped at the Chateau of the former dukes of Clermont-Tonnerre. Inside the courtyard of that chateau the family's motto is inscribed. It reads: 'Si omnes, ego non', which one may roughly translate as: 'If everyone else does it, then I won't'. That is a thought well worth remembering: but do be careful. Don't be *so* different that you place yourself outside the mainstream of commerce.

William James the philosopher once quoted a carpenter who said: 'There is very little difference between one man and another; but what little there is, is very important.'

Be similar, but not identical might be a good maxim when looking at positioning. Look at the strong points of your competitors and see if you can come up with some unique twist which will mean you have everything they have – and a little bit more.

But what if you don't have any clear position in the minds of your prospects and customers, or – even worse – you are perceived as being inferior in several respects?

The first thing you can do is to offer a better product or service. That will almost invariably have a greater effect than anything else. The second thing to do is to ensure that whatever you do say about yourself is believable. You will remember my observations earlier about British Rail. Woolworths used to say in their commercials, 'The wonder of Woolworths'. Everyone in the country knew that the wonder of Woolworths was that anybody went in there at all – their stores were such a mess.

This was counterproductive. It reflected poor thinking about positioning. And such poor thinking is very common. Sometimes you can look at an individual advertisement and see that poor positioning is bound to make that advertisement fail.

Some years ago a company offered two monogrammed dressing gowns at a good price in the colour supplements. I thought the ad was unlikely to succeed, partly because the creative execution was not very impressive. A good product can always overcome that, but not if the positioning casts doubt on the company's veracity. In the advertisement for these dressing gowns, the company advertising was described as 'Britain's leaders in leisure goods'. They had never advertised before. This alone would get horse laughs from the readers. Secondly, to reassure the customers, the company was described as a subsidiary of Tate & Lyle, the giant sugar combine. Why should anyone think a sugar company knew anything about mail order or leisure?

The sad thing was that the company actually supplied many of the pack premiums to major advertisers. There was a good position there waiting for them if they only told the truth. They could explain that they knew all about buying good value products, that they supplied famous companies, that they had a big warehouse which could get the goods to you fast.

But they didn't bother. They used their imagination instead of telling the truth.

Research your positioning

Once you have decided on possible positionings for your product or service, it's sensible to research them and see which of them your target market finds credible and appealing. For instance, one of our clients sells a wide range of kitchens, bathrooms, bedrooms, doors, windows and the like to the public through retail outlets. We wanted to find out what the right positioning for them could be – and then reflect it in their advertising.

Accordingly, a number of lines were written, each reflecting a different position. I am going to give you these lines with a brief indication as to how consumers reacted to them. This should prove salutary if you ever feel tempted to boast or misrepresent what you offer.

1 'The best DIY store in town' – consumers appreciated that the stores were not DIY outlets, so this was seen as inaccurate.
2 'The ideal home improvement store' – consumers thought this dealt only in superlatives, which were glib and self-congratulatory.
3 'The store for top quality home improvements at value for money prices' – consumers thought this was not distinctive; it was over-used phraseology; nor did it appear credible – people expect to pay a premium price for quality.
4 'The home improvement store where service really is personal service' – the idea of service was good news, but not enough; products had to be good, too. In any case, this claim was seen as something other stores like Marks & Spencer could make.
5 'Find out what "the trade" has always known' – people had mixed feelings about the trade. Some thought of it in association with craftsmanship; others thought of cheap workmanship and cowboy operators.
6 'The store traditionally used by the trade' – here the same negatives aroused by the previous trade line came up, though in a better sense because of the use of the word 'traditionally'.
   One problem, however, is that the line implies such products need proper experience to install.
7 'Made to last by us. Sold direct to you' – this conveyed that the company was personally involved in the making of the products, as opposed to being an importer. Moreover, the line was seen as patriotic, because it clearly meant these were British goods. It also conveyed craftsmanship, durability and the good value you get by buying direct. Readers also appreciated that the line was to the point, not gimmicky. This line came out on top.

Successful companies tend to have a clear positioning from which they rarely if ever deviate – and then only with great care. I make no apology for reintroducing American Express. It was positioned single-mindedly for many years as 'the world's most prestigious financial instrument for business travel or entertainment'. This positioning came out in everything American Express did. For instance, the letter sent out to solicit new members which began: 'Quite frankly the American Express card is not for everyone ...'. This reflected the positioning so well that for many years in most countries of the world it was the most cost-effective direct mail used.

Positioning important to all

Even the smallest enterprise can benefit from thought about positioning. Here is the copy for an advertisement run by a small hotel in the West Country. Almost every word reflects very accurately the positioning of this hotel.

HOT HOME-BAKED ROLLS

Wine-laced dishes with freshly picked herbs. Scrumptious puddings with thick local cream are served in the beamed restaurant of
our small Georgian Hotel. Two miles Exmoor and coast. Phone
owner-chef Dick or Kay Smith, WHITE HOUSE HOTEL, Williton,
Somerset TA4 4QW. Tel: 0984 32306. Try a 4-day

BARGAIN BREAK

& save £30 per couple

You immediately feel the hotel is special. It is old fashioned. You get
good food. The people who run it do the cooking themselves. They even
answer the phone themselves – they must *care* about their business.
Their establishment is clearly positioned as opposed to a big impersonal
modern hotel. (And incidentally this excellent little advertisement even
contains an offer.)

One of the big questions about positioning is whether you should
position something as bought and appreciated by everybody or as
something to be aspired to and enjoyed by a few. Both positionings are
perfectly reasonable. One will make sceptics think that if everybody is
using it, then it must be good. The other, conversely, will make
prospects think that if only a few people have the taste (or money) to
enjoy it, it must be good.

Take American Express. If the American Express card is not for
everyone, it follows that you will not necessarily see it honoured in
every retail outlet. So, when competitors fault American Express – as
they do – by pointing out that their card is acceptable in more outlets,
the positioning itself helps defend you against these attacks.

Our agency's experience around the world is that the most important
thing to test is probably the positioning. Positioning can vary depending
upon the state of the market. A New England stove company found that
at the time of the mid-1970s' oil crisis stoves were bought as *efficient* log
burning alternatives to oil. This type of stove, which had previously
enjoyed less than 5 per cent, seized 50 per cent of the market for heating
in rural areas.

People became more sophisticated; the stoves sought further distribution; the oil crisis receded; and the positioning of the stove changed.
Split-run tests revealed that in this new, selective market, people were
more interested in the *looks* of the stove. As the stove began to
penetrate urban areas, split-run tests found that even referring to it as a
stove was a mistake. It became positioned as a 'fireplace'.

Sometimes the name alone of a product of service can imply
positioning. For instance, our client North West Securities finances
companies making capital acquisitions. They call the service they offer
'The Money Programme'. That title implies money *making* as well as
money *lending*. It makes more of a promise.

Positioning in tough markets

Positioning obviously becomes extremely important where competition in a market is fierce, especially if the differences between products are minuscule. A typical example is the mail order catalogue industry.

The NEXT company broke into the mail order market effectively by doing one thing: they promised to deliver goods to the customers within 48 hours, at a time when everyone else in the industry was talking about 21 days. This in itself said more about their dedication to serving the customers than anything else. At the same time they positioned themselves apart from the competition in something they said: instead of calling their catalogue a catalogue, they called it the Next Directory and gave it a distinctive visual style.

In the United States the Spiegel company, a very poor fourth in the catalogue industry in 1976 – and which looked like going nowhere fast – changed everything in order to conform to a new positioning. There was nothing to recommend the position they occupied at that time: dowdy, cheap, and selling just about everything to anybody who was prepared to buy. The architect of the transformation, Henry Johnson, decided he would reposition Spiegels as the store which combined the shrewdness implicit in buying direct and thus getting good value for money, with being chic. As he put it: 'It's smart to buy from a catalogue, but chic to buy from Spiegel.'

Based upon this thinking Johnson and his team completely restructured the range of merchandise offered, getting rid of items that were dull, dowdy, widely available elsewhere, or in some cases inconvenient to handle – like cut to size carpets, floor-tiles or garden huts.

Because they wished to move to a new upscale customer who was looking for added value rather than cheapness, they dropped items which sold primarily on price – even if they were selling in considerable quantities. As Johnson put it: 'We were going to become target marketers.'

They introduced high fashion items, designer clothes by people like Kamali, Liz Claiborne, Yves St Laurent and Pierre Cardin. Everything they did fitted in with the new positioning. They started charging for their catalogue. If it was free, how could it be desirable? As people planning to meet the individual needs of sophisticated people, they had to target more precisely. So they started breaking down their catalogue into mini catalogues aimed to meet particular needs.

It was spectacularly successful. Spiegel have pursued this positioning ever since. Today, 12 years later, they are running advertisements showing that celebrities like Bianca Jagger and Priscilla Presley buy at Spiegel.

In short, as I have already emphasised, what you say about yourself will never have as much impact on the way you are seen by your customers as what you *do*. Nevertheless, sometimes doing and saying can be combined very effectively. Indeed, the best advertisements and mailings generally *talk* about something that you are *doing*, as opposed to those which boast about what you think you do.

One instance of this is a campaign run by the Schwab company in Germany – a campaign created by our Frankfurt agency which proves once and for all that the Germans have a great sense of humour.

Each of the advertisements makes a free offer to readers if they will conform to some unusual, sometimes even bizarre, requirements. For example, in one advertisement the reader is offered a free washing machine if the family has more than 11 children. Ordinary people are advised in the same advertisement that they can buy the same machine from Schwab delivered, fully guaranteed and insured to their home for so many Deutschmarks. If they are over a certain height, they can have a free jogging suit with their initials on it. Once again, the general public is advised to buy the said jogging suit from Schwab. (In this particular advertisement, incidentally, a picture of a dog was featured, wearing a jogging suit. Some wag wrote in and ordered a suit for their dog, which the company duly made for them.)

This campaign, apart from generating inquiries, says something to the reader about the company: this is not just the usual inhuman catalogue company. A campaign like this will also influence the *employees* of the company a great deal. It is rarely appreciated that your customers are twice as likely to read your advertisements as other people who are not customers, and your staff are likely to do so to an even greater extent. They are probably influenced more than anyone else by what you say in your advertising – and your positioning.

Changing the rules

Another fiercely competitive business is that of the book club. The original concept developed nearly 60 years ago has hardly changed at all. Offer a very low-priced selection of three or four books for the opening order to recruit a customer, and then ask that customer to *commit* to buying a certain number of books at a higher price. Possibly the only significant development has been that of aiming certain types of book club at certain types of reader, eg a military book club, or a gardeners' book club, or a thriller book club. Attempts at positioning have been perfunctory to a large extent.

One exception which proved triumphantly successful was the case of the Quality Paperback Club in the USA which changed the rules of the game. By offering paperbacks they were able to eliminate the long-term commitment. The offer was three books for a dollar – you then buy as few or as many books as you like. This marketing thinking led to a successful new company. One, however, which came to full bloom only when it was positioned properly.

The initial advertising was relatively successful, but responses doubled when a campaign was produced (and you will not be surprised to know it was produced by us, in New York) which treated the customer as an intelligent person. Something which is implicit in the idea of the Quality Book Club.

A series of advertisements was run featuring famous literary figures. The one featuring Vladimir Nabokov, for example, had a headline set in Russian with a picture of the writer. Underneath was the English headline: '(Translation: 3 bucks. No commitment. No kidding.)' And in the coupon the line ran: 'OK. Send me 3 books for 3 bucks. Nyet commitment. Nyet kidding.'

An advertisement featuring Hemingway had the headline: 'Tres Libros por Tres Dolares and a Farewell to Commitment. No Bull.' Another successful advertisement ran: 'QPB. The book club that doesn't put pressure on its members.' Underneath was a cartoon which showed a devil poking a man towards two doors. The signs on the doors read: 'Damned if you do. Damned if you don't.' Under this picture, once again, ran the line: '3 books. 3 bucks. No commitment. No kidding.'

This particular campaign *halved* the cost of recruiting a member. The offer was not changed; the product was not changed; only the positioning and the way it was expressed: a book club as something to appeal to intelligent people, done with verve and style.

General advertising and positioning

If you look at the kind of brief which the general advertising agency will use to initiate creative work, it often has under the heading 'Objectives' two subheads. First, what the advertising is intended to make the prospect *know*. Second, what the advertising is intended to make the prospect *feel*. The thing it does not very often contain is a third heading saying what we want the prospect to *do*. Thus, much general advertising is an exercise in positioning.

The difference between what we, as direct marketers, do and what the conventional advertiser does, is that we want to *inform* people, we want to make them *feel*; but above all we want them to take some *action*.

It goes without saying that the positioning must be right. Indeed, there is ample evidence to show that the relationship between the position set up by the conventional advertising and the action demanded by the direct marketing is crucial.

In a number of cases, particularly in the United States, commercials have been run using a 'head and tail' which are the direct marketing element asking for some form of action, sandwiched around a core which is effectively a re-statement of the positioning commercial created by the conventional agency. Hardly surprisingly, this is highly effective.

Some of the points I have made in this chapter may strike you as blinding glimpses of the obvious. All I can say is that I have seen some very intelligent people make some dreadful mistakes over the past 30 years because they thought they were too clever to need to master the basics of our business. For my own part, I have found that occasionally reflecting that people do need a good *reason why* before choosing your product has made my task easier. And I have seen millions wasted by people who didn't appreciate that advertising is *salesmanship*.

I have also found that searching for the *unique selling proposition* is particularly sensible, not only when creating a promotional piece, but when deciding whether a business is likely to be viable or not.

My belief in the idea of *positioning* is total. By consistently conforming to your positioning you will have marketing which is targeted accurately, and you will start to occupy a clear place in the minds of your customers and prospects: a place from which it will be very difficult to dislodge you. In other words, you will begin to enjoy something very rare in business: a feeling of security.

Yet I am constantly astonished at how few people do bother to seek out the right positioning, or to find out how their prospects and customers see them today, with the object of improving the way in which they are seen tomorrow.

Of course, people in any specialist area love to make things sound more complicated than they are, just as the old mediaeval doctors had their hocus-pocus.

When I came to London to seek my fortune, having been falsely informed that the streets were paved with gold, I had to teach a trainee copywriter in my first job. A daunting task, not aided by the fact that he was undoubtedly much cleverer than me. His name was Gopal Krishna Menon, and we became good friends. He enlivened many hours telling me about his uncle, the famous Indian politican Krishna Menon.

I recall asking him on one occasion what he thought of the Indian mystics who were just then becoming prominent, it being the early 1960s. He looked at me in his portentous way, and replied: 'They are my fellow countrymen trying to make a living. I never knock another man's racket.'

I suppose you could simply call positioning finding your niche in the marketplace. A good old expression we all understand. But that wouldn't sound quite difficult enough – though it sounds like commonsense to me.

Commonsense also applies, I believe, to the planning of your direct marketing, which is our next subject.

6

How to Plan Clearly

'If I was you I wouldn't start from here.'
   Traditional rustic reply to a request for directions.

'Beware of making five-year projections, unless
you're thinking of leaving the company after
four years.'
   Stan Winston, Ogilvy & Mather Direct, New York

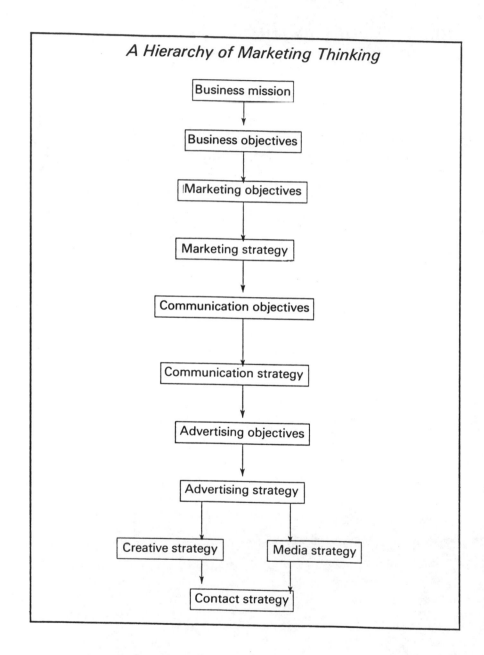

Figure 6.1. *A hierarchy of marketing thinking*

Once you have learned what your position is today, and where you would like to be eventually, you have to determine how you get there. You have to plan.

If you think the need for a plan is obvious, and therefore that everybody plans carefully, then ask yourself about the advertising most companies run year after year. Why, you may wonder, is there so little consistency in most cases? Could it be because people have *no* plan? Or because their advertising is created without any reference to the plan they have? Or possibly their business objectives change every year?

If you think this sounds improbable, let me tell you about the time I had to address a conference on this very subject – how to plan your marketing. The first thing I did was probably what you would do: I tried to find out what was going on. What sort of plans were people making currently? And with what objectives? How did they approach this important matter?

I was surprised at the responses I got. I had expected to discover that people's planning was perhaps less thorough than they thought it should be; or that they set objectives which were too ambitious; or that planning gave rise to heated dispute, even discord, within their organisations.

Nothing of the sort. Most of the people I spoke to had no formal business plan whatsoever. The whole thing was done by guess and by God. This may be another facet of that English amateurism I referred to at the beginning of this book.

Most of those who *did* have plans gave two reasons for them. One was: 'We have a plan because I have always had to do one every year.' The other was: 'We have a plan because head office in America insists we have one.' Few evinced any great enthusiasm for planning.

One man who is the head of a major advertising agency group said: 'I have banished these planning documents from my business. In my last job, I spent all my time making plans. Nobody ever seriously evaluated them afterwards to see whether a plan had been successful, and if so why; or if not, why not.'

A somewhat extreme view, you might think. But another authority, the head of Porsche Cars in America, said that when he was asked to submit a plan, he naturally consulted other chief executives to learn what they thought. The general feeling was that because of the unpredictability of life nowadays, it's almost impossible to make a plan which allows for what might happen in the future. For instance, two occurrences which have had a dramatic effect upon our economy, neither of which was predicted, were the oil crisis of the 1970s and the Stock Exchange crash of 1987.

Nonetheless, I believe that with all its faults any plan is better than no plan at all. As circumstances change, you can adapt your plan. If you have no plan at all, you are operating in a very unsafe way. And if your plan is in your own head, what happens if you get run over?

You need a written plan which is carefully thought through. However, clear planning is so contrary to human nature that all the endeavours in the world seem unable to enforce it. Our frivolous minds seem to prefer the erratic path, to go scampering after every enticing little thought we conceive.

The importance of planning has been recognised to such a degree in the advertising business that there is now a vogue for a new type of individual: the *account planner*. A colleague of mine has defined this person as being 'the customer's representative within the agency' because he or she will try to establish what the prospect or customer wants, how they think, how they should be approached, and what effect the advertising has on them.

The account planner is a hybrid. He is not an account handler, though he will spend time with both the client and the creative department. He is not a researcher, though he will often commission and evaluate research. He is a thinker: it's his job to make sure things *are* properly planned. This job used to be done (and still is in many agencies) by the account handlers, working in concert with the creative department, the research department and the client.

Eleven steps to success

Winston Churchill said on the subject of writing: 'Use simple words everybody knows, then everyone will understand.'

You may have realised that I have a *passion* for simplicity. This is because I do not find it easy to understand new ideas quickly, but if I have simplified them enough in my own mind, I can communicate them quite well. This approach suits me, and I have found it suits most other people, too.

However, before giving you my simple recipe, let me outline the *formal* approach to planning in direct marketing. I am indebted to my partner in London, Rod Wright, for the sequence shown on p 109.

You must start with your **business mission**. What are you trying to achieve? From this you will be able to establish what your **business objectives** should be over the planning period. For example, in 1992, Europe will become a single trading area. This gives companies opportunities to branch out more easily into other European markets. It also poses problems. Are other people going to come in and steal the market share you have at home?

In preparing a plan for the next five years, therefore, no major European company can really ignore 1992. Suppose your business mission is to become the world's pre-eminent office systems company.

As 1992 approaches you may have to adapt your business objectives to allow for the way you think your Italian or German competitors are going to behave. Whereas previously you might have been determined to drive them into the ground in your own home market, you might now simultaneously wish to protect your position in your own country, whilst gaining a foothold in their home markets.

From these intentions you will derive your **marketing objectives**, and flowing from them your **marketing strategy**. Thus, in your own country your objectives may be to protect your present customer base whilst also trying to recruit as many new customers as possible. In the markets where you wish to gain a foothold, you might have objectives such as setting up an effective sales and distribution network so as to be able to recruit new customers and service them properly.

Your marketing strategy to achieve these things will depend upon your original business mission. If you wish to be pre-eminent, have you decided that this position will be achieved through low prices? Or should you maintain a high margin, but add value, and thus be perceived as a company that concentrates on quality, not price?

I'm going to assume the latter, because all indications are that it is by far the safest position to occupy. This brings us to step five: your **communication objectives**. They might be to tell your customers and prospects that you care more about them, which is why you give them added value.

Your **commmunications strategy** – step six – may well be to build a database of customers and prospects, which you can use to initiate a long-term relationship. This relationship will centre upon communicating the added-value message we've just mentioned to *individuals* (and you will notice that here the emphasis which we as direct marketers place upon the individual comes into play).

The next step, of course, will be your **advertising objectives**: what precisely do you want your advertising to achieve? What do you want your customers and prospects to *know* about you, to *feel* about you? And what do you want them to *do*?

Because you've followed such a logical sequence, it's all fairly simple by now, isn't it? You want them to *know* you're a company that doesn't offer bargains; it offers added value for your money. This demonstrates in a practical way what you want people to *feel*: that the company cares about them. And, of course, what you want them to *do* is to initiate a relationship with you if they are prospects; and to cement further the relationship they have with you already if they are customers.

The **advertising strategy** would be to convey certain messages through selected channels. You might choose television and public relations to project the image you are aiming for. Sales promotion and special offers in advertising could add names to your database. Then you might use direct mail and telephone to build a stronger relationship with each individual – and, of course, make sales.

Your next step – number nine – is your **creative strategy**. How ought you to say the things you wish to say? What tone of voice are you going to adopt? What type of creative executions do you feel are appropriate?

Your **media strategy** will be considered at the same time. If you're going to go on television, which channels? If you're going to use PR, which publications do you want to get coverage in? The specialist press? The national press? The same thing will apply to how you might wish to build your database. *Where* are you going to make your offers?

Finally – the eleventh step to success – comes your **contact strategy**. At what points in the relationship between you and your prospect and customer are you going to communicate? When and how will you use the media you have selected to reach each prospect or customer?

Here, once again, the emphasis you as a direct marketer place upon individuals as opposed to masses is critical. Take two people you wish to sell to. From studying the database, you may discover that one is much more likely to respond to a certain offer than another. Or perhaps that one is more likely to influence an ultimate purchase than another. That means you can afford to spend more money to contact and communicate with that particular individual. This, in turn, will influence your contact strategy.

Let me give you a simple example from real life. In Belgium we wished to sell a new copier to customers who had obsolescent machines. A most attractive offer was made to our prospects; an offer so appealing that we felt it worth not simply mailing but telephoning these people in advance of the mailing to tell them this offer was coming. The response rate was so high – in some cases over 50 per cent – that it certainly justified a follow-up on the telephone, and even a second mailing after that.

Your contact strategy will, of course, be influenced not merely by the appeal of the offer but by other decisions you have made earlier on in your planning process. In the case history just mentioned it was extremely important to the client that the obsolescent copiers be replaced.

In fact, any part of the planning process must be viewed in the context of all other parts of that process. To take a simple instance, replacing obsolescent copies may be a goal which flows from your business mission as much as it does from your marketing strategy. This will give it a high priority. It might even pay to lose money on such an exercise: to put in place a very expensive programme. On the other hand, if it were of low priority then a much less intense contact strategy might be called for. Possibly just a single mailing.

Five questions you must answer

You can plan as much as you like, but to make your plan *work* you must look at things from the point of view of the people you are addressing. You should be viewing your own company and your own objectives from their perspective. It is from their perspective that any communication must be planned. If what you do does not make sense to them, to those vital individuals, you are heading for trouble.

If you look at it with them in mind, here are five simple questions I think you should be able to answer.

1 **Who** are you trying to influence?
2 **What** are you selling?
3 **Why** should your prospect buy it?
4 **Where** will you find your prospect?
5 **When** should you speak to them?

To adapt an old saying: this is all so obvious, anyone could have thought of it ... but surprisingly few people do.

Over the page I have illustrated two advertisements for a marking gun, a little machine that prints price labels onto supermarket cans. They both appeared in the same publication. They are interesting because they demonstrate how easy it is to ignore some, if not all of these important questions.

The first advertisement with the drawing at the top actually appeared in colour, so it cost more than the second, in black and white. Yet it pulled only a *fraction* of the number of inquiries.

The reasons for this are:

- It is not clear immediately **what** the product is. The art director has chosen to use a close-up drawing which makes it look like some strange ship's prow.

    Even if the confusing illustration were removed, the headline would not tell you what the product is, because the headline is a contrived piece of work which conceals the nature of the product.
- It is addressed to the wrong prospect: the **who** is wrong.

    The copy makes the point that this type of gun can go round corners, thus making the job of marking easier. But the person who marks the cans – almost invariably a junior employee – does not buy the guns.
- Because it is addressed to the wrong person, the reason for buying – the **why** – is wrong.

In the advertisement we created (in black and white) for the same product it is *instantly* clear what the product is, and what benefit it confers on the prospect, who is the supermarket owner.

The advertisement was in fact written by my former partner, John

By paying attention to the first three of the 5 W's, the second ad did ten times better than the first. You can see WHAT the product is, WHY it should be bought, and it is aimed at the person WHO is the best prospect.

Here you can't see instantly what is being sold. The benefit is aimed at the user of the marking gun – not the person who buys it. In the next ad, the message is to the profit-orientated manager.

Figure 6.2 Pitney Bowes advertisements

Watson – one of the best copywriters I know. It got ten times as many replies as its predecessor. The reason, I think, is that John did a lot of research into what goes on in supermarkets as a result of bad marking. He also examined (or as he always says, 'interrogated') the product itself very carefully to see how it worked. And he thought carefully about the motivations of anyone wishing to buy such a product. Quite clearly, money is the major issue. In addition, of course, he was able to tell a much longer and more convincing story than was told in the first advertisement.

Apart from the factors I have mentioned above, which revolve around the creative thinking before the job was done rather than the execution itself, I think another 'W' has been ignored in *both* ads. And that is **where** to reach the prospect. In my experience direct mail is almost invariably a more effective way of getting responses from people in the grocery and supermarket industries than is advertising in the trade press.

What is more, if I am right, then the mailings could have been *timed* to fit the journey cycles of Pitney Bowes salesmen. The **when** would have been better handled. Indeed, if a proper database had existed at that time, the company might have known what *kind* of supermarkets would find these guns most appealing; at what times they were most likely to buy; and even who the relevant influencers, specifiers and makers of the ultimate buying decision were. Thus the whole exercise would have been carried out infinitely better.

The first W is the most important

You will not be in the least bit surprised to hear that of all the five Ws, in my view the *first* is the most important. Everything else is to some degree a matter of fact; but 'Who' involves individuals, and they can never be neatly categorised. Yet thinking carefully about what makes them do the things they do is vital. And sometimes the answers are most surprising.

A few years ago I was particularly struck by an article in a Sunday paper about a Japanese company. They had a real problem with the slipshod typing coming from their UK office. Requests, directives and exhortations had no effect. The girls in the Tokyo office had the idea of adopting a *personal* approach to this problem. They sent signed photographs of themselves to their counterparts in the UK. They started to make friends. And this direct, personal link did the trick.

People don't care about impersonal companies. They care about other people. And they make decisions for emotional reasons rather than rational ones. I can't implore you strongly enough to think about people and what they are like.

I spent a very frustrating day some years ago driving to see a totally uninterested prospect on the south Coast. But I got something out of it.

Talking to the man I went with, I learned that he had once worked for Sir Charles Higham, a legendary pre-war advertising figure. I asked him what this famous man was like.

'I once took him a piece of copy. He looked at it and put it down. Then he pointed to the wall of his office where there was an enormous blow-up of the FA Cup Final crowd. "Those are the people you are writing for. Now go away and do it again."'

It would seem that advertising tycoons are quite similar whichever side of the Atlantic they come from. Fairfax Cone was one of the founders of Foote, Cone & Belding. Apparently whenever he saw a piece of copy he didn't like he would look over his glasses at the writer and ask: 'Would you say that to someone you know?'

It is all about *people*. From thinking about them you arrive at what will persuade them. You cannot make them do what they don't want to do, or change their beliefs: you have to go along with what they want.

When I was speaking at a conference in Monte Carlo in 1982, one of my co-panellists was the beautiful Marie Dumont. She had written (like a true Gallic intellectual) a very acute rationalisation explaining why she had been successful in selling magazines to French women. 'You must be able to sense the way women are feeling at a particular moment . . . to catch that sentiment and to ride with it,' she said.

How true! We cannot *create* feelings. We must learn how the tide is running in people's minds, and float our messages on its surface. But *how* do you find out what your customers are thinking? One of the best ways is the most obvious, yet how many do it? Read their letters. Sometimes this will tell you more about them than any staged focus group or research project.

Keep in touch

Ours is an interactive business. You will be amazed how much people like to communicate. This is particularly true of the English. A Dutch bulb grower wrote to all his customers throughout Europe, politely saying he hoped their gardens were doing well. From most countries he got the odd reply. From England, he got letters by the thousand.

If you're starting up on your kitchen table, you will naturally read the mail. Don't stop doing that as your business prospers. Keep in touch. If you're not in the mail order business, then make a point of meeting your customers. This is something which in my experience the majority of senior executives don't do nearly enough.

By reading correspondence, you can learn the most surprising things. I once wrote advertising for a headache relief powder. One letter we got was from a woman who used it to soak her tired feet. Whether this would have led to a whole new advertising approach I don't know – but that letter told me a lot about my customers.

Sometimes, meeting customers can be a more hair-raising experience than you might imagine. In the 1960s I worked for a fashionable advertising agency called Papert, Koenig & Lois. My Creative Director was a well known US copywriter called Joe Sacco. He was extremely keen on people going out to see the customer. I well recall arriving in a rugged part of London's East End and trying to explain to a very large man at eight o'clock at night that I had come to talk to his wife about washing machines.

From Joe I learned the importance of translating people's ordinary needs into the emotional messages that make them buy. I also acquired a deep distrust of judgements made by advertising and marketing people. Joe had been largely responsible for a detergent campaign which, universally execrated by sophisticates, was nevertheless the most successful ever: the 'White Knight' campaign for Ajax detergent. Research revealed that women hated dirt and saw their lives as a constant battle against a rising tide of filth. If only they could make it all disappear as if by magic . . . if only someone would come along and do the job for them!

In the White Knight campaign, that's just what happened. To the chant of 'stronger than dirt', a champion on a white charger dashed everywhere touching things with his lance, and turning them white. 'Abysmal! Ludicrous! Puerile! Insulting!' cried the advertising pundits. 'Stunning! All records smashed! A miracle!' said the sales figures.

The campaign transformed the balance sheet of Colgate Palmolive. For the first time ever, they suddenly became real competitors to Proctor & Gamble and Unilever. It succeeded everywhere in the world, in all sorts of transmogrified versions, like the White Tornado – a sort of climatic detergent – and the Missisippi gambler – a dream-like figure wearing a white suit who waltzed round the kitchen with the housewife, obliterating dirt.

If the research on this concept had been accepted literally, then the campaign would have been rejected as too fanciful and far out. If the experts had been listened to it would never have got to first base. I believe this is also true of the Marlboro cigarette advertising – probably the most successful campaign in its category ever run.

So look at the research, and listen to the experts by all means – but neither will be as important as your ability to understand your customers and their emotions, and apply that understanding imaginatively.

How to understand your customers better

Julius Rosenwald, the great merchant who begat the mighty Sears empire in America, said that he wished he could stand on both sides of the counter at once. What a wise observation; for it is only if you can look at things from the customer's point of view as well as your own that you can understand how to sell to them.

For many of us this poses a problem. The more you succeed in business, the greater your income becomes and the more your personal circumstances change. Thus you become more and more removed from the market. (In fact, now even the new recruits to our industry tend to come from highly educated middle class backgrounds – the kind which militate against any understanding of ordinary people.)

I have already suggested you should read the incoming mail from your customers, and meet them whenever possible. Here are three other intelligent things to do – particularly if you fear you may be moving in an increasingly rarefied atmosphere:

1 Talk to your salesmen or telephone girls; sit in on their sales pitches, listen to their conversations with customers.
2 Go shopping in a street market at least once a month. While you are at it go and sit in a crowded pub and listen to ordinary people.
3 Invest regularly in group discussions amongst your customers, or street interviews. Get your creative people involved in these. Even if you have no specific objective, I am sure you will be surprised at what you learn.

By doing all these things you will undoubtedly find it much easier to understand all those people out there, what it is they want out of life, and how to talk to them in language they understand and appreciate. You will also be vastly entertained.

One of the things you will certainly learn is that people very rarely devote as much time to speculating about the wonders of your advertisements and mailings as you do. Indeed, they are almost entirely indifferent to them.

For this reason, they do not spend much time trying to puzzle out what you're trying to say. So if you don't make it extremely clear what it is you're selling right from the start you are on a hiding to nothing.

What is the product?

One instance of this, which in fact pointed up a number of other rules, like 'don't be too clever', came in the case of two advertisements for the same product. It was an industrial type of vacuum cleaner being sold off the page. The price was good, and the product had the unique characteristic that it not only vacuumed up dirt; it could also pick up small pieces of debris, such as glass or stone, and even liquids.

One advertisement for this product had the headline: 'The Jet Stream eats almost everything. Only £54.95'. And above it ran a line of captions saying: 'Devours dirt'; 'Scoffs leaves'; 'Guzzles water'; 'Gulps glass' over some very imaginative cartoon drawings. Many people in our agency at that time thought this advertisement was so clever and creative that it would sell extremely well.

Another advertisement for the same product had as its headline: 'Now, a high-power vacuum cleaner that picks up liquids too. The Jet Stream 850 from Shelton. At only £54.95, it actually costs less than ordinary cleaners'. The copy went into great detail about the product, and a series of photographs showed the machine in action.

The straightforward – even dull – approach was astonishingly successful. The clever approach was so disastrous that the gross sales did not even cover the cost of the space. Why? Because the successful advertisement told you instantly what the product *was*. It also gave you a couple of good reasons for buying it in the headline. And the information was presented in a way anybody could understand quickly.

The unsuccessful ad had a headline which was meaningless unless you knew what was being sold. In addition, an important element in the successful advertisement lacking in the unsuccessful one was that it *showed* clearly and convincingly with photographs what the headline said the product would do – I call this 'word-picture lock'. The other advertisement did *not* show clearly what the product did. It also relied on cartoons, which may have been entertaining but were not as believable as photographs.

Since these advertisements ran I have seen the results of a series of studies which show that if a picture and a headline do not reflect each other and the product, consumers simply do not understand what is being advertised. And if they don't *understand* what is being advertised, it is very unlikely they are going to *buy* it.

In fact showing a thing and saying what it is at the same time is usually the best way of communicating. I remember years ago reading that words and pictures working together are up to five times as effective in communicating ideas as either on its own. When you begin to plan your communications, one thing you must devote a lot of time to creating is this one compelling combination that conveys the essence of your product or service and its benefits.

You can probably think of famous examples of this yourself. The best I can summon to mind at the moment is the famous graphic used by Hertz for many years of a man magically descending into the driving seat of a car, with the line 'Hertz puts you in the driver's seat'.

Flop into success

A much simpler example dates back to the start of the THB&W agency in 1977. In those days, we were takers-in of other people's dirty linen. If someone had a hopeless product, we would ask them to give it to us and see what we could do in the hope of getting all that business. It was good training in a hard school.

One company gave us a product they were about to sell off as a job lot.

The product was described in the existing advertisement as a 'Regency Ensemble'. Could you tell what that is? I couldn't.

In fact it was a carved beech case which contained a set of dials: a clock, a thermometer, a hygrometer and a barometer. All with a regency-style pediment atop. The existing headline made the bathetic statement: 'Functional things can be beautiful, too.' The writer had obviously not thought too long about the problem of how to describe it. He had simply given up.

Knowing the company in question, a bunch of cheapskates, I suspect he hadn't been given too much time to think about what he was doing. Consequently, he had not given much consideration to the people he was aiming the ad at. They were relatively uneducated customers who wouldn't recognise an ensemble if it came up and kicked them in the teeth. It was a word they would never use.

The new ad we prepared revived the product for another year. But it was not remarkable: it simply told people what the product was. The main headline ran: 'The "Regency" 4 Instrument Clock Forecaster.' And in an overline it described each of the functions it performed. It *showed* the product and *told* you what it did. Word-Picture Lock.

This advertisement attracted attention as well as money. It was parodied by 'Punch' magazine. This is the headline they ran:

THE CHIPPENDALE 4-MODE HOME COMPUTER

The overline ran:

Hand-worked luxury for the discerning, sophisticated few – at prices just a fraction of those you would have to pay in Hollywood, Belgravia, Paris, Honolulu or parts of Rome.

This was followed by:

Wake up to the technological miracle of an appliance lovingly fashioned by Black Forest craftsmen in solid, natural, satin-look, creamy-beige balsa – and embellished in 100% tin.

I once showed this parody to a prospective client. He gazed solemnly for a while, then said: 'I don't think it will ever do well.' I formed the conclusion that the man was solid balsa from the shoulders up. We got his account but he proved difficult to deal with. People with no sense of humour are one thing you don't need to add to all your other problems.

Why such vagueness?

Why *do* people fail to describe products or services accurately? I think the reason is composed of one part sloth, one part cowardice and one part presumption.

Sloth being the unwillingness to spend time working out how to describe something accurately. Cowardice being a lack of faith in what is being sold, leading to the belief that if you come right out with what it is, nobody will want to buy it. And presumption because the writer *presumes* people know what you are selling simply because there is a picture of it, or a vague description.

Some may. But many won't. And if so, you have automatically lost a high percentage of your potential sales.

A very common fault is that the writer takes refuge in word-play, thinking this will substitute for information. This is rarely the case. You must work out how to describe what you're selling, and do so as precisely and briefly as possible. If it sounds boring, say it in a more interesting way, or get someone else to do the job – someone who *believes* in the product or service. At some point you will *have* to tell people what you're selling. You might as well get on with it.

The average advertisement is seen for a few seconds. If you were to start in the morning when you get up and count the number of advertising messages you're exposed to, it runs into hundreds. Every poster. Every commercial. Every newspaper ad. Every magazine ad. Every bus side. Every sign in a shop window. They're all screaming for your attention. And that's not including the mail and door drops that reach you every morning.

Accordingly, you want to know *instantly* what the product or service is. What's it all about? What's in it for you?

The last is the most important. Sometimes the most effective communication may not in fact start by showing the product or describing it. It may start by concentrating on its benefits. In any case, until you have clearly defined and written down what it is, you will have a problem.

This demands that you subject the product or service to rigorous examination. Look at it. Play with it. If it's a piece of merchandise, drop it on the floor. Tear it apart. Analyse it. Think about it. List all its characteristics, then look for the *buying* proposition. People often talk about *selling* propositions but I always prefer to look at it from the customer's angle. In terms of benefits, not attributes.

Thus, the attribute of a car may be that it will go in seven seconds from 0–60 mph. But the buying proposition – the thing that will turn you on – is the exhilarating sensation of power and speed you experience; the ability to overtake quickly; to get away from the lights faster than the next car; or accelerate out of trouble when you see someone coming towards you as you overtake.

Who knows where or when?

The remaining two Ws are concerned with your choice of media, and your timing. **Where** and **When** will you meet your prospect? They are covered to some degree in the chapters on media and database. In some ways these questions are more easily answered than the other three Ws: Who, What and Why.

There is one maxim I would like to emphasise to you, because it is far too little appreciated. It is this: your customers want to buy when *they* want to buy – not just when *you* want to sell.

One of the great US mail order success stories is the LL Bean company which sells outdoor clothes and tackle. In a period when they increased their number of catalogue mailings from two to thirteen per annum, their sales grew tenfold.

Many direct marketers communicate with their customers too rarely, in the fond belief that for some reason they will all be in a mood to buy exactly when the six-monthly catalogue or special offer comes out. This is a somewhat arrogant assumption. It may be true that most people are more likely to purchase a number of things just before Christmas or in the springtime. But don't put *all* your faith in this.

A better way of looking at it is that if you give your buyers more opportunities, or excuses, or reasons to buy, then they will. Study of them and their characteristics will help you produce appropriate rationales. Here are a few examples.

- 'It is now a year since you first became a customer of ours. I would like to thank you for your association with us, and as a gesture, make the following offer to you.'
- 'I see it is your birthday next week. We have, therefore, taken the opportunity to review your investments with us, and come up with some recommendations which we hope will prove appropriate, based upon what we know about you.'
- 'The budget is coming up, and it is likely that the Chancellor will radically alter the system for tax relief. This is, therefore, a good opportunity for you to . . .'
- 'Although *you* are one of our best customers, we have never had the pleasure of dealing with your wife. Accordingly, may I suggest . . .'

You probably get the idea. The more you communicate, with good reasons to communicate, the better you're likely to do.

Moral: you may easily be able when planning media to find out **where** to reach your customers, but don't underestimate the number of occasions **when** you should hit them.

Where your money will do most good

In this chapter I have looked at planning from two very different points of view. From within, as it were; starting with your own organisation's objectives; then, from outside: how what you do affects your customer.

Clearly, your customers are only affected (or not) by the communications you finally make. The customer is not interested in – or even aware of – all the effort and planning which leads to those communications. Yet this process is not carefully conducted, then those communications will not do the job they should. That being the case, where should you direct your attention, your time and your money to gain the greatest benefit?

The answer to that, in my experience, is almost invariably *not* where most companies often do lavish most of their attention, which is frequently in two areas: concern about how much it's all going to cost; and concern about the minor details of the communication which finally goes out.

Take the case of a client of mine who wrote lamenting the prodigious *fee* he was having to pay for a new mailing pack. You will not be surprised to know that despite the air of lordly impartiality I have tried to preserve in these pages, I was just as interested in the subject of money as he was.

My initial reaction (biased perhaps) was to point out what a splendid investment it was, and what a wonderful mailing pack it would be. This argument, based largely upon my own belief in the excellence of our work, struck me, upon reflection, as somewhat weak. Accordingly, I thought further about what the investment he was about to make could achieve, and whether it was money well spent. Let me therefore outline to you what could happen to the mailing we were discussing and see what conclusions one might reasonably come to.

This mailing was planned as part of a series of tests. It was being sent out in the first place to 50,000 prospects. If it did better than the existing control mailing, it would become the new control. That meant it would then be rolled out to over a million names this year, and next year it would be used again. If, at that time, it continued to do better than any tested alternative, it would be rolled out once again.

As it happens, this particular client is international. This other mailing could then be adapted for use in many other countries. In fact, quite possibly millions of pounds could be spent on this particular mailing – *if it proves good enough to beat the existing control.*

And if it *did* prove to be that good, it would generate millions of pounds of additional profit. But initially the main point of argument revolved around a few hundred pounds more or less. Now I am not suggesting for a moment that businessmen should not be concerned about getting good value for money. I think it's very important. But it is even more important that that concern should be directed properly.

A hundred extra pounds – even a few thousand extra pounds – will enable the agency to apply more resources to this particular problem, think harder, concentrate more on that mailing. That time, bought by that money, could well make all the difference between having a new control mailing or just another run-of-the-mill effort.

If the agency looks at the job and says: 'Well, there's only a limited amount of money; we can only spend a certain amount of time and effort on this,' and the mailing isn't as good – and doesn't do as well as it might do – then what will happen in the end?

The answer is simple: possibly more money will have to be spent to achieve the results that might have been reached. Maybe hundreds of thousands of additional names will have to be mailed. Or, quite possibly, a new mailing will have to be created. Indeed, if you reflect upon what that mailing *might* have done, in terms of its worldwide and long-term potential, that initial saving could be exceptionally shortsighted.

Fight for time

Now you may be thinking that I am talking about a very special case for a particular company where large sums of money are involved. Not at all: the principle we can derive from this little story applies no matter what size your company may be.

What I am talking about really is not money, but time and effort. In my view you are best advised to apply most of your time and effort *early* in the direct marketing process. Because if you don't, you will almost certainly end up spending a great deal more *later*, trying to put right the results of doing things on the cheap to start with.

The moral is that simple. Fight for as much *time* as possible, as much *effort* as possible by everybody in the early stages of your programme. Fight for investment in research. Devote money and time into considering your positioning. Into discovering more about your prospects and what they want. Into learning about the likely reaction to your mailing packs. And when creating and producing that creative material, look for the best, not the cheapest.

You will be astonished how much time and money you will be able to find when, in the end, the work that you skimped fails. All because you didn't give sufficient consideration to getting it right in the first place. You will be amazed how much frantic effort you have to devote into developing new offers (often in a hurry) because the one you threw together to start with, without thinking carefully (or paying enough), flops.

A famous author once observed: 'That which is written without effort, is generally read without interest.' My experience is that that which is *planned* without effort, is generally read without much interest either. And very frequently that which is done on the cheap can cost extremely dear in the end. As an American colleague of mine once said to me memorably: 'What you end up with is four monkeys in a back room churning the stuff out.'

7

Media: A Different, More Flexible Approach

'Statistics are a highly logical and
precise way of stating half-truths
inaccurately.'

    NASA archives

'He reclined in a somnolent posture.'
    Stanley Holloway, referring to Wallace,
       the lion that ate Albert

If you have spent much time in agency presentations, you will be aware that when the media man stands up many clients adopt a somnolent posture.

Media is not an easy subject to make interesting – indeed it is not even easy to make comprehensible. But it is very important, since the correct selection of media is often the prime determinant of success.

Moreover, if your background is in conventional marketing it is vital that you understand the significant difference in approach to media employed by direct marketers as opposed to general advertisers. You may have to forget some things you have always taken for gospel.

Five major differences

The professional direct marketer's approach to media differs in five ways to that of the general advertiser. All these differences stem from the three 'Graces' of direct marketing which I enumerated earlier.

First of all, you speak to individuals rather than masses; second, you test to discover what works and what doesn't – and adapt accordingly; third, you think in terms of a continuing series of communications.

Here are the five differences you should bear in mind:

1 The various media do not enjoy the same relative importance conventional marketers assign them.
2 The effectiveness of media is often evaluated differently.
3 Schedules and budgets have to be designed to make allowances for a great deal of testing.
4 The concept of repetition is viewed in a different way.
5 The effect of space size is regarded differently.

Let's look at these important differences one by one.

Different weight

The relative weight assigned by a direct marketer to each medium will be almost the reverse of that given by a general advertiser.

The mailing list – be it a rented one, for instance, or a selection of names from a particular database – is the medium you will rely on most. Other media, which you would scarcely mention in general advertising, are very important, too. Door-to-door drops, take-ones and inserts are typical examples.

The telephone now plays such a significant role that it is the largest single promotional medium in the United States, with $42 billion expenditure per annum on the last figures I have available. However, this includes both outgoing communications and inbound communications. In some countries unsolicited outbound telephone communications are forbidden. Therefore the role of the telephone will vary according to the legal situation in your country.

Television, in many countries the number one general advertising medium, is usually a secondary medium for the direct marketer – though its use is growing fast.

The potential of television has scarcely been exploited in most European countries because of the very limited amount of commercial time available. In the United States, on the other hand, television is a major direct marketer's medium. Radio enjoys even less attention than TV nowadays, though in the 1940s and 50s in the USA it was described by a knowledgeable friend of mine as 'hot as a pistol'. However, it remains a powerful medium, particularly for generating leads for financial services.

In particular, a new type (well, really an old type that has re-emerged) of programme is making major inroads. This is also true on television. This is the advertorial: a programme which may last for as long as half an hour dealing with such matters as how you can become inconceivably rich by following the advice of an advisor. Or, for that matter, how you can improve your golf game beyond all recognition, or even catch monster fish with a flick of the rod. Programmes on how to dress better, or make-up better, or even how to buy jewellery, all do well. It is often forgotten that consumers are far more thirsty for useful information than many advertisers realise. We are often so intent on *selling* what we have, that we forget that helpful facts often do the best selling job of all.

Posters – a major medium for general advertisers almost everywhere in the world – are of relatively little interest to us.

In short, if your background is in general marketing, you must rethink your priorities when you become a direct marketer: just about the only equivalent medium in general and direct is the press.

Individual impact versus cost

A simple way to look at the various media is to relate them to how much it costs to reach an individual. Not surprisingly, the more it costs to reach each individual, then by and large the greater the impact will be on that individual.

Thus, if we describe personal selling as a medium, then it is certainly the most expensive one. On the other hand, generally speaking, nothing will have greater impact on a prospect or customer than another human being talking to them face to face.

The telephone, the most expensive 'advertising' medium at our disposal is the one which has the most impact next to personal selling. After that, we have direct mail – not as expensive as the telephone, but still a potent communication because it reaches individuals and can, of course, be personalised and tailored to fit the information obtained from your database or rented list.

Next, we have the insert – the chameleon of the business. That's because an insert can be used in so many ways and can appear in so many guises. It can be something that you include in one of your regular communications. Or it can be sent out with some merchandise. Or it can be bound into a publication. Or it can be free-standing in a publication. It can even re-emerge as something stuck through your door, or placed as a 'take-one' at point of sale.

Nearly all these types of insert will attract less attention from the individual than a direct mail shot, but usually more attention than – for instance – a full page press advertisement. Of course, when it is used as a 'take-one', it is almost impossible to predict what impact an insert might have – it depends almost entirely upon exactly where the material is sited.

Nevertheless, generally speaking I would say that all the media I have listed so far have a greater impact in terms of reaching the individual than TV, radio and the press. On the other hand, of course, all those three media are relatively inexpensive in terms of reaching large numbers.

Obviously all the instances above are general guidelines, not universal truths. For instance, the poster is probably the medium with least individual appeal, but you have to make allowance for particular cases. A poster on a highway is almost useless to the direct marketer – it's virtually impossible for the passing motorist to respond. But a poster at a place of work can have considerable individual impact.

Figures not the only indication

In making your media selection you will obviously consider the demographic make-up of your prospects or customers – their location. their physical and financial characteristics – and also their psychographic characteristics: what kind of people are they?

The calculation then ought to be quite simple: how many of the right type of people can you reach for a given sum in a particular medium? This is – put very simply – the way in which general advertisers tend to make their media plans before proceeding to the equally important matter of how good a deal you can get from the particular medium to reach those particular people.

Direct marketers have learned, however, that the media which appear to give the greatest number of likely prospects do not always prove as responsive as they ought. Some media appear to attract more responses than others, even though they may seem to have near identical profiles. You can take two newspapers which ought in reason to deliver a similar type of prospect in similar numbers for a similar cost, yet one will prove to be far more effective than another. These are facts you will learn only from experience and from studying your results. Moreover, they are constantly changing, as publications change. This means you must be unusually sensitive to what is happening day by day. You must be alert, and ready to alter your plans.

Fortunately, because you are *measuring* your results you don't have to rely on guesswork or computer analysis. But this does place unusual demands upon the direct marketing media planner. Perhaps greater in some ways than conventional media planners face.

Test budget

As a general advertiser, you may plan how you are going to spend your budget at the beginning of the year, place the ads or commercials . . . and that's more or less it. Retail is the outstanding exception, of course, where frequent swift change is called for. But in most general advertising you may, for example, have an autumn and spring campaign, but there is relatively small requirement for change. (I once spent half an hour listening to one of our clients complaining bitterly that his mainstream agency had been running the same ad, fundamentally, for 15 years . . . and collecting 15 per cent every time it ran. I wish it were that easy for us.)

In our business, we know just what the results are of each mailing or ad. We are constantly trying new approaches. New sizes. New formats. New lists. New publications. For this reason, it is always wise to set aside a percentage of your budget for testing. You must have loose scheduling, too. You must be ready to switch your money around dependent upon the results you are getting. Such and such a publication may suddenly stop pulling as well as it did previously. A mailing list that used to work well for you last year may suddenly flop. Another may suddenly start improving. Or for that matter the market for your particular product may suddenly turn sour. You must stand ready to change your plans instantly.

In summary, the very idea of a fixed sum to be spent each financial year or season is not sensible for direct marketers. The issue is: how much can I afford to spend to acquire a prospect, or to produce a sale from a customer? And within reason, as long as you can meet that figure and you have the money available, then keep spending.

Conversely, if you suddenly find you are not getting the cost per response you want and can afford, then you have to find either a more effective communication, or a more effective medium – and pare your spending until you have done so.

Winning the battle

Marketing is a form of war. You are trying to gain and retain 'territory' in the form of market share or – as I prefer to think – individual customers. This sort of thinking led many years ago to media men thinking in terms of 'domination'. The idea was that you could dominate a particular medium either through repetition, or through big spaces.

In fact, in the 1950s the Ted Bates agency in the United States conducted a number of studies which tended to indicate that once you had covered a certain medium to a certain degree you were better off spreading your net further and going to other media than spending more money to dominate existing ones.

Much earlier, some interesting research was conducted in the United States in a related area, which ought to influence everybody's thinking. In 1912, a man called Shryer studied what happens when you repeat advertisements. He learned that if you run an ad a second time immediately after you have run it a first time, it does not get better results. It generally does worse.

Almost every direct advertiser finds this to be generally true. Perhaps the only exceptions I have come across have been in financial advertising where the credibility of the advertiser was important. Until prospects had seen the advertisement once or twice they were worried about whether they ought to do business with that particular company.

Yet how many times have you heard space sellers try to persuade you to take a *series* in exchange for a discount? You probably recall the pitch: 'People may not notice it the first time. But if you keep running it, they will eventually get round to replying.' The truth is that your prime prospects, the *cream* of your market, will tend to reply to the first ad. To get the same level of response again, you'll probably have to wait a little while until more prime prospects emerge.

This does not mean you can't repeat ads. It merely means you ought to carefully consider the right interval between repetition. And what is that? Well, it depends on three factors:

- the size of the ad (the smaller it is, the more often you may repeat);
- the interest of the product (the greater the human appeal the more frequently it will run); and
- the circulation of the medium (the larger the circulation, the more often you may repeat).

Of course, you must use your intelligence in following these guidelines. For instance, my former partner Brian Thomas (at that time marketing manager at a major catalogue company) was offered a full page in a major national newspaper – the *Sun* – one day after he had already scheduled an ad. Knowing the fall-off would be heavy he was very reluctant to run it, particularly because he had no time to alter the copy. However, the paper was desperate to fill the space and offered him a deal he could hardly refuse.

To his surprise, the second ad pulled 80 per cent of the results of the first. This was far higher than he expected. So although the response did fall as the rules say it should, by seizing his opportunity he did well.

What happens when you change the size

The other way to dominate a medium is, of course, by buying large spaces. We have to go back to the work of a Mr Strong in New York City in 1914 to learn what a dubious idea that can be. He published a book which showed that, on average, in terms of response, if you assign a rating of 100 to a full page ad, then a half-page carrying identical copy in the same place in the same medium does not pull 50. It pulls about 68.

A quarter-page pulls about 49, whilst a double-page spread will only pull about 141. That means a quarter-page is *twice* as responsive as a full page.

You may wonder whether those old greybeards in the 1900s knew what they were doing. Well, the same research has been repeated since. By Vic Schwab, the famous copywriter who ran Schwab and Beatty, one of the first good direct advertising agencies; by Gallup, and by Daniel Starch & Staff. They all came up with the same result to within two percentage points.

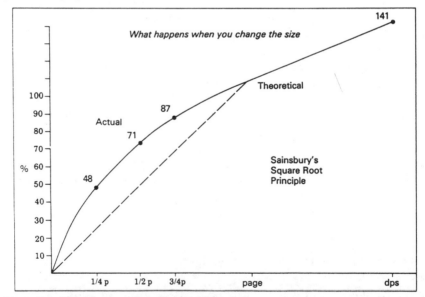

Figure 7.1. 'What happens when you change the size'

This graph demonstrates what research has shown about space sizes. The important thing to remember, though, is that for a smaller space to be cost effective, the content must be exactly the same as the bigger space.

So beware the lure of large spaces unless you need a large space to tell your story fully and you make use of *all* the space. However, it's important to remember that long copy very often tends to outpull short.

So you may need a larger space to do an effective selling job. On top of that, there have been exceptions which prove the rule: cases where simply taking an ad and making it larger has proved not only more effective in *total* numbers of responses but *pro rata*.

Once again, only testing will discover the truth for you and your particular product, but these guidelines generally prove to be worth following. Certainly, it's not wise to start with an unnecessarily large space to tell your story.

Much of what I have said does not square with the way conventional marketers plan their media, particularly in respect to these last two points. But these figures are not based on opinion, they are based on results. Conventional advertisers, who don't have to measure their results, believe in 'impact' and 'prestige'. Happily, their beliefs fit their pockets. For is not the easy way the most profitable? It's much easier to take large spaces, repeat them frequently, write short copy and change it once a year, isn't it?

The media recipe

The media you choose will obviously depend on your objectives, and what you are selling. You certainly cannot divorce creative considerations from media planning. If you are selling a set of records, there is a strong argument for considering radio which allows you to use sound. If you are selling a complex financial product, then you will need room to tell your story. You'll probably be considering a flexible medium like direct mail.

But if you are in any substantial way of business, you will almost certainly be considering more than one medium. This is where we come to the media mix – or recipe. This is the judicious selection of the right media in combination to achieve the right effects.

Thus, a car company might use television or posters simply to communicate awareness of a particular product and show off its looks. They might then use national press and magazines to convey more detailed information, using the local press – perhaps backed up by direct mail and radio – to encourage people to come in and test drive a car. Direct mail and telephone can be used to stimulate loyalty and repeat sales.

From reading this book so far, you will know where direct marketing should fit into your overall marketing objective. And since you are looking at how you treat an individual, rather than the way you reach masses of people, you ought to consider carefully the *sequence* of communications most likely to get the best results, bearing in mind how much you can afford to pay to get a lead or a sale.

Suppose you were introducing an expensive new business product. You would want in the first place to make sure you were reaching the right people. You might test the telephone against a question-naire mailing to identify the appropriate decision-makers. You might simultaneously announce to them that you are about to make a special offer which they should keep their eyes open for. You might then send out a mailing detailing this offer. And, if your response were high enough to justify it, you might send out a follow-up mailing or even telephone call shortly after the mailing came out to give it greater impact. This is all part of the strategy mentioned in chapter six.

Once you have these people's names on file, you would then be thinking how quickly you ought to re-contact them, and how often, because obviously they might not be ready to buy your product when you first approach them. Other considerations might be conducting a test of the appropriate trade press to see whether couponed advertising would prove as cost-effective in locating the right decision-makers as the telephone or direct mail. (In my experience it never does.)

Timing critical

Another factor to take into account would be timing, not merely in terms of what is the best time to sell a particular product or service, but how you should co-ordinate the timing between two different media. For instance, it is always a good idea to time direct mail to coincide with major general advertising pushes.

The timing and type of media you select will, of course, always be determined by the situation of the individuals you are approaching. Thus, when successfully promoting the British Automobile Association's very competitive car insurance rates, MSW Rapp & Collins in the UK faced a simple problem: in this country only a certain number of people are in the market for new car insurance at any given time. To run a national campaign over a finite period would not make sense.

The objective was to 'trawl' for prospects – to catch them at the time when they were likely to be considering their forthcoming car insurance decision. The solution was to devise 10-second television commercials which just said: 'Looking for a good deal on car insurance? Call us now.' This seemingly simple solution was one nobody had thought of before. Previously, people had been running free offers in advertisements to collect people's names and then re-contact them at the time when they were considering car insurance.

What I am trying to point out is that media planning is very much a *creative* process. The best media people are keenly aware of it. The worst remain chained to their sets of figures. The best work is produced when the creative people and the account planners, the media people and the client all get together and consider the problem from *every* aspect, and thus come up with a plan which takes advantage of the potential synergy between the different approaches to a particular problem or opportunity.

Having considered the background to the subject, what are the media available to you; what are their relative strengths and weaknesses?

The seven media at our disposal

1 Direct Mail

I am constantly amazed that I managed to make a living for so many years in this business without knowing nearly as much as I should about direct mail. I was very lucky.

As I have already pointed out, direct mail is probably your principal medium. It is particularly useful for testing, and for building the long-term relationship with your customers as individuals which you are aiming for.

As I have also indicated, direct mail is the most expensive medium open to you after the telephone, per person reached. On TV you can measure hundreds of impressions for every pound spent. In direct mail you can reach two or even three people for a pound. But they will, if you plan properly, be the right people. People you can speak to *personally*. And with direct mail, as you will see in our chapters on testing, you can test an infinite number of variables.

Other advantages include:

Selectivity
You can target with great precision, using the information available to you from your database or what you know about the list you have rented, and you can use personalised printing techniques to add impact.

Flexibility
You can, of course, choose when you mail, but more importantly, you can control what goes out. It is not a medium with only two dimensions like the press. You are not restricted to a limited space, or time as on TV or radio.

So, having a careful eye to the costs of posting, you can tell as complete a story as you wish when mailing to people, using any kind of illustrative technique or device (like a pop-up) you like. And It is also very easy to vary direct mail packages for testing purposes, in terms of the number of pieces enclosed and the messages on those pieces.

Big results
If you were lucky enough to sell one £50 product just once to one in a thousand (0.1 per cent) of the many millions of people who read a major national newspaper, you could retire for quite a long time. Even one in 10,000 readers (0.01 per cent) responding would be very satisfying.

Compared to that, direct mail produces enormous percentage results, though these don't always mean instant wealth.

What sort of results? Well, for years the magic figure of 2 per cent used to be quoted by people who didn't know this business. Where this figure came from I do not know. But let me give you some idea of the sort of results you can sometimes expect.

A major UK catalogue company could quite easily expect between 10 per cent and 15 per cent response rate when offering a new catalogue in a mailing.

Where you are simply offering the opportunity to enter a competition and win something, you can expect much higher results. Twenty per cent is not at all unusual. Fifty per cent is not unknown. This applies to consumer and business-to-business.

In fact, basing your thinking on some putative response rate is not good. One of our clients in the Far East was outraged when our agency only produced a 45 per cent response rate. He felt his product was so marvellous that 80 per cent or 90 per cent should reply to it. Some optimist.

The issue to address is: how many responses do I need to reach an acceptable break-even, based upon the financial criteria I have already set up? The answer to that will depend entirely upon your own business and the tests you conduct.

However, I digress. The important thing to remember is that direct mail can be very profitable when approaching relatively small numbers of people compared with the press. And the big percentages make it an obvious test medium. Above all, it is the way you normally reach your most important group of people: your own customers.

The one-piece mailer
Another fast-developing format. Changes in printing technology have led to the design of machinery which can, with one pass, create pieces which, after folding, act as complete mailings in themselves. In effect, you have a very low-cost mailing all made from one piece of paper.

A one-piece mailer can be used as an insert or as a pure mailing piece. Its variety of applications makes it a potentially very powerful weapon.

However, the principal advantage of this kind of format (which includes the ability to *personalise*) is that you can incorporate a letter, order form, brochure ... even a catalogue if you wish. All printed at once, from one sheet of paper. When you tear open the outside envelope, out they all tumble. Very involving.

We have tested these mailers in various ways. They rarely (in my experience) work as well as the conventional mailing in an envelope in terms of percentage response. But because they cost so little, they can be more effective, particularly when you are going for inquiries or sales requiring a relatively low commitment.

The answer, again, is to work out how much a sale is worth to you, and use the more cost-effective format. You could be pleasantly surprised.

The co-operative mailing
A medium which, so far, is relatively underdeveloped in most countries. But I think, with the postal costs we have to pay, it is bound to develop much more.

Incidentally, postal rates in some countries are so high that it can pay to mail in bulk from elsewhere. This gives you a creative edge, too. On more than one occasion we have been able to mail from the US to customers in this country with gratifying results, whilst our Milan agency on one occasion sent a mailing to retailers from the US which was highly effective.

The co-operative mailer which goes out to a specified list can take the form of a 'card deck': a number of cards of a particular size all put in one envelope. This is particularly effective for selling business books. People love to pore through these cards and make a selection.

Another form of co-operative mailing is a long strip divided into spaces and folded into a concertina to get it into an envelope. This too is a very cheap way to reach a well targeted group of customers and has proved very effective for business-to-business, particularly for getting inquiries.

If you do have the opportunity to go into a co-operative mailing like this, then make sure the offer you are making does not conflict with one that someone else is making. Unless, of course, yours is a better offer; in which case you will do even better than if you were out on your own.

2 Door to door drops

Door-to-door has many of the virtues of direct mail, but in less degree. By definition, it is less selective, since the logistics of delivering to a particular list using door-to-door would make it uneconomic normally.

Obviously, this medium is suitable if you are in a door-to-door selling business: double-glazing, swimming-pool installations, home improvements, for instance. You can arrange your canvassers or salespeople to follow up immediately after a drop has been made.

What are the advantages of door-to-door?

May be half the cost
Door-to-door is obviously cheaper than direct mail since you have no postage to worry about and no list to buy. It could cost as little as half as much.

Less control

Unfortunately you can't always be sure what people who are supposed to stick literature through doors actually do with it. There are many hair-raising stories of vast quantities of leaflets being furtively slipped down drains. For this reason, the more reputable companies have inspectors who monitor the activities of those who do the job. Moreover, the Post Office offers this service.

Therefore, make sure you are dealing with a good company. I recall a while ago having a drop scheduled for a client which was supposed to go to the financial area in the City of London. He was somewhat surprised – and we were embarrassed – when one leaflet arrived in Berkeley Square, Mayfair, several miles away from the City.

Quality controllable – but . . .

Of course, the *quality* and *content* of a door-to-door piece can be controlled. You have the same flexibility in that respect as with direct mail. But the results will be much, much lower.

Ernest Palfrey, an alumnus of *Reader's Digest*, conducted several tests a few years ago which directly compared door-to-door with direct mail. He sent out identical packages using the two alternative means of delivery.

. . . Less effective

Door-to-door was 52 per cent less effective than direct mail. This, of course, does not even take into account another important factor: direct mail can usually be addressed to the specific name of the recipient; door to door can't. And, of course, you can find appropriate lists of people with a special interest in your offer which, of course, would enhance response significantly.

My advice is only to use door-to-door for products of pretty universal appeal, or because you have need for large numbers of leads regardless of cost. An interesting sidelight, by the way, is that in some countries the postal service is so appalling that door-to-door becomes extremely attractive.

Dr Alberto Foglietti in Italy discovered a few years ago that door-to-door in one Italian city was *more* effective than the post. Another puzzling piece of information is that the Italians seem to like receiving direct mail more than any other European country according to recent statistics. Perhaps this is attributable to their sheer delight at receiving anything whatsoever through the post.

Door-to-door magazines.

One particular door-to-door activity of great interest is where a magazine (usually full of offers) is dropped through household doors.

It has been used in this country to some degree, and can work very well. In Scandinavian countries it is one of the most popular media of all.

Postcode classifications

In some countries it is possible to target both direct mail and door-to-door drops more accurately as a result of databases developed from information available in the first place from census statistics.

These statistics enable a particular list or a particular locality to be broken down into relatively small groups of households which are *likely* – but not certain – to have characteristics in common.

The principle involved is quite simple. First of all demographic information is extracted from the electoral register. This will provide information on household composition by size, sex, age, mobility, and the length of time a particular household has lived at an address.

In addition to this, it is possible to identify the likely type of building presented by the address, be it an apartment, a detached house or a farm, for example. Other significant information can be overlaid, such as the result of any financial searches which have been conducted by the courts.

To give you an idea of the sort of thing I mean, let us take one particular database of this type. This is the Mosaic Database developed by CCN Systems in the UK. On this database you will get the address, postcode (and the number of other houses sharing that postcode) as well as demographic data such as the composition of the household, type of address and any information available from the 300 census variables which tell you something about this type of address.

The only thing that this sort of database will not tell you is information you can only obtain from your own dealings with a particular house-hold. For instance, if you are a credit card company you can take a particular postcode and calculate the likelihood of the people in that particular area being amongst your card carriers. In this way, you need only mail those areas you are interested in – be it the ones where people are more likely to accept your card and are therefore better prospects, or contrarily, those where you have poor penetration and wish to improve it.

Since I am not a world expert on this subject, I will simply advise you to look very carefully into this sort of database which in my view is a very valuable tool – particularly so when planning proposed outlets for retail chains, such as banks. You can, for instance, very quickly estimate where you are best advised to site branches to give maximum effective penetration of an area without overlapping nearby other branches.

3 Newspapers

Newspaper readership varies widely throughout the world. For this reason newspapers can be more effective as a medium in some countries than in others. For instance, in the UK and Japan – both small countries – the newspaper is a very valuable medium indeed.

In America, on the other hand, until recently there has not been anything you could really call a national press with comprehensive coverage, though *USA Today* is beginning to offer something very similar to this. I have no doubt that new technology is soon going to make it possible to produce a much more effective national press in that country and other large countries.

Another reason for the power of the press in the UK in particular is that we simply seem to like reading newspapers. The last figures I saw indicated we were the world's most omnivorous consumers of them.

Project fast
The press is powerful, pervasive, and quick to pay out. In a business based on testing, this last is a characteristic hard to overemphasise. You can test one week, and two weeks later you can proceed to roll out a successful advertisement based upon your results with a fair degree of certainty.

Test availability
Moreover, there is quite a degree of availability for testing, both in terms of A/B splits and geographical breakdowns.

Uncertain quality, not enough colour
You do not control the quality of the print in the press, so for certain products you may find that it is far from suitable. Until recently colour facilities were very limited in the press in many countries, but colour availability is now increasing as a result of new technology.

The press has one additional benefit: it is usually less costly to test than direct mail, TV or inserts. And the ability to project fast enables you to make swift and profitable tactical decisions.

4 Magazines
Magazines, in which I include the colour supplements many newspapers incorporate, are another important medium with significant advantages which counterbalance the problems of the press – but with one major disadvantage. This disadvantage is so important that I shall give it first.

Long copy dates may invalidate test
You may have a lead time of weeks before you can actually place an advertisement in a magazine. Add to this the time it takes you to conceive, plan and prepare such an advertisement and you can have a major problem with a magazine.

This is because sometimes a product which looks very good now can be quite out of date by the time you run your ad, particularly when we are talking about technological products.

I recall, for instance, a camera offer made by one of our clients which represented unusually good value when we prepared the ad. Between the time the ad went to the publication and the day it appeared prices for this type of product had dropped so fast the offer turned out to be no more than average in price terms, and the ad lost money. This is not unusual at all in product categories like that. Pocket calculators and computers are others to be chary of.

Better reproduction

Of course, a magazine will usually offer you better colour facilities than the national press. Because you don't control the production of the magazine you can (and should) make sure somebody goes down to look at the work on the presses. You are about to invest quite a lot of money. And if you don't do that, you certainly ought to keep a very sharp eye on the proofs.

I utter this advice with particular emphasis to agencies. Clients tend to get very, very excitable indeed about the reproduction of their products. I imagine this is probably because it is one subject which anybody can be an expert on, assuming they have good eyesight. In reality you don't have to worry too much because I have found time after time that appalling reproduction has had very little effect whatsoever on results, even for products where you would think looks are very important. Indeed, I have come to the conclusion that the public is purblind.

Pulls over long period

Magazines keep pulling in responses for months, and even years. I remember preparing an advertisement to sell swimming pools for my late brother. Two years after it ran in a publication with only about 50,000 circulation it was still producing replies.

Often a good test medium

Magazines tend to offer a fair range of test facilities both in terms of regional and A/B splits. Some offer outstanding opportunities in this area.

Let me quote for you what is offered by the *US TV Guide* – the largest publication of its type in the world.

- 106 separate geographic editions, which can be purchased individually, ranging from 58,000 to 2,500,000 in circulation.
- A guaranteed weekly circulation (1987) of 16,400,000 copies reportedly adds up to pass-along readership figures of 39.3 million adults and 7.2 million teenagers.
- Because it prints two-up, you can get perfect A/B splits of black and white ads in 74 editions.

- The four-colour sections in the front and back allow for perfect A/B splits in eight major markets.

So, it is difficult to imagine a more perfect medium for testing. Nor one which at one fell swoop, once you have tested, you can roll-out to such an extraordinarily large number of people at the same time.

Inserts for tests
The magazine insert is – as I point out in my chapter on testing – a favourite format of ours. It offers almost unlimited test opportunities. You could test ten different inserts in one publication if you wished.

Total control
Because you control the quality and content, you can use any creative technique you like, without fear that some printer at the publication will screw the reproduction up.

I regard the insert as peculiarly valuable for another reason. This is that the insert, by its nature, is something of a hybrid. It isn't an ad; it isn't a mailing – it has characteristics in common with the two. Once you have found an insert that works effectively, it is not difficult to develop it into a mailing or into an ad, whichever you prefer.

Use many ways
The insert you place in a magazine can easily be used in other ways. As a bounce-back in your own merchandise when it is sent out; as a billing stuffer; as a 'take-one' in retail outlets; or as a piece to go out in other people's mailings or fulfilment packages.

Many of the most successful direct marketers employ inserts as their number one medium. And they seem to work whether you are dealing with a relatively up-market clientele, like American Express, or with a relatively down-market clientele, like our former clients Odhams Mail Order, who sell cookery cards and the like.

Many formats
The insert is not only an effective medium; it is also one which is growing and developing fast.

Different formats, sizes and shapes will produce very different results. For instance, stitched-in or bound-in inserts tend to work better than loose inserts. Moreover, some formats have now been developed which can incorporate rub-off sections to reveal prizes, or even a built-in envelope. These formats tend to overcome inertia and do better than the standard format.

One form of insert which enjoys considerable popularity and success, particularly in the US, is the multi-page free-standing insert. These creations look rather like small magazines. They are delivered inside your Sunday newspaper, and at the time of writing they offer advertisers something like a 50 million circulation.

They are particularly effective when used by packaged goods companies for making money-off offers, self-liquidators and premium offers. They are also used by mail order companies for making direct offers, and catalogue companies to obtain leads. Because they offer a wide range of regional editions, they are valuable for companies wishing to reach particular demographic targets.

They have something in common with the door-to-door magazines and cooperative mailings I have mentioned elsewhere. Indeed, the same sort of companies find that they work.

5. The Broadcast media

The importance of the broadcast media varies depending upon the country and the stage of development reached in radio and television.

For instance, radio is a highly developed medium in the United States and Australia. In the UK, on the other hand, radio stations vary in quality greatly. Some offer very good coverage; some do not. Some attract great loyalty from their listeners; some don't seem to.

Television, on the other hand, is a popular medium in every country, but the regulations governing the availability of commercials vary widely. For instance, in the United States you can watch television around the clock and there is a wide range of channels to choose from. This gives great opportunities to the TV advertiser for negotiating keen rates. Consequently, direct response television works extremely well there.

In the UK there are only four channels – of which only two are commercial. And these channels do not broadcast 24 hours a day. The result is a shortage of TV time; and that which is available is over-priced as compared with other markets. Indeed, a 1988 report suggested that this relative high price was actually costing the country literally billions of pounds in unnecessary expenditure on the part of advertisers.

This report led to considerable furore; but whether it is true or not, it is unquestionably very difficult to get the right spots at the right time in the UK. However, cable and satellite TV are likely to change all this.

My own experience of television as a direct marketing medium dates back to the 1960s, when I worked for CPV, the agency which handled the British Army recruitment campaign. The army considered TV would be ideal for its prospects. It inaugurated something which has been used a great deal since: linking TV with the press. This was not a predetermined decision: it was stumbled upon by accident.

In the first place we used the standard TV format of that time – the 30-second commercial. Our client soon found out, as many others have since, that 30 seconds is not long enough to *sell* anything. The reason is simple. In 30 seconds you simply don't have time to convince anyone of anything important, let alone give them the time to get a paper and pencil and take down the response details.

What could have been done at that point – but was never thought of – was to run very long commercials. What was done was to feature the press ads in the commercials, asking people to look for the ads and respond to them. This proved highly effective. In the UK this form of TV back-up to advertising, mailings or door-to-door drops is still very effective.

In one case where a very heavy door-to-door drop activity took place in the North, a 30-second back-up television commercial apparently increased response by 50 per cent. In my own experience, television campaigns backing up direct mail activities and door-to-door drops have increased response by anything between 20 per cent and 40 per cent for different clients selling different products.

To create such a commercial you do not need to be elaborate or clever. You simply have to draw people's attention to the fact that an offer is oming through their door and make it quite clear what format the offer will take, so that it is recognised immediately. Spots as short as 20 seconds and ten seconds have been found effective in achieving this.

The secrets of success on TV have been best covered in a book by Al Eicoff of the Chicago agency Eicoff & Company (an Ogilvy subsidiary) in his book *Or your money back*. Much of the information I give here is contained in much greater length in this book – Eicoff has conducted research which confirmed a number of facts I already knew, but which he was the first to explain the rationale for. For example:

You need time

The technique I have described developed in the 1960s was, of course, using TV as a secondary medium. I have also mentioned the use of TV by the Automobile Association to get inquiries.

You can, of course, do the same thing with radio. But whichever of the two media you wish to use, if you want to sell then you have to remember you need at least 15 seconds to tell people how to reply.

Eicoff believes you need two minutes to create an effective selling commercial. On the other hand, my French colleagues have conducted tests which have proved (to their satisfaction at any rate) that a good job can be done in one minute.

Demonstrate, repeat

The ideal product is one which requires demonstrations, visually or in sound. Thus, records and books have done well in these media, and household gadgets.

These media are fleeting. You cannot (unless you have a video tape recorder) turn back and see or hear the commercial again: and who listens or watches for the commercials?

This means you need to repeat the commercials a number of times to get real attention. Typically you would run a burst of commercials over a six-week period, then rest for four weeks before trying again. But, once more, this depends on *your* experience with *your* product.

Off-peak works

In dealing with TV and radio, many people have found that *off-peak* spots do very well as compared with the same money invested at peak time.

I have three theories about this. I was very pleased upon reading Eicoff's book to realise that his research confirmed that two of them at any rate appear correct.

- At off-peak you are not competing with the all-dancing, all singing £50,000 extravaganzas put out by the big packaged goods companies. You're up against the dull efforts of the local department store. And, often, old re-run shows. People are happy to stop watching a programme and start buying a product.
- Late at night or early in the morning many people are at their lowest ebb: less able to resist your blandishments.
- Anyone listening to radio at two in the morning may have little else to do with their time save reply to your offer. (I have no research to back this up, just my own belief.)

Shop around . . . extensively

TV and radio reach a huge audience; in terms of cost per thousand impressions they are the cheapest media of all.

But on TV, production costs are staggering if you are not careful. If you shop around carefully though – I suggest more carefully than with any other medium – you will be surprised what you can achieve in cost savings.

There is, hardly surprisingly, constant complaint in the UK and the USA about the astonishing costs of producing television commercials. I am not surprised. I suspect advertising agencies (and clients, too, for that matter) are somewhat gullible when it comes to costs.

This was brought home to me when in 1987 I had to make a training video for our own agency. The video was produced to a high standard by a reputable production company and when completed lasted 52 minutes. It wasn't a particularly complicated video – basically me sitting at a desk talking, with lots of cut-away shots to demonstrate various points I was making.

I asked an experienced creative head who had done a lot of TV how much she thought this video must have cost. 'I suppose you could have got it done for as little at £20,000', she replied.

The actual cost was £4,000. Having made quite a few commercials over the years, I find that if you really want to it is usually possible to make them for a lot less than many people might imagine.

In radio, though, production costs are exceptionally low. Even the most gullible of individuals can see that simply sticking someone in front of a microphone and recording them cannot cost all that much money. Moreover, radio offers great opportunities. It is a medium in which you literally have to create word pictures. I think it is much under-utilised in many countries.

6 The telephone

This is a fast growing medium. which arouses such strong feelings that in some countries unsolicited telephone calls have been banned.

However, it is an extraordinarily potent medium. In 1980 *The Times* was moved to refer to it in terms which (by their standards) might be described as hysterical enthusiasm. 'The most cost-effective marketing tool invented lies on desks up and down the country.'

It has the value of immediacy, with all that that implies in terms of reading results fast. It is *interactive*: apart from face to face selling, it's the only medium where objections can be stated – and overcome. By the same token, you can establish what the best appeals are for your product.

It is therefore a very useful research medium, especially when, for instance, you are following up unconverted leads for a product. You will not only find out how people feel: you will also sell. Indeed, I have lost count of the number of times I have said to people who have been asking me why I thought a particular mailing did not work: 'Why don't you ring a few of the people and *ask*?'

One of the major benefits of the telephone is that your customers like it. The average catalogue company may have 70 per cent or more of their sales coming in on the phone. Our research into businessmen's inclinations shows that almost exactly the same percentage said they would prefer to inquire about new products on the telephone. The fact that people like to use the phone and call you gives you additional possibilities.

Create more sales

When a call comes in, you have an opportunity. Be it an inquiry, an order or even a complaint, it often represents a chance to create more sales. (It is not often sufficiently realised that someone who cares enough to complain does so because they have a real *need* for the product. They can be sold far more easily than someone who has shown no interest at all, as long as you are polite and helpful.)

In conjunction with the intelligent use of database information the telephone can be extraordinarily powerful.

Let me give you an example. Supposing somebody rings in who has bought maternity clothes from you. When they ring up you can pull up their details on a video display unit, discover what they bought last and talk to them about the possibility of selling them baby clothes, cot, and all the other paraphernalia associated with a new birth. The same sort of technique can be applied in almost any product area.

The telephone is very expensive, of course. It might cost you £5 to reach a particular decision-maker in a company. First of all to find out *who* you should be talking to, secondly to find out whether they are *there*; and thirdly to ring them later when they *are* there.

But cost is relative. Although a phone call is expensive, it can quite frequently get five or six times as many sales as a mailing selling the same product or service. Indeed, on occasion a telephone call can get several times as many sales as a mailing would, even if it is directed to a list of people who have been previously *unsuccessfully* mailed.

Let's face it, paying five pounds to talk to somebody on the phone may seem dear. But how about spending £150 on a sales call to the same person?

Many, many times a telephone campaign will pay where salespeople can't. Indeed, there are cases where customers *don't want* to see a salesperson. They are too busy. They will always either pick up the phone or answer the phone and do business with you as long as you're polite.

In the case of one of my clients it was discovered that for a particular financial service the customers not only preferred to deal with telephone salespeople, but the actual *sales result per call* was greater than that of a personal call. For that reason, I would suggest you give a great deal of thought to the potential the telephone offers.

Gets attention
The telephone has unique attention value. It *demands* a response.

I quoted earlier the remarkable amount of money spent in the United States on telephone marketing. I was surprised when I read that figure, until I remembered a statement which we ran in an advertisement: 'It uses no petrol. It gets decisions from 4, 6 even 12–15 people every hour. It's never sick. It says exactly what you want. It works.'

The client in question, Robert Leiderman of British Telecom Telephone Marketing, has a very beguiling way of describing just why the telephone works. 'When did you last leap out of the bath and run downstairs to look at a television commercial?' he asks. Yet we all do that sort of thing when the telephone rings.

I am also indebted to Robert for his way of describing the fundamental difference between just making telephone calls and telemarketing.

You've already got phones and some people who are underutilised. So you test it by using what I call the Linda method. That's L-I-N-D-A,

LINDA. This is usually the first step in starting a telemarketing campaign. You take a sample of about 50 names put them on your secretary's desk, and say 'Linda, I've got a job for you. Call these people in the next three days and sell them our widgets.'

Now Linda, who has worked for you for the last 15 years, knows the product backwards, forwards, inside out, and upside down, and she's helped you look at your direct mail and space, so you know Linda is not going to say something wrong. Three days later, she comes back and tells you the results – she actually spoke to 30 of the 50 people, and got 20 to say 'yes'.

'Incredible', you reply, 'a 67 per cent response! That's a lot better than two per cent by mail.' Linda, though, being a realistic and helpful person, says: 'Well, it is a 67 per cent response of the people I spoke to, but since there were 50 people, I'd really have to say it's only 20 out of 50.'

'I can live with 40 per cent. What a gem you are, Linda. Not only have you proved how successful the telephone is, you've found a way for us to hit our targets, and saved me from making a mistake on my projections.' Then, you give her a fiver, to show your thanks.

Based on this little test, you decide to contact 30,000 consumers in the next month, before rolling out to your 150,000 customers. So, you do some quick calculations: 30,000 x 40 per cent or 12,000 orders on your test.

Then you look at the list and see that there are no telephone numbers on your file, so you send them to someone for looking up and you find that only 50 per cent have a phone. Well, 6,000 orders ain't bad either. So, you have 15,000 names.

Linda goes crazy. She is not about to call 15,000 people.

So, back to the numbers. Fifteen thousand names at about 12 completed every hour is 1,250 hours. The calls can be made, say, for six hours a day, so you need 208.03 man-days. Or, on a five day week, 41.67 man weeks. Now, since your full plan needs to be approved within three months, you need numbers quickly, and you want the test completed within one month or 4.3 weeks.

That means you have to find ten people to do the job. So, you find the ten people – who are willing to work for a month – have Linda tell them how to do it, and wait for the orders to roll in.

Unfortunately, they don't. The whole thing falls flat on its face.

Tempting as it may be, don't fire Linda. She was good. The problem is that you didn't test the telephone. You tested Linda. And to get the same results with other people, you would need people with the same skills, the same gift of the gab, the same product knowledge, and very often, the same high salary that goes with all that.

A properly designed telephone marketing programme does not

rely on Linda or a whole room of Lindas. It relies on a *system* which incorporates the best elements of the person who knows the product, the person who knows the communications channel, the person who actually delivers the message, and the person who is asked to buy.

By putting these different elements into a telephone campaign, you limit your variables – as you do in other direct marketing methods – and have projectability. Surely, you wouldn't ask your postman, who talks to many of the people on his round, to write a special letter to each one – you'd never know why you got the results you got. How can you project it? How can you be sure the right message is delivered? Certainly the same is true by phone, when it is used as a 'verbal letter'.

A brilliant little story, I think you'll agree, which makes the point beautifully.

7 Posters

The only time we have ever used outdoor posters for one of our clients was when we were offered them free. But as a secondary medium, I believe they have their place. Thus, if you were planning a huge door-to-door drop, you could schedule posters in that area. Or, if you were a charity, you could run posters when you were doing your annual door-to-door collection.

For that matter, if political parties were clever enough with raising funds by direct mail, they could schedule posters to coincide with their efforts in areas they thought particularly favourable to their views.

The perfect poster
The problem with posters is that the perfect outdoor poster has about five words on it, plus the brand name (or, even better, *including* the brand name).

They are designed to attract the fleeting attention of drivers – and as such, are a menace, apart from being a blot on the landscape. But five words are hardly enough to deploy any kind of meaningful argument. So a poster cannot be expected to do more than attract an enquiry, on its own. This is how, for example, La Redoute, the big French mail order firm, uses them to generate catalogue enquiries.

Some kinds of poster can do a good job: the kinds that people have time to read, like underground posters. We find them very effective in attracting enquiries on the telephone.

The media of the future

Many years ago, somebody who travelled to California commented: 'I have seen the future and it works.' The same applies to some new media.

It is fearfully difficult to predict what is or is not likely to happen in our business because so much depends upon technology. And if the future can be gauged from the past, then only one thing is sure: the developments I imagine will prove crucial won't; those I never dreamed of will.

However, here are examples of developments I consider already represent serious new media.

The use of video tape in mailings

This has developed to such a degree that our agency encouraged Winfried Hirschle of Middlesex Business School to conduct a study into its effectiveness. Clearly, a videotape coming through the post is not an everyday event, and can hardly be ignored. More to the point, for certain types of product, the ability to *demonstrate* means video is likely to make a considerable impact.

The study concluded that where the product in question was something which people were very *familiar* with visually – eg a car that had been heavily promoted on television – the impact of this sort of communication, whilst great, does not necessarily pay off in the resulting sales. People are already familiar with what they are seeing and, in the end, it all comes down to 'do you like the car when you drive it?'

On the other hand, where a product is little known, or entirely new, or is of a highly technical nature, then this form of communication obviously makes a lot of sense.

Interactive, personalised media

I find it almost impossible to understand how some of the new media now emerging work. However, their *potential* is quite clear. Let me give you what I see as being the most remarkable example of what I am talking about.

In the United States ACTV are about to start offering a remarkable new service on cable television.

Some of the experiences subscribers will be able to have strike me as less than breathtaking: for instance, they'll be able to play Black Jack with on-screen opponents, or challenge them to trivia tests. They could even confide the details of their love lives to an expert and receive advice on relationships. Much more interesting from a marketer's point of view is the fact that during the station breaks they'll see commercials specifically targeted at them as individuals.

In effect, interactive TV allows the viewer to talk to the television through a remote control device. For instance, when an expert asks you: 'Where did you meet the person you're dating?', four choices appear on the screen:

1 Through friends
2 At work
3 At school
4 At a Singles Bar

Should the viewer press No 4 on the remote control, an expert appears on the screen shaking his head sadly: 'Unfortunately', he says 'studies show that relationships that begin that way may not work out. I am worried.'

On the other hand, if the viewer taps 1,2 or 3 the announcer rejoices and predicts a more rosy outcome.

Here's another example showing how an advertiser will be able to use specific data to determine who sees which commercial. If a host on a show asks: 'Do you own a dog?', only those who say 'Yes' will see a dog food commercial. If the host asks: 'Do you make over $100,000 a year and live in Manhattan and own a dog?', only those who reply 'Yes', 'Yes' and 'Yes' will receive a commercial for an expensive kennel.

Fascinating, isn't it?

I am not going to go much further into this – and I would like to acknowledge that the information I have just given you I lifted shamelessly from an article in *Advertising Age*, written by Lenore Skenazy. But I think you are beginning to get the idea. Through this sort of medium people can not only interact with the programme on television: the entire selling process can be matched to them – including the ability, literally, to order direct off the screen.

This ability to have a truly interactive medium whereby the customer can respond to a range of alternatives and select a product fitted to him or herself does represent the future. The creative challenges all this is going to summon up are such that I find it difficult to envision them.

Of course, any new means of communication is a medium. You can put direct response ads on matchbox covers, bus tickets, for that matter camel sides. Some have more merit than others. I am not entirely convinced of the merits of the camel side, but unquestionably matchbook covers work extremely well for advertisers trying to generate low interest inquiries for products or services of general interest – eg Join the Army. I can also see that putting advertisements inside taxis will work under certain circumstances.

I will only make one sure prediction after all this. And that is that no matter how much these new media develop, the old ones will not die away: people will still want to read through things and look at pictures. These new media will simply represent fresh and challenging opportunities.

The fax machine

It is a surprising irony that in some cases people find the fax machine a more desirable communications medium than the telephone. Despite the fact that it has less humanity.

However, it does have certain substantial advantages – advantages worth paying for now that fax machines are rapidly diminishing in price. For instance, when you can actually see something on paper, it can be conveyed much more precisely – it doesn't take as much time to transmit information which verbally you might waffle on about. When it reaches you through your own fax machine it tends to attract your attention more than the mailing would. Because it is in writing, where it involves some sort of contractual obligation it can be legally binding. And finally, of course the fax can be used off-peak thus giving you a very low rate per communication.

Successful media selection

Don't be a pioneer

In our sales equation 'W × 5 = SALES', the last two Ws are: *where* are my prospects, and *when* should I reach them? These are media questions.

To aid you in the task of determining the answers, you must turn to past precedent. You'll temper this with common sense, naturally, and look carefully for any special factors which may have affected your results. You must also refer to the many statistics available in print. Plus, of course, any research you have available.

In most countries there are extensive readership surveys in addition to the figures that the media print to prove (to their own satisfaction, anyhow that you should put every penny you've got with them. All these will act as a gloss on your own past results and aim at helping you to make the right decisions.

But what if you are a newcomer? Then you must *observe*, and *copy*. You must get on as many mailing lists in similar product areas as possible. Get copies of all publications you think may be relevant. (How do you get on a mailing list? Buy a product or make an enquiry.)

You must spend some time studying where it is that *other* people spend their money. And, as always in life, make sure those people are capable of making the right decisions.

There is actually no substitute for spending a great deal of time sifting through publications to see where and when your competitors (or, if it's a new product, similar products aimed at similar people) spend their money.

In the UK, for instance, MEAL is a service which tells you, in exchange for a subscription, where and when companies are spending their money. Such information tends to be very partial though. For instance, it often does not cover the local press properly. One of our clients has been consistently misrepresented for years as spending far less than they actually do because of this.

For that reason, you have to read these statistics with great care. They are in some ways not as valuable as seeing the actual publications. Apart from anything else, you see not only *where* people are placing their money but what precisely they are *doing* with it. What sort of advertisements they are running.

Evaluating the use of mailing lists is much more speculative. But you can build up an overall picture. If a soundly based company runs ads *consistently* in a certain publication, or *repeatedly* mails a certain list, then you should try it.

Rule of three

What do we mean by 'consistently'? Well the old rule is: one insertion is a trial. Two is to confirm the first result. And three means it worked, so you should try it. The same applies to repeated mailings.

But beware of one thing. That big, well-established organisation may have more money than you. They may be able to pay more money for each initial order, in order to make money long term. So judge your results with that in mind. And for goodness sake, adopt a sceptical view. Lots of smaller companies (and even the occasional large one) aren't reading their results as carefully as they might. They could be living on their fat – and you can't afford to do that.

An instructive story on this subject (and a very sad one) was told to me by my old colleague Gene Griffin in New York. I asked him why a big company that had been in business for many years in the US had suddenly gone broke. They had always seemed exceptionally professional in everything they did.

The answer was that the founder had contracted a terminal disease. He didn't care any more, poor man, and the company went into bankruptcy.

So, follow, but with caution. And whatever you do, never pioneer unless you have to. The best place to put *your* market stall is where all the others are.

Where you will do best

I gained my education in space planning and buying when I was running the marketing of the Bullworker. It was a valuable education because I learned everything bit by bit.

I discovered in the first place that the best media for me were, not unnaturally, publications with a heavy sport or health orientation. These publications would produce inquiries for the product five times more cost-effectively than the second most effective type of media which were general-interest weekly magazines. These in turn tended to do about 50 per cent better than the daily newspapers.

Since I was working on share of profits based on reaching a target number of sales, I could not simply rely upon the relatively small numbers of inquiries produced from the health magazines. Because they had relatively small readerships they tended to 'tire' very quickly. Nor could I even reach my targets by advertising in addition in the general interest magazines. I had to make the national press work.

This proved quite difficult. To start with I found the only spaces that would pay out for me were little bargain spaces in the pages which run every Saturday in the British national press offering lots of gimmicky items. Even this was not bringing in enough sales.

I then tried running advertisements in the body of the paper. They did not pay for me. I finally got the breakthrough I wanted when I started testing ads on the sports pages. I found that my ads would only pay off if I could get a position on the back page – the most prominent of all the sports pages. Elsewhere it did not do well.

In the process I developed additional knowledge about what could work and what could not work. I discovered that in the publications which did very well – the health and general interest magazines – I could afford to run bigger spaces. Indeed, in the former I ran full pages, whilst in the latter I built up a big editorial style ad.

So you will have gathered that apart from the publication itself, position is vital. An ad which does well on the sports page may flop on the leader page. An ad which stands out, and therefore succeeds, when placed amongst the earlier pages of a magazine, may fail through not being noticed when placed four pages from the back. Indeed, that is precisely what we found out for one of our clients. Eighty per cent of their successful ads were near the front of the publication. Their unsuccessful ones tended to be towards the end.

Here are some guidelines on what works and what doesn't.

- The front of a publication is better than the back. The front page is best (if available) followed by the back. Then the inside-front right. Then the inside-front left. Then the inside back-right. Then the back left. After that it tends to be in order going from front to back.
- Right hand pages do better than left. And it is generally agreed that pages facing editorial do better than otherwise – though one piece of research I saw a couple of years ago suggested this was not the case. I have to say, however, that it was for a particular magazine, and I suppose once again the answer is *test* and find out what does best for you.
- Any ad in magazines or newspapers which is next to the letters pages, TV programme pages, or horoscopes does well.
- Gutter positions do worse than outside positions. The gutter is the fold that runs down the middle of the paper when you open it out. You want your advertisements to be on the outside edges of the newspaper, not the gutter.

- Any ad which is surrounded by matter (so you can't cut the coupon out easily) will do worse than otherwise.
- Special positions are usually worth paying extra for.
- If there is a feature directly relating to your product, then a medium that is not normally worth going into may prove profitable. Thus, if you are offering finance to people, then a home improvements feature might do well for you.

Once again, as in every other aspect of our business, these are only general rules. Results may vary according to many other factors. And a good position won't save your lousy ad.

In mailings, one thing is obvious, and it's almost all you need to remember. If your mailing hits a prospect just after someone else offering a similar product, it can't help. Unless, of course, you are offering a better deal. But such clashes are to be avoided.

When you will do best

'When should I run my offer?', is the final question to ask.

My experience is based upon the western hemisphere. For this reason the monthly listings I am going to give below apply to our climate. However, whatever the country, here are two commonly accepted facts: the first is that you will generally do better in winter than in summer; and you will *not* generally do well during public holidays. (Obviously, there are exceptions, like seasonal products which appeal in the summer months.)

Thus, here and in America, for most advertisers the best month is January, and then February. The sequence after that is difficult to place exactly, but September would probably be next, then March, October, April, November, August, May, and – the poor months – June and July. Then, death on skates: December.

Equally, the days of the week vary, as I have noted in the chapter on testing. Tuesday seems to be best for many people.

Sometimes, because you can get a very good price from the media, bad months can become good months. And the same applies to public holidays, with the exception of Christmas (only holiday advertisers seem to do well at that time). I recall negotiating for Bullworker a very good deal on Easter Saturday and Easter Monday with the *Daily Express*. We got our best-ever results in a national paper. And one of our clients puts nearly *all* his money into August, because he gets good deals.

Experience – and chance

I don't think I can repeat too often that it all depends on your experience . . . and on *chance*.

Some years ago I had an interest in a company whose marketing I controlled. What happened is a cautionary tale. The company was importing its product from Germany. We tested with enormous success, the *Sun* newspaper. Indeed, the results were so outstanding that I made that paper our main medium.

In April/May of the year in question, three things happened. First: the pound dropped 20 per cent against the deutschmark. Second: results that year (for everyone I spoke to) dropped dramatically at the end of April. Third (and I should have waited to find this out): the conversion rate to sales from enquiries in the *Sun* turned out to be much lower than in other media we had been using, which was exacerbated by the overall slump in results.

You can imagine the combined effect. Utter disaster all round.

So as you see, timing in media selection can be of inordinate importance. All media planning should be conducted on the basis of pessimism, moderated by gloom, with a healthy dash of caution.

Proven principles of negotiation

This leads me to the very special area of *negotiating*, which can make nonsense of everything I've just said.

There is one overriding principle of negotiation. A principle which has been proved, in controlled tests, by Dr Chester Karrass of the Californian Centre for Effective Negotiating to hold true: **The person who asks for least (or offers least) will always come out best in a negotiation ... assuming his offer is not so ludicrous as to make it insulting**.

As long as you are pleasant and not too aggressive never be afraid to make an offer you think is outrageous. This is so important not only in media buying, but in buying or selling anything, including your product or services. I will give you one or two examples from my own experience.

Many years ago, I became involved in a series of negotiations to obtain the rights to a central heating system which converted an ordinary coal fire into a most effective heating method. My partner (and mentor) in this negotiation was a man called Fox, who had worked all his life in the toughest business on earth: the rag trade.

The system in question had been developed by a big engineering company who had no idea of how to sell it. They had lost a fortune trying. It had cost £50,000 to create. Fox and I went to see them.

He said he wanted to make an offer. They asked how much. He said: 'I'd rather not tell you, because you might laugh and end our discussions. You tell me how much you want.' People hate to make the first offer, as well he knew, and he had already made them realise he was not going to pay a lot. They then insisted on him telling them the figure. Once again he demurred. They realised this really *was* going to be a low offer. They insisted. He said: 'Are you sure you won't just end the discussions when you hear what it is?' They then reassured him. He said '£2,000.'

They were stunned: 'But this thing cost £50,000 to develop.' Nevertheless, their expectations had been brought right down.

He said: 'What are you going to do with it? You might as well dig a big hole in the ground, and bury it for all the good it is to you.' This brings out another important principle: always study your opponent to establish what his own position is. Fox knew they didn't know how to sell the unit.

In the end we got it for £5,000.

Don't worry about refusal

My late brother worked in another tough business, property, and used to operate the same sort of system, but in a more systematic fashion. I asked him how he managed to make such a profit on taking a property and doing it up to sell it.

'Very simple,' he replied. 'I look at about ten or 12 houses that seem suitable every month. On each of them I put in a very low offer that's bound to give me room for a profit. Nine out of ten will say no. Sometimes they will *all* say no. But I find there's usually somebody who has good reason to sell. The right price is what people will take. The big mistake most people make is to fear being turned down.'

So another rule of negotiating is that if you don't ask, you won't get.

You will be surprised, if you approach the media with an eye to their position as much as your own, what good deals you can get. You may be sitting worrying about making an offer that will be refused. At the other end the man may be praying for *any* kind of offer. What have you got to lose? Only a good deal!

Remember, a newspaper is like a railway train. Each day, it runs whether the seats (or advertising pages) are full or not. So if you make it easier for them, they will often make it cheaper for you. In this way, everybody is happy. And that is the *best* form of negotiation, because you are not just negotiating: you are establishing a relationship.

Ten good deals

Here's how you can help yourself, and help the media. The obvious opportunities come first.

1 Volume discount
You'll usually get a better rate if you promise to spend at a certain level.

2 Series discount
Almost every medium offers a discount for taking a series of ads.

3 Run of week discount
You may prefer to go in on a certain day of the week. But the publication may like to have an ad ready to slot in on *any* day and give you a discount for the privilege.

4 Standby discount
If you have an ad standing by with the publication which they can drop in whenever they've got a problem, you should get a big discount.

5 Distress discount
This is the miser's favourite. Have an ad ready so that when they call you (and you let them know you are always interested if the price is right) you can negotiate a rate just short of daylight robbery.

6 Rate protection guarantee
Rates go up, but rarely, if ever, down. When negotiating, try to get the publication to guarantee you the rate at the time for a given period. It could be a big saving.

7 Special position free
If you have a good enough relationship with a medium, you may be able to get a special position (or time) with no premium. It's got to be worth it. And there's no harm in trying.

8 Specified day free
You can do the same with the specific day you want.

9 No payment for solus
A solus position on the page is usually worth paying for. Try to get it free.

10 Soft period discount
When space is hard to sell, and easy to buy, that's known as a soft period. You should make hay then.

Finally, there's the *perfect* deal. The PI or per inquiry deal. There are few times in life when you can get something for nothing, but this is the next best thing.

You know how much you want to pay for an order or inquiry. The publication (or list owner) knows how much he wants for the use of his medium. If you can agree with him that you will pay so much per sale or inquiry, and he'll take it, then what could be more perfect?

Several TV stations in the UK were trying this method with direct advertisers for a period until an outcry from other advertisers forced them to stop. However, in most areas you will find somebody willing to have a go.

PI is the perfect way to *test* a new medium. The sales rep will tell you what a marvellous medium he is offering you. You will wonder. The best way to find out is to do a PI deal. In the end it will be to the interest of both parties. If only all media would do it, media buying would be so simple!

But one word of advice. No matter how well you negotiate people down, don't boast about it. Keep quiet, and protect your deal.

8

Your Greatest Asset

'Father, Mother and Me,
Sister and Auntie say
All the people like us are We
And everyone else is They.'

    Rudyard Kipling

'The one thing our industry does not lack
is computer people with the personal characteristics
of a Messiah plus a willingness to dress up a
perfectly ordinary mailing list maintenance system
and call it a "marketing database".'

    Ian Goodman
    Southwark Computer Services

A measure of how quickly direct marketing has changed in the five years since this book's first edition is that the word direct marketers probably use more than any other was hardly mentioned in that book. That word is *database*.

In those days, people talked about *lists* – as they had done for many years. Now, the simple (and inexpensive) list has been cast into outer darkness and replaced by the sophisticated (and sometimes very expensive) database. In fact, one of the leading UK experts on this subject once asked me: 'At what point, Drayton, do you think a list becomes a database? What *is* the difference?'

Lists were relatively inexpensive because everyone understood what they were, and thus what they were paying for when they compiled or rented one. 'Database' is a word many do not entirely understand. A very profitable industry has evolved to cater for this ignorance, with predictable results: many people spend prodigious sums, even millions, without gaining a great deal of satisfaction.

But, I have good news for you. If you start by thinking about lists, you will end by understanding databases and what they can do rather well. Indeed, I hope to reassure you: you probably understand a great deal more than you may have thought.

The value of a name

I refer elsewhere to Jerry della Femina, who once said he thought advertising 'the most fun you can have with your clothes on'. This displays a worrying ignorance of good music and fine claret, but I know what he meant.

Working in our business is not as worthwhile as being a conservationist or a surgeon, but it is fun, and you get involved in some interesting areas of life. For example, I once spent some time writing copy for a racing tipster service. It all came about through a couple of friends, one of whom gambled professionally, and the other of whom already ran a tipster service.

I learned a number of things from this activity, including the fact that one of Britain's most respected businessmen started out as a tipster. I also learned that the average professional gambler is not too hot at running any kind of service, let alone one which requires you to be at the office first thing in the morning to give people tips.

But the most interesting fact I learned was that the name of one regular purchaser of racing tips was worth £1, making the value of a list of 1,000 such names £1,000. To put this in context, at that time the pound sterling was worth about three times as much as it is now and even the most expensive list would have cost you no more than £50 per 1,000 to rent once.

I tell you this to emphasise that if you can find the right people to talk to you can hardly fail. The most wonderful mailing on earth will die the death if it goes to the wrong names. The worst mailing on earth can sometimes succeed if it goes to the right ones. This is because marketing starts with people. I shudder to think how much money has been thrown away because insufficient thought has been given to the people who are being spoken to. If you don't know who you're talking to, you're unlikely to make the right offer, let alone gauge why they should want to buy whatever it is you're selling. Your creative work will almost certainly be wide of the mark.

This is true even of the most broad appeal possible – like a sweepstake. Almost everybody likes the idea of winning something for nothing. But in some cases people are put off by this sort of approach. One of our major clients who operates in almost every civilised country on earth has hardly ever been able to make a sweepstake work properly. Their type of customer simply isn't interested; or to be more exact, does not find that sort of approach from them appropriate – an important distinction, obviously derived from their positioning.

The problem is that, particularly for people accustomed to general advertising, it's easy to think of a list as a *medium* like a newspaper. Yet in fact, of course, direct mail is the medium; the list is the equivalent of the readership of a newspaper. More importantly, a mailing list, if carefully compiled and properly analysed, will reveal a far greater number of variables than you might consider when trying to learn about the readers of a particular publication, or the viewers of a particular TV programme.

List experts sometimes utter a rather dull, but nonetheless very relevant expression to recall us to the most important truth about lists. They say 'Lists are people'. And – you might reasonably reply – so are the readers of a newspaper or the viewers of a TV show. I think the point to bear in mind here is that these people can all be approached as individuals – to return to the besetting theme of this book. And the point about individuals, as I indicated earlier, is that if you can learn enough about them and their needs, you can meet those needs better, and get closer to perfect marketing.

The relative importance of the list

The role of the list as compared with the other factors involved in a mailing is well illustrated by the results of some tests we conducted a while ago for one of our clients.

Mailings were sent out to 12 lists, all of which we thought likely to succeed. We also tested three prices, two ways to pay, different times for mailing, alternative ways of responding and several creative approaches. The best combination of all these factors produced a result 58 times as good as the worst combination. And by far the most important factor in these tests was the choice of list – as you can see from the following abbreviated figures.

Typical mailing test results

Factor	Difference between best and worst
List	× 6.0
Offer	× 3.0
Timing	× 2.0
Creative	× 1.35
Response	× 1.2

Let me emphasise that we did not have any clear idea in advance which of the 12 lists would work best. As a matter of fact, the winner was something of a surprise to me.

This book is not the place (nor am I the person, for I have little sympathy with the subject) to go into the fine and dreary detail of list buying, holding and maintenance, though I hope to give you some helpful advice. But you will have gathered simply from looking at the mailing test results above that the role of the list lies at the heart of the direct marketing business. Let me now transfer your attention for the moment from the list to the database.

Nowadays, people generally hold their lists on computer. It's easier. And the computer is getting infinitely less expensive to buy and run. I read a couple of years ago in *Direct Marketing Magazine* that 'Since 1960 the cost of computer mainframe storage has plummeted roughly 20,000 times – whilst speed of operation has increased by a factor of about one million. There is now a 50 per cent gain in efficiency per annum.'

This enables you to build (increasingly cheaply) a new kind of list: a database.

There is currently a lot of talk about databases, not all necessarily well-informed. Indeed, one expert, out of curiosity, recently asked a group of his colleagues to *define* 'database marketing'. They all gave different answers.

This gives you some insight into the confusion surrounding this word. Yet, in my view, a database is only a *list* of customers or prospects incorporating relevant information about those people. This information enables you to target your messages in a way which is much more interesting to your recipient – and therefore likely to be far more profitable to you.

One publication remarked a few years ago that the importance of the database is such that it believes the *primary duty* of a direct marketing agency is to build its client's database. I think this a sweeping and inaccurate assertion. After all, the agency must also be able to help the client exploit that database in an imaginative and profitable way. A database is an *enabling* tool, nothing more. It is your skill at analysing the information on the database and using it to construct more effective communications that will determine your success.

Be that as it may, once you understand the principles of list evaluation, you are a fair way to understanding all about databases. In fact, the idea of building a database – of acquiring information about your customers or prospects which you can note down in conjunction with their names and addresses – is not new at all. I am indebted to a friend, Roger Millington, a keen historical sleuth, for an example of database-building which dates back quite a while.

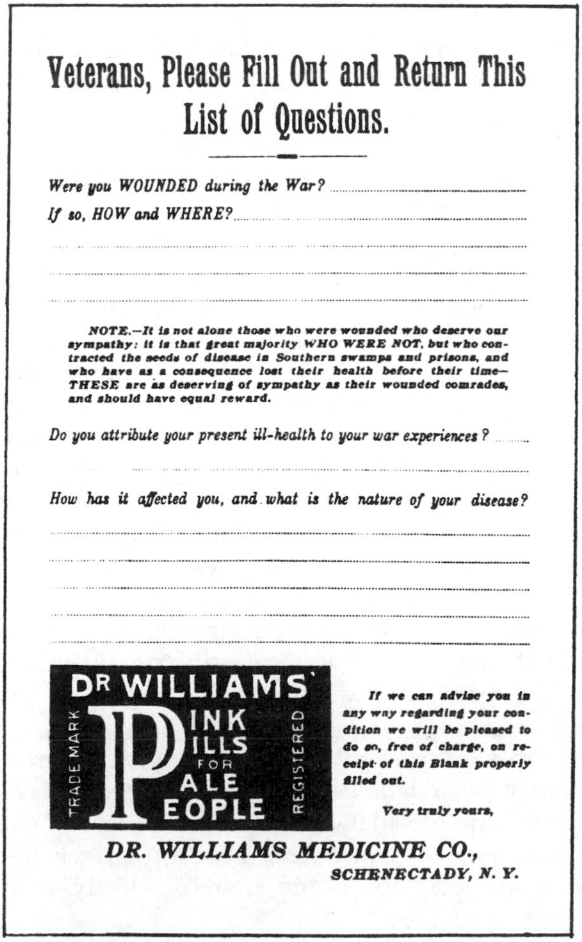

Veterans, Please Fill Out and Return This List of Questions.

Were you WOUNDED during the War? ....
If so, HOW and WHERE? ....

....

....

NOTE.—It is not alone those who were wounded who deserve our sympathy; it is that great majority WHO WERE NOT, but who contracted the seeds of disease in Southern swamps and prisons, and who have as a consequence lost their health before their time— THESE are as deserving of sympathy as their wounded comrades, and should have equal reward.

Do you attribute your present ill-health to your war experiences? ....

How has it affected you, and what is the nature of your disease?

....

....

....

....

DR WILLIAMS' PINK PILLS FOR PALE PEOPLE
TRADE MARK   REGISTERED

If we can advise you in any way regarding your condition we will be pleased to do so, free of charge, on receipt of this Blank properly filled out.

Very truly yours,

DR. WILLIAMS MEDICINE CO.,
SCHENECTADY, N. Y.

Figure 8.1. Dr. William's Pink Pills. This example of database building goes back to 1868: there's nothing new under the sun

It is the case of a company with a medical product asking respondents to give details of their injuries or illnesses as a result of their war experiences. Obviously, this would enable them to target those people better: to offer them the right products.

It was not particularly difficult for the company in question because they made Dr William's Pink Pills for Pale People, which had the uncanny facility of being able to cure everything from the common cold to cancer. Probably they merely adapted the communications they sent out – based upon the information their respondents supplied – without adapting the product.

What is most interesting about this example is, of course, that it dates back over 100 years, to the period of the American Civil War. Not only is there nothing new under the sun, there is not very much new in database: simply greater technological proficiency as a result of the computer.

Let us now return to the fundamentals of the mailing list.

Three simple facts to start with

All understanding of mailing lists starts from three simple facts.

1 Lists may be conveniently divided into two kinds: your own, and other people's.
2 Your own list should always give you better results than anyone else's.
3 The best lists to rent or buy are those which are most similar to your own.

I think this is fairly simple. But in case you have any doubt, let me explain that by 'your own' list I mean any list of people who have transacted business with you or had a contact with you, and thus know you.

In business, people prefer to deal with people they know. This is particularly so in the mail order business where customers have to have confidence in the vendor. To send you money for a product they don't have in their hands they have to believe you are reputable. If they've done business with you before, they are going to be that much more confident.

But you will be interested to know that the same thinking applies whether you're talking about mail order or any other form of marketing. For instance, one of our agency's major clients uses salesmen. They have discovered that it is four times easier to sell to existing customers than it is to sell to similar prospects who have not done business with them before.

So the important thing to remember is: if people have done business with you or had contact with you previously, their names and addresses are valuable.

In the mail order business, it is reckoned that a mailing to your own list will be about three times as effective as if it were sent to someone else's list on which the names had similar characteristics.

You will, I am sure, have nodded in agreement at all this. It makes sense, doesn't it? The customers you wish to get are likely to be very similar in nature to those you already have.

Predicting success

Gordon Grossman, a former marketing director of *Reader's Digest* in the US, is one of the most intelligent commentators on the subject of lists. In December 1982, an article of his: 'Foreshadowing response: the muscle in your merge' demonstrated in the most startling way how important it is to remember the fact that new customers' responses can be predicted from old.

Grossman noted that if you compare the lists that are working for you currently with ones you are thinking of testing, you can predict with a high degree of certainty which lists are likely to work.

When people rent lists, you have to complete a computer run to eliminate duplication – known in the trade as 'merge and purge'. Having removed this wasteful duplication the average mailer carries on. Not Grossman, because he takes a look to see how *similar* the lists are. He points out that in his experience: (1) if the duplication factor between the two lists is 25 per cent, your mailing has about an 86 per cent chance of succeeding; (2) if it is under 10 per cent the likelihood of success is about 3 per cent.

Your ability to place on a database relevant information about the people you are interested in, to analyse what you have learned and then exploit it, determines your success in direct marketing. Here's a simple example which shows how *little* the thinking has developed since Dr William's Pink Pills were saving lives (or not, as the case may be) 100-odd years ago.

I've already mentioned our client, North West Securities. You may recall that they raise finance for companies to acquire capital assets of one kind or another – machinery, cars and so forth. A mailing is sent out to prospects which asks them to reply to a simple questionnaire. The questionnaire gives information about what assets the prospect is planning to acquire over the next 12 months, how much they estimate they will cost, what makes and models they are considering, and when they intend to put their plans into effect.

This is all enormously valuable ammunition for the company offering the finance. It also makes a lot of sense for the prospect. He knows that he is only going to be approached by the company *at the right time* to talk about something *he is already interested in*. At the appropriate moment, the company can speak to him and offer a better service than it could without that information.

The importance of analysis

Every piece of information which is relevant can help you in building up a picture of your best prospects or customers and enable you to do a better job for those people. And the principle applies whether you are talking about business-to-business or consumer marketing. Moreover, the information you use to enrich your database can come from many sources, internal or external. And many methods can be used to acquire it.

One method is looking at who has responded to your previous communications, and discerning the characteristics they share with other respondents. The converse is equally true: you can see who does *not* respond. In this way, you can target your communications to those most likely to respond and eliminate those least likely.

This means that you can take a list of people which as a whole would not be profitable for you to mail and by eliminating the least responsive names, cut down the size of that list and make it profitable to mail the remaining names. In effect, you transform failure into success. Alternatively, you can make a list which is *already* profitable *more* profitable.

You can use generally available information to enrich your knowledge of the people on your database. For instance, in the public domain there is often information about particular residential areas: what sort of people live in them, what sort of accommodation they inhabit. This is usually available through Post Office or census statistics.

You can also acquire information from your order forms; often simple but valuable data, such as whether people have telephones or not, how old they are, how many children they have and of what sex and age. By comparing this information with the responses you have received from other customers you can predict likely responses from those people. Every shred of information helps build up a picture of the people you are talking to and their probable behaviour.

For those of you who like to blind your colleagues with science, the phrase 'regression analysis' can be used to fine effect when discussing this subject.

For those of you who like to impress your colleagues with good profit and loss statements, I should state that generally this technique – though attended with a degree of cost – tends to generate more profit than such costs: indeed, you can *double* your profitability.

Of course, unless you have your list properly organised, with every possible factor about your buyers incorporated into the database, such analysis is very difficult.

For instance, we once learned for a particular service that our best prospect was likely to have an ethnic surname or, if English, was likely to have more initials than average, was likely to be a professional person inhabiting a house rather than a flat, and a house with a name rather than a house with a number. Information like this can, as I said, enable you to transform unprofitable mailing lists into profitable ones simply by eliminating the names less likely to respond.

In short, success in direct marketing is likely to be attained by creating a database of customers or prospects as economically as possible and then mailing or otherwise communicating with them as profitably as possible, based upon what you have learned about their likely responsiveness. And the more you know about them the better you will do.

Twelve criteria for evaluating lists

Here are 12 points to consider when assessing a list's value, in *rough* order of priority – based on the way the classic direct marketing company looks at lists.

1 Are they your customers, or someone else's?
If they are someone else's, one way you can get a better response is by persuading the list owner to write an endorsement of your product to go out with your mailing.

2 How much money did they spend per transaction?
Obviously, the £1,000 buyer is likely to prove a more lucrative prospect than the £10 buyer. Equally, when you come to communicate with him or her you will use a very different tone of voice.

3 Have they bought recently?
Recent buyers will always do better than others. In the US they are sold as 'hot-line' buyers. Often, when other names will not work on a list, people who have bought recently will work. In one company I was involved in at one point, whereas we were failing to convert customers by mailing them after six weeks, we were wildly successful by mailing them immediately after a purchase.

4 Have they bought frequently?
In the same way that recency is important, so is frequency.

5 How up-to-date is the list?
People sometimes move home. They move jobs more frequently. Unless the list has been mailed recently and the 'gone-aways' have been cleaned out, it could be full of out-of-date names. Business-to-business lists can be particularly poor. I recall a list which we discovered was 50 per cent inaccurate although it came from a very reputable source.

6 Are they mail order buyers or not?
Some people like to buy through the mail. Some don't. So a list of retail

buyers or competition entrants will not be nearly as good as mail order buyers – though a list of your own competition entrants will almost certainly do better than a list of somebody else's buyers.

7 Were the sales for cash or for credit? What sort of credit?
A cash buyer would be a better than a hire purchase buyer. But a credit card buyer should be better than a cash buyer. And a charge card buyer should be better than a credit card buyer. They generally have a higher socio-economic rating.

8 Are they buyers, or just enquirers?
Normally buyers will be better for you than enquirers. Sometimes, though, when renting outside lists, you may find enquirers work better.

9 Is it a list of people who have established a business relationship with someone?
Or it is a compiled list, taken from printed records of some kind, like the telephone directory? Compiled lists are not nearly as good. Moreover, if they have dealt with someone, that enables you to approach them by referring to that relationship. This establishes a reason for writing – very valuable.

10 If it is someone else's list, how similar to your own are the people on it?
By age. By socio-economic background or, if this is business-to-business, by type of company. This is, of course, quite apart from whether they have bought the same kind of product. The best list for you is a list of people who have bought an identical product to yours. (You may find this hard to understand, but, as Shakespeare said, 'The appetite grows by what it feeds upon'.)

11 How often is the list mailed?
You may be surprised to learn that the best lists are those which are mailed often. The people have got into the habit of responding to offers. If a list has only been mailed once in the last six months, the people on it seem to languish.

12 Is the name as well as the title of the person on the list, if it's a business list?
Some lists may only have the company name on them. Make sure you're getting the detail you think necessary. In my experience rather than settle for what are likely to be inaccurate personal names you are better off going for the title.

If you take all these criteria and apply them intelligently, you should find assessing the likely responsiveness of a list much easier. Indeed, by looking at a list or database and thinking about it attentively, you will frequently come up with the offers and even the products you should be marketing. After all, what you sell, the offers you make, and how you make those offers all start with studying the customer or prospect.

Thus people who paid £145 cash through the post for an exercise bicycle might read your new £12 a year publication on fitness. On the other hand, a list of subscribers to your publication on fitness are not proven mail order buyers who spent good money recently: they might not be at all prepared to pay £145 for an exercise bicycle – let alone through the post. You would approach your test with fewer expectations.

But let me repeat: your entire business should revolve around considering the individuals on your database or on the people you wish to recruit as new customers and thus enrich your existing database. Considering those individuals will not merely help you formulate the right offers and the right products to offer; it will enable you to *communicate* your message more effectively. As a copywriter, I always find information about the people I am about to write to and how they have behaved in the past – and indeed *anything* I can find out about them – is immensely valuable in helping me do a better job.

Even scrutinising the names and addresses on a list can sometimes tell you a lot. People with upper class names and smart addresses are different, clearly, to those with working class names living in cheap neighbourhoods. It is *particularly* worth your while to read customer correspondence, as I suggested earlier.

Know how people behave

Perhaps a little story will illustrate how very profitable it can prove to think carefully about the people on a list.

Some years ago some enterprising folk opened offices in Manchester and printed a lavish catalogue full of attractive consumer durable goods. They mailed the catalogue to a large list of people who had bad debt records. All the goods offered were available on low deposit.

Because they had thought about the nature of the list, the mailing was extremely successful, pulling some £60,000 in deposits, so my informant told me. A few weeks after the mailing had gone out, the entrepreneurs vanished with the money.

This is quite the most successful approach to the problem of bad debt that I have heard of. It also illustrates one of Sir Francis Bacon's maxims: men behave as they are accustomed.

You should never forget this when making fresh offers to customers you have recruited, for generally speaking they will respond well to the kind of appeal that attracted them in the first place. Thus, to take a simple example, people who were recruited via a sweepstake offer will respond to that sort of offer later, and so on.

How to build a database

There are only two ways in which you get people on to your database. You may know enough about them to identify them as prospects for what you're offering. You therefore place them on your database and start communicating with them until you find it is no longer worthwhile, because they are clearly not going to respond. Or they identify themselves by replying to communications of one kind or another – advertisements, commercials, take-ones, or syndicated questionnaires (more about this in a moment).

At conferences, people often say to me: 'We don't have a database; how do you build one?' Being a bit of a smart Alec, I always reply: 'Surely you must have a list of customers? Even if it's only to send out bills? Surely you must have a list of your staff? This is your database. All you have to do now is enrich it by adding information about these people on to it.'

Although this is a bit of a simplification, it is true. Most people actually have important lists under their noses which will form the basis for their database and either fail to see their value or don't realise the names are there just for the compiling.

A while ago, somebody in the very competitive business of photographic developing came to see us. He spent most of the meeting telling us what a hot shot company he had. At the end, we asked him what he did with his database. 'What database?' he asked. 'The list of all the hundreds and thousands of people who send in for free films,' we replied.

'Oh, those. We take their coupons and use them to send the film back – it saves money,' he replied. 'Making a list would be far too expensive.'

Anyone who thinks that a list of satisfied customers is not worth the xpense of compiling is being very shortsighted indeed. And when you are in a highly competitive – even cut-throat – business like the one this gentleman was in, you should be particularly anxious to communicate regularly with the customers to retain them.

So the first place to look for lists which can build you a database is in your own backyard. Some of the sources are so obvious it's easy to overlook them.

Trapping customer names

Gordon Grossman, whom I have just quoted, once wrote an article with the pleasing title: 'If your customers won't make you rich, then who will?'

It's vitally important that you trap the name of every customer you have, or have had in the past. They will come in from your direct advertising and mailing obviously. But what if you're just starting out on direct communications? Then you must look elsewhere.

- Get everyone who deals with customers to record their names and addresses. Your telephonists. Your receptionists in the showroom. Your complaints department. Your service people. Your sales people. Your marketing people.

- If you have retail outlets or agents or a chain of dealers, get them all to do the same.
- Do you offer a guarantee? Get those names and addresses on file.
- What about your past records? Invoices you have sent out, old customers (a lapsed customer is one of your very *best* prospects), past enquiries.
- Do you attend exhibitions or shows? Collect names there.
- How about competitions? Build in a reply device to capture the names of entrants. They should be useful, too.

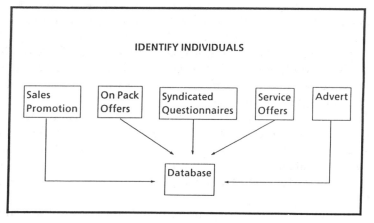

Figure 8.2. Identify individuals

I have included a little chart which shows you how names come on to a database. Unlike most business charts, I can understand it, so I hope you will. You may be puzzled by the phrase I referred to before: syndicated questionnaire. I believe this is something you really should be well aware of, because in my view it may represent a significant element in the future of direct marketing.

The concept is simple, like most brilliant ideas. It is brilliant for several reasons, not least of which is that it will eliminate to a large extent the need for you to build your own database. It is in effect the business of creating *proprietary* databases which contain all the information you need to target accurately the people you want to reach.

This is how it works. Consumers are offered incentives – often free or discounted samples – usually in exchange for completing a questionnaire. These questions cover the characteristics of the household, and the individuals within it, in considerable detail. What they buy, what brands, when they buy, how often they buy, what their hobbies and interests and habits are – almost everything you need to know. With the aid of this information you can target very accurately.

For instance, suppose you are selling Brand A coffee, you can then offer households who buy Brand B free samples of your brand and thus attempt to convert them. To households already using your brand, you can make a different offer. Perhaps one which encourages them to buy a greater quantity.

This offers you what is potentially a *guided missile* for your marketing. You are able to target your competitors' customers and make them compelling offers. And it works. In the case of a pain reliever in the United States, one brand was able to persuade between 50 per cent and 75 per cent of the customers of a competitor to try their product.

Like most new ideas, this can give rise to vain hopes, if not considered carefully. The truth is that most sophisticated marketers are aware that just to get your prospect to sample your product once is only the first step on the way to brand loyalty – that nirvana of the sophisticated marketer. Nonetheless, it is a very important first step.

If you offer to customers a series of incentives which persuade them to keep trying the product, then you really are getting somewhere.

I am only familiar with this form of database building in the consumer area, though clearly it would apply for business-to-business as well.

What should go on a database?

Your database is only as good as the information you hold on it. The more relevant the information, the better the database.

You need to know more about what kind of people they are; what area they live in; how many people live in the household; how old those people are; what sort of a house they live in. Depending on what it is you sell, you may want to acquire other information.

For instance, one of my favourite advertisements over the last few years was a series of pages for Fancy Feast cat food, with the engaging headline: 'The richest cats in the world and how they live.' The reply section asked for such useful information as: "How many cats do you have, how old are they, what are their names, what cat food do you buy, and how much?' Information like this is obviously of critical importance to that company.

Indeed, *everything* relevant you can learn is likely to make your endeavours more successful. Suppose you wish to sell home improvements. You will obviously be better off appealing to certain types of people living in a certain type of property. If you wish to sell children's toys, you want to find households with children of the right age, and so on.

Equally, as you have already learned, if these people have either bought from you or received communications from you in the past, that must go into the database. *If* they have bought, *when* they bought, *how recently* they bought, *how much* they paid and how they paid – all valuable ammunition to help you build a dialogue and create a relationship with your prospects.

The same thing applies when you are dealing with business-to-business.

Let's examine the type of information you might want to hold. It will probably fall into the following categories:

- purchase history;
- value/date of last sale/frequency of purchase/product range;
- company profile;
  business type/size/credit rating history;
- marketing data;
  source of name/promotion history;
  (i.e. mailings/telephone calls/sales visits)
  expressed interest in other products or services.
- You need to know who the influencers, specifiers and purchasers within a company are, so you can address each individually, addressing his or her motivations. That's because the majority of purchase decisions are made by more than one individual.

If you know what interest a customer might have in other products or services you offer it enables you to cross-sell. This is obviously desirable, but few people do it as well as they might, simply because they lack this information. But what happens when you do have it? Some time ago, the Trustee Savings Bank announced unusually good results. The reason given by informed observers in the City was that they had developed unusual skills at cross-selling. 'Around the world the bank has been held up as an example of what you can do when you know your customer base', said one leading analyst.

If your business relies upon personal selling, a rich database enables you to manage your sales force leads in a sophisticated manner, thus helping you monitor and control all your sales activities far more efficiently. Because you are constantly acquiring more knowledge about people as individuals, you can manage your database to identify your key prospects.

As we have already learned, those prospects will be the ones whose characteristics most nearly match those of your existing customers. Thus, retailers can examine regional distribution and identify the best areas for potential new outlets by analysing what they know about their existing customers.

We suggested to one of our clients, for instance, that by analysing the geographical distribution of their best customers and prospects, they could convince retailers that a market existed in their area. In this way they were able to persuade them to join a preferred supplier scheme.

Obviously, building a database requires careful planning. Sometimes costly errors can be made. For instance, a few years ago the Automobile Association discovered that when planning its database originally it had neglected to include information about the makes of cars members had, and how long they had had them.

Markets where there are 'no databases'

Some of my colleagues in less developed markets say to me: 'There are no proper databases in my market. In fact there are hardly any decent lists. Nobody knows how to put databases on computer.'

Is this an insurmountable problem? Of course not. As I have already pointed out, people were using forms of database a hundred years ago. Certainly marketers like *The Reader's Digest* were using the database principle before the introduction of the computer. The computer is just technology which enables you to create a database more easily. Moreover, if your clients don't have databases, then start creating them. If you're a client, start creating your own.

The computer is not such an awesome mystery after all. You might be encouraged, when contemplating possible mistakes, to realise that the big companies are *constantly* screwing it up gloriously. It may be that you have little to lose and much to gain by attacking the problem yourself.

But you will need specialist help. That is precisely what I sought when writing this chapter. I went to a leading expert on the subject, Ian Goodman, a director of Southwark Computer Services. Ian gave the following examples of computer problems during deduplication.

Simple overkill
Mrs J Smith
Janet Smith
The computer compares these two names at the same address and decides they are duplicates. In fact they refer to mother and daughter. What if Mrs Smith is a bad credit risk, but her daughter isn't?

Invalid marketing information
The computer discards Janet Smith after crediting her history of purchases to Mrs J Smith, who now appears to be a splendid customer.

False name creation
The computer creates a non-existent person by amalgamating the names into Mrs Janet Smith.

Sequence-dependent overkill
A Mr John Smith, Motoring Ltd
B Motoring Ltd
C Mr John Brown, Motoring Ltd
The computer compares A with B and decides that A=B. It marks B for suppression. The computer then compares B with C and decides to mark C for suppression. Thus only A will be mailed.

Same name, different companies
Mr J Smith, Motoring Ltd
Mr J Smith, Cars Ltd
Suppose both records refer to the same address. Either they refer to the same person who works for a group of associated companies, or they refer to two different people whose companies share the same business premises. How does your computer cope?

Synonomous titles
Mr John Smith, Managing Director, Health Care Ltd
Mr David Jones, MD, Health Care Ltd
Perhaps the company has joint managing directors. Perhaps one of these records is quite old, referring to a person who has retired. What does your computer make of this?

False title creation
Mr David Jones, MD, Health Care Ltd
Does your computer 'improve' MD to managing director? Or does it realise that Mr Jones may be a doctor?

Sequence straightjacket
Computers rarely demonstrate any flexibility about the way they sort names and addresses into geographic sequence prior to deduplication. The tiniest spelling variation in two otherwise identical names and addresses can play havoc with a computer sort, forcing the records so far apart that the computer cannot spot the duplicates.

Suppose the computer is sorting by street name. Consider *Alder Road* and *Older Road*. Imagine the number of other street names which may be sequenced alphabetically in between!

Tie-breakers and heart-breakers
Suppose the computer resolves its sorting problems and notices the two addresses for Alder Road and Older Road. How far will the computer go to test if one of these names has been incorrectly spelt? Consider the possibilities.

- Alder Road exists, but Older Road does not;
- Older Road exists, but Alder Road does not;
- Both Alder Road and Older Road exist;
- Neither Alder Road or Older Road exist;
- It is possible to match either street name with another street in the locality, after allowing for a different kind of spelling error. For example, Alder Street.

The computer might resolve these conundrums by referring to a gazetteer of all known streets in the given locality, using any given postcode as a tie-breaker. But it does not take too much imagination to see that the rules required to break the tie are extremely complex, being variably dependent upon both the given names and addresses and the particular mix of real street names recorded in the gazetteer in the given locality.

How far does your computer go in resolving these problems? What protections exist against incorrect address correction?

Ian ends with a statement you might like to consider when developing your database: If 99 per cent of direct mail managers do not know the answers to the above questions, and 99 per cent of computer people are equally uncertain, then only 0.001 per cent of all computer deduplication work involves people who know what they are doing!

Where to find the best new customers

Just as your own customers are the best people to make you money, they are the best source of new customers. Always spend time and thought on ways of encouraging them to give you the names of possible new recruits. This activity – known variously as 'Member-get-Member' or MGM, and 'Friend-get-a-Friend' – tends to be the most cost-effective of all ways of getting new customers.

It will normally pay you to offer incentives in exchange for the names of customers' friends. (The incentives only being received when the new name actually makes a purchase.) Usually it pays to offer the new recruits a gift, too. That way they do not feel exploited.

This activity of stimulating your own people to give you names is surprisingly neglected. I think it is so obvious that people tend to dismiss it as something they will get round to when they've solved their *big* problems, such as the design of the new corporate logo. Apart from collecting and exploiting testimonials, it may be the most neglected marketing ploy I can think of. Yet I can imagine few circumstances (save perhaps recommendations to a clinic for unsociable diseases) where it would not work, and I know of no easier way of measuring your profits.

It's normally a licence to print money, because the communication that solicits the new customer goes out as part of your regular commerce with existing customers. It rarely requires more than a simple leaflet, sometimes less. Unlike a mailing or an ad soliciting new members, you have no need to spend too much time persuading people your product is good; your satisfied customer is already convinced. In fact, the most cost-effective example I have ever seen (which I mention in another chapter) consisted of a simple one-line request on an envelope flap, offering no incentive at all. *Nothing* could be less expensive; I have never heard of *anything* as cost-effective.

So, write it in letters of fire over your desk: 'I need an MGM programme because it's money for old rope.'

Pass on the message

While I am on the subject, what about the converse: what can you do with people who won't buy? Your customers will help you recruit new customers; what about those who aren't your customers? It is by scavenging around in piles of what appear to be otherwise useless commercial debris – like non-customers – that you can sometimes find little nuggets of gold.

Therefore, never forget to put a small message in your communications suggesting to recipients that if they are not interested themselves, they pass the message on to someone they think may be. A good place to do this is behind the window on an envelope in a mailing so the message appears when the contents are removed.

In business-to-business mailings it's particularly important to do this sort of thing. That's because although it generally pays you to mail people by name, this is not always true: sometimes the additional cost is too great to justify the additional response. Often people move positions within organisations, or from one company to another so that you may be better off mailing to a title. This is not generally the case. It depends on the industry.

Often, it may not be at all clear who the real decision-maker is in the case of your product or service. That makes it particularly important that if you mail the wrong person they pass the message on to the right person.

Never assume that people will do it automatically. However, if you point out to them that the better a job of informing their colleagues you can do the more it will benefit their company, they may be more than happy to help you.

Compiled lists

Evaluating whether people are likely customers or not is something I have covered already to some degree, but I have not dealt with the tedious business of *compiling* lists of names of likely prospects.

Generally speaking, you are only likely to do this if you have a subject which is rather rarefied – one for which there is no list available from a broker to suit your purpose. Even then, though, it may pay you to go to one and get him to compile it for you. He may do it cheaply in exchange for the right to hold the list and derive revenue from renting it out to other users. You obviously make sure you retain the right to restrict rental to people you approve of, ie non-competitors.

But if you do have a pool of fairly intelligent people willing to pore through business directories and put lists of names on to word processors for a pittance, then by all means compile your own lists. Your sources for this heartbreaking task will be some (even all) of the following: telephone directories, trade directories, membership lists of relevant associations or clubs and any private lists you can beg, borrow or otherwise lay your hands on.

It is frequently worthwhile compiling your own list in business-to-business. Business products are becoming increasingly sophisticated, and inside businesses there are functionaries who did not even exist a few years ago. Like – an appropriate case in point – a data processing manager.

Sometime the value to you of reaching a named executive can be great enough for it to pay you to *telephone* companies to find out the right people to talk to. You'll also pick up valuable information on how buying decisions are made.

The list industry

When I first became involved in this industry, there were many occasions when one had to compile one's own lists. Now, happily, such measures are becoming less frequently required.

In those early days, too, the industry was infested with jolly pirates offering to sell (or even *steal*) your lists. Some of these have now left the business; others have 'gone straight' and become pillars of the industry.

So today, although the list business worldwide is not nearly as highly developed as in America, it is becoming fairly well-organised. As long as you take sensible precautions you can normally rely on getting what you have paid for.

Some of the rogues I knew in the 1960s whose pockets were stuffed with illgotten cash must be stunned to see that there is now even a List Brokers and Managers Association in the UK. They must feel rather like aged gunfighters did when the law came to the Old West. In their day, the business was often conducted over bars, with the unit of exchange purloined postal dockets. These would be filled in with fanciful numbers and shown to the gullible clients as proof that their mailings had gone out.

Nowadays, if the thrills and spills have diminished, there are still quite enough things that can go awry to keep the adrenalin flowing.

In the United States, the list industry is divided between list managers and list brokers. A manager will look after lists on your behalf, whilst a broker is a middleman. In most other countries such fine distinctions have not really caught hold. Most brokers will manage; most managers will broke.

Any broker can normally get hold of most available lists, so it really comes down to finding a broker you think is efficient. In a nascent industry, this comes down to trial and error, and consulting your friends.

You can go direct to the owners of the lists, too. There are two directories that give you lists of the lists available: one is published by Benn, the other by Gower. Neither can keep pace with the changing marketplace. Now, British Rate and Data have come out with a List of Lists. In the US there are many such sources. In less developed markets, none.

Use an expert

Although you will end up paying one way or another for his services, I think it's worth going to a broker.

The number of things that can go wrong with the way names are held (eg what kind of computer tape is it held on?) and with whether you get what you paid for (eg the number of names on the list, or the number actually still alive and kicking) is such that you should make sure you have someone else to worry about it. And of course to *blame* when things do go wrong.

I will only give you two words of advice on this subject. First, make sure you are not paying *two* sets of commission rather than one. Sometimes the broker you are dealing with may be charging a commission and the one who is managing the list may be, too. Let them split their earnings, not double them.

Second, take the time to go into every conceivable detail about the lists; or to make sure that the broker has done so. Other, more technical books deal with this at great length. They are worth studying if you can't afford an in-house expert. Happily we have more than one person in our company who has forgotten more than I'll ever know about the subject.

All I would urge you to bear in mind is that this is a world on its own, with more possibilities for foul-ups than you can imagine. All the criteria I listed earlier in this chapter apply, plus questions such as whether the computer can provide an *n*th selection for testing? . . . Are the names in postcode order or in alpha sequence? . . . On what kind of labels will they appear? . . . Does the owner insist on mailing himself? . . . How recently were they mailed? . . . How soon can *you* mail them?

Every question contains the seeds of a sleepless night if it hasn't been asked and answered, I promise you.

The cheapest way to rent is: don't pay

Many sophisticated direct marketers believe list rental is good for three reasons:

1 Having your list mailed regularly keeps it 'clean' by taking out the gone away names, as well as making it more responsive.
2 Mailing list rental income is easy money, for the overheads are minimal, and the revenue almost entirely profit.
3 The activity nourishes the industry generally by giving everyone another source of sales.

Unfortunately, there are also good reasons for *not* renting out your names. Some companies use their lists so much they are worried that additional use by outsiders would kill the goose that lays the golden eggs. Others are just naturally cautious: they fear they will have their names stolen. Personally, I would take the money and take the precautions.

One way to overcome this problem (particularly with a competitor, who may be worried about his precious customers) is to *exchange* names – possibly names of lapsed customers. That way, you pay no rental, and everyone feels secure. Another is simply to keep the mailing of the list under your own control.

Renting out your own names

It is perfectly possible for list rental to make the difference between profit and loss in a modest business. The average rental today in the UK is about £50 per 1,000 names. If you only have a small list of 100,000 names and you rent it out just once a month, the pickings are quite toothsome. Under such circumstances only good reasons of corporate policy (or reactionary masochism) can impel one to non-rental.

But you must take precautions. You must seed your list with trap names – the names of people who work for you, or are associated with you, to monitor what goes out. And, of course, you must let those who rent the list know that your list is so protected. Equally, before letting anyone use your list, make sure they show you what they are sending out.

Other sensible precautions include storing a copy of your list elsewhere, in case of fire or theft – indeed, anything you would normally do with something of value. Simply think about the list not just as some *names*, but as a precious business asset and act accordingly. Maybe just by calling it your *database* you will treat it with appropriate respect.

Incidentally, one consequence of renting out your list is that you get to see other people's packages and learn how they are doing.

The most crucial element

Mailing lists, or even databases, may seem at first sight rather dull. Yet I am particularly keen that you assign great priority to the subject. This is possibly because, as I have already admitted, I suffered for many years through knowing far too little about it. More important, these are *people* we are talking about.

Thinking deeply about the people you mail or telephone is vital. For example, if by analysis you can make unprofitable lists profitable, and profitable lists *more* profitable, this affects your business right down the line.

You can, for example, afford to mail a greater number of outside lists, thus enlarging your business base. You can also make more money from your own database. First by segmentation, secondly by communicating more often, and thirdly by delivering more potent messages.

In testing, it is the *people* – the lists – that make the biggest difference. In creative, the same: how well you understand them will determine your results. In choosing the correct position for your business, once again, your knowledge of people is critical.

The database, or list, is your treasury of people. What you do with that treasury will determine the future of your enterprise. And what you can achieve will be determined by how well you understand those people.

9

Where Ideas Come From and How to Express Them Persuasively

'Genius is one percent inspiration and
ninety-nine percent perspiration.'

Thomas Edison

'Everything that is written merely to
please the author is worthless.'

Blaise Pascal

The birth of an idea

You only have to look at your children's drawings or listen to the odd little phrases they coin to know that man is born with a creative urge. Yet sadly, in most people this urge seems to vanish as they grow older.

Many 'primitive' societies seem far wiser than us in the way they nurture this quality. For example, I have in my home some masks and statues from New Guinea, tapa cloths from Samoa and aboriginal paintings. Artists like Picasso learned much from this kind of art, and the artistic impulse – seen in acts like body painting and tattooing – seems more widespread in their communities.

But we 'civilised' folk in pursuit of such worthy ends as direct marketing usually allow this inherent ability to atrophy. We have come to think that to be 'creative' you have to be a specialist. Yet, who has not used the phrase: 'I've just had an idea'? The question is: was it a good idea or a bad one?

Those who don't do it for a living tend to imagine giving birth to ideas is a matter of flair; of letting the mind wander where it will. This is a myth. Your imagination flourishes best when guided. You are more likely to have good ideas if you go about it in the right way. I am not saying everyone can be a great writer or painter. But when someone asked Johann Sebastian Bach the secret of his genius, he responded: 'Anyone can be a genius if they work as hard as I do.' But work hard in what way?

I have already mentioned James Webb Young, the American copy-writer. He became a successful mail order operator after he retired from J Walter Thompson, so he would seem better qualified than most to advise you on how to get ideas in this business. In fact he wrote a book on the subject.

How do great artists, writers and musicians find and develop their ideas, he wondered. He did a lot of research and found out their methods were often very similar. From them came the book, *A Technique for Getting Ideas*. Much of what he learned is encapsulated in the following three steps.

1 Master your subject

You must be thoroughly familiar with the subject. David Ogilvy once stated that before he set about writing any advertisement he looked at all the advertising that had been done for the particular category of product for the previous 20 years. You may not have the time or resource to go to such lengths, but the point he was making is important.

Suppose, for instance, you have to write about something pleasant like a tourist destination. First, steep yourself in knowledge about it.

From this knowledge will come your raw material. Learn all you can about the people, the places, the amenities, the local customs, the beauty spots. Compare it with alternative destinations. See what its strengths are. Take note of its shortcomings, too.

It is from the *truth* that you will create good work. Your imagination can never dream up anything to beat the truth. This process of learning is vital. It will determine your positioning.

Think about your prospects. Read any market research there is available. Speculate about those wishing to visit the country. What kind of people are they? Why would they wish to go there? Make lots of notes. What would *you* like about going there? What would disappoint you? Talk to your colleagues and ask their views. Jot down any ideas you may have (no matter how odd).

I chose this example – a tourist destination – because I spent years working on such accounts. Two examples show how taking the facts and positioning the destination carefully on that basis can prove very successful.

Thirty years ago, when the Greek National Tourist Office set about selling Greece, four benefits stood out:

- There were miles and miles of unspoilt beaches.
- The weather was exceptionally pleasant.
- The people were unusually hospitable.
- There were outstanding historical sites.

Comparing these facts with other destinations and with what tourists liked, it emerged, for instance, that prospects were not interested in learning about antiquities – though they appreciated beauty. So the advertisements showed famous sites, but did not talk much about them.

This, of course, was an English advertising campaign. I believe that had we been writing to a French or German audience research would have revealed different inclinations.

However, to return to my story: we learned that our prospects loved sunshine and beaches. What is more, at that time French hoteliers were building a reputation for rapacity; the Italians were becoming known for a very imaginative approach to preparing their bills; and Spain was full of half-built hotels, with – in those that *had* been built – waiters who had often got jobs in exchange for building skills.

Accordingly, a campaign was devised based upon the positioning (and the slogan): 'Greece greets you warmly.' Every ad also ran the line: 'Summer in Greece lasts from April to October'. And every ad mentioned the hundreds of miles of unspoilt beaches in Greece.

The campaign rightly won many awards. More importantly, it produced an astonishing number of enquiries and sales. Somebody at head office must have got bored, because they stopped running it after a few years. They were foolish. I do not know who wrote it, but it was a brilliant solution to the problem. The advertising has never since been as good. In the years since, Greece has become one of the most popular of all European tourist destinations.

I worked for some time on the British Travel Association account. The only thing I learned from that was that if you put a very large FREE next to a picture of the brochure, you get a lot of replies. Mind you, this is well worth knowing.

Another tourist destination which has been promoted brilliantly is Singapore. Singapore is very small, unbearably humid, and there are no real beaches. On the face of it, the only good reason to go there is for shopping or business. However, if you are travelling between Australasia and Europe, Singapore is as good a place to stop off as any.

The city is inhabited by four different races: the Chinese, the Malays, the Ceylonese and the Indians. Each has retained its own culture. So it has been sold as a place where, in a few square miles, you can experience all those four cultures, whilst having a break from your trip across the world.

The cleverness of it is that the advertising does not try to sell a two-week holiday in Singapore. It points out that you can see it all in a few days. It is based on the truth, and is thus wildly successful.

Campaigns like this can only be created because somebody has *started* by mastering the facts, which leads us to the second step in getting good ideas.

2 *The inner game*

Your brain is a computer with so many connections that by comparison even the mightiest man-built computer is the size of a pea. So your brain is perfectly able to do all the analysis and synthesis you need to get ideas – if you have faith in it.

You must have heard people say: 'I have no idea where that idea came from. It just came.' Well, a lot of what we achieve comes from the subconscious. Indeed, in a totally different field, many top sporting coaches have come to believe that if you just let your brain and body run on 'autopilot' and stop concentrating consciously, you will do better. One of my former colleagues who is a pinball fanatic told me this works for him.

Whatever the truth, it seems that in getting ideas the same principles apply. At a certain point you must let your subconscious take over.

Once you have stored up all the facts about your problem in your brain, and talked to other people about it, and written down anything that has occurred to you, just relax. Move on to another job. Don't struggle, just forget that particular problem. But set a mental 'alarm clock'. Tell yourself you need to look again at the problem on Tuesday morning. Then let your subconscious worry about it. On Tuesday morning, sit down and see what ideas come to mind. You could be pleasantly surprised.

This method does not guarantee success. No method can. But many people find it works. The secret seems to be relaxation. I find that going for long walks seems to help. (So did Beethoven, which makes me feel good.) Mozart played billiards. Some like lying in the bath, or having a drink. Apparently the philosopher Descartes conceived his great maxim 'I think, therefore I am' whilst sitting in an oven in Poland. I suggest you do whatever you find most relaxing to help your brain get to work.

3 Use sounding boards

One of the principal benefits of working with others is that you can talk to them about your ideas. When you have an idea or some alternatives, discuss them with your colleagues, your secretary or even potential customers. They will always see the benefits or drawbacks more clearly than you.

Many people are most unwilling to do this. We identify strongly with our ideas. They are our creatures. It is hard to expose them to the bitter wind of criticism. However, you are not creating for yourself, but for others.

A word of warning, though. Make sure when asking for others' reactions that you don't ask leading questions. I used to provide a lot of innocent amusement to my colleagues by the way I phrased my requests for comment. I'm so delighted with getting *any* idea that I tended to say something like: 'I've just had this fantastic idea. What do you think?'

Only close friends (or unfeeling wretches like my associates) are willing to tell me the truth – that my brilliant idea has about as much chance as a snowball in hell . . . that nobody would understand it . . . or, more than once, that I hadn't even made clear what the product was.

So phrase your questions carefully. Don't incorporate the desired response in the question. 'Can you understand this?' Or: 'Would you buy this product?' Or: 'Is this credible?' Or: 'Do you think this is worth the money I'm asking?' Particularly valuable is: 'Have I missed anything out?'

Of course, some kinds of people seem to get better ideas than others. They are better prepared. If you have what is known as a 'well furnished mind' you are likely to do better. Read a lot (anything and everything). Watch TV. Go to the cinema. Visit art galleries, shows, exhibitions. Travel.

Above all, be *curious*. 'Questioning is not the mode of conversation amongst gentlemen,' said Dr Johnson. But it is amongst successful copywriters.

I am also inspired by example. Watching any supreme performer in any field fills me with greater keenness for my own endeavours. It doesn't matter what they are good at, I find it makes me want to go out and do better myself. I have watched street traders, violinists, singers – they all inspire me if they are really good.

The key word is *awareness*. Don't be dull. Be alive!

Being able to come up with ideas is only one part of the process of persuading people to want to do what you want them to do. You have to put your ideas on paper.

Writing is not an airy-fairy pursuit. It is just hard graft. Twenty-five years ago I wrote a novel. When people asked me what it was like, I remember answering that it was very hard on the fingers (I am a two fingered typist, and didn't have an electric typewriter). It is also hard on the nerves. Especially when you are confronted with that first blank sheet of paper.

I recall working in one agency where one of the writers just couldn't come up with ideas. Day by day he came in later and left earlier. Finally he disappeared. Some years later I met him in Regent's Park. He was working as a telephone operator. His case is not unusual. People talk, for instance, of 'writer's block'. Even great authors fear it. For example, F Scott Fitzgerald was obsessed with the fear that he had within him a source of inspiration – a kind of well – that would one day dry up.

Nearly every good creative person I know has this awful feeling when first confronted by a problem that *this time* they won't be able to cope. I certainly do. Times without number I have smiled confidently at a client, promised I could handle the task – and gone away filled with despair, wondering if I was up to it.

If you are not a writer or an art director, you may imagine that this feeling of panic is confined to 'uncreative' people like you. Well, now you know it isn't.

Getting organised

I have given you a sequence based on how other people get ideas. But you may rightly ask: how do you *marshal* your ideas? How do you start?

The great appeal of working in a creative environment is that it is not like working in a factory, producing so many car panels a day, or so many mouldings. But the drawback is that what you are doing is hard to measure or evaluate. Nobody can look at the number of words you have produced and say: 'Ah, that's 20 per cent above target, have a bonus.' And you can't just switch a machine on and get on with it each morning. You have to start your *own* little machine, and discipline yourself. It's not easy.

To succeed in creating effective selling communications, you *need* discipline. Anthony Trollope used to get up every morning and write for three and a half hours before going to work in the Post Office. Dickens succeeded by writing to the demanding formula of a monthly serial. Certainly you shouldn't feel too proud to work in a disciplined way.

Throughout history, great creators have been confined and thus forced to exercise ingenuity, either by convention or by self-imposed guidelines. In mediaeval times writers, musicians and artists were usually obliged to work on religious themes. Otherwise, they could not eat, for the church was the major source of patronage. The great composers of the classical period wrote within rigid structures: the symphonic form is quite a strait-jacket. Chinese and Japanese poetry for thousands of years has been produced to very precise rules.

I am not suggesting that producing advertisements and mailings is great art. But I can tell you that, having written just about every kind of communication, commercial or otherwise, over the past 25 years, that they *all* demand some kind of discipline. They all benefit from a proper structure.

There are a number of formulae you can follow if you want to ensure that your work follows a logical sequence. However, the most famous is also the best in my view. It is certainly one that has stood the test of time. Here is how it was expressed in a book called *The Inner Side of Advertising*, written in 1920 by a former advertisement manager of the *Daily Mail* called Cyril Freer:

> Here are the component parts of a good sales letter:
> The *opening*, which should attract the reader's attention and induce him to read.
> The *description and explanation* should hold his interest by causing him to picture the proposition in his mind.
> The *argument* should create the desire for the article offered for sale.
> *Persuasion* should bring the reader around to your way of thinking by seeing how the article is adapted to his needs. This is followed by:
> *Inducement*, which gives him an extra reason for buying, and in conclusion you have –
> The *climax*, which makes it easy for the reader to order, and assures that action by causing him to act at once.

This formula is variously known as AIDA or AIDCA. If you want to remember it, then recall the name of the opera by Verdi.

AIDCA stands for Attention, Interest, Desire, Conviction, Action.

It stands to reason that in order to give people your message, you must first attract *attention*. Having attracted attention, you must *interest* people in what you have to say. But this is useless if they do not *desire* what you are offering. And even if they desire it, they must be *convinced* what you say is true.

All this is wasted effort if you do not then get them to *act*. But before considering this formula in more detail let's look at how your prospect or customer is exposed to your communications.

Context is everything

'Circumstances alter cases' is a legal maxim which it is well to bear in mind. That which is relevant today can be supremely irrelevant a year from now, or even a week from now. It is the inability of poor creative people to adapt to circumstance which makes for a lot of poor work.

The most obvious example of considering the circumstance is that of adapting the *tone* to match the advertiser and the audience.

Equally obvious are cases where the whole communication is based upon the circumstance: eg a mailing on the occasion of someone's birthday, a new year, or the anniversary of their first doing business with you.

When considering how somebody will react to your message, simply consider what makes sense. Thus, the other day I received a letter from my optician. It had a very good opening: 'It hardly seems a year since I saw you last!' They wanted me to come in and have my eyes tested again.

This excellent opening, however, was useless for two reasons:

1 I didn't actually *know* anybody at that opticians – yet they were writing to me as though I did.
2 The thing wasn't properly signed by anyone – there was just a meaningless squiggle at the bottom. A good example of misapplied creativity.

Considering circumstances carefully can make for breakthroughs – either because you come up with a new offer, or a new way of presenting the product to a particular audience.

A few years ago American Express introduced the Gold Card. It was a radical concept; simply saying to cardmembers that there was now a Gold Card for those who were rather more important than Green cardmembers was sufficient to get sales. In the UK the appeal of the Gold Card was bolstered by giving cardmembers access to a line of credit. This worked extremely well – but not everyone responded, obviously.

Here is the opening to a follow-up letter which I wrote to offer the card.

> You may recall my writing to you some while ago inviting you to apply for The Gold Card – which gives you access to benefits greater than those available to Personal Cardmembers.
>
> You will, I believe, find these well worthwhile: particularly the £10,000 *unsecured* overdraft facility, which many Cardmembers certainly find invaluable. This overdraft, which is available through American Express Bank Ltd. can be yours *in addition* to your present banking arrangements.

Of course, it didn't take long for the banks to come up with their own gold cards. What could we do then?

The answer was to make a more competitive statement. Here is the opening to the letter I wrote with that in mind:

> You may recall that I invited you a while ago to apply for Gold Cardmembership.
>
> As you are aware, there are now other 'gold cards' – indeed you may possibly have been offered one; so you may well ask: 'Why the *American Express* Gold Card?' It's a good question.
>
> The Gold Card is designed to give certain Cardmembers a complete *range* of privileges; exclusive privileges which will make your life easier and more pleasant. Indeed, we have recently introduced several *new* benefits, which is why I am writing to you now.'

Both these mailings were extremely successful but, as you can see, they depended upon the context at the time.

Let's take an example of using what you know about your customer to communicate more accurately. I once had to write some copy for a company, Ace Gifts & Cards, which recruits agents who sell to other people – usually friends and neighbours.

The only thing clear to me about the prospects was that they were people who wanted to make extra money – or save money for themselves and their family. And the best prospects were likely to be sociable people.

The list being mailed was one of people who had recently moved home. The audience was not very sophisticated, so we made the personalisation very overt – each personalised section was marked in yellow. We found this simple device lifted response.

Here's the opening of the copy:

> How to make money as you shop –
> and make new friends around Chalk Lane
>
> Dear Ms Berger,
>
> Hello! How are you enjoying life at No. 18? Let me tell you about a new idea that could make (or save) you money as you shop . . . help relatives and your family with their gift problems . . . and even make friends amongst your new neighbours.

One of the things I had discovered was that the majority of sales were made not from a desire to make money, but simply from a desire to save on the commission.

Let me give you another instance where circumstance was all important. I was asked by the Save the Children Fund if we could persuade people to leave them legacies. This struck me as difficult. The same problem had been attacked quite simply by other charities offering a free booklet in advertisements on how to make your will. This seemed to me a good idea, but to succeed it depended upon people actively responding to an advertisement dealing with a very delicate subject – death. The idea of writing a mailing with the same objective I found daunting.

I spent a lot of time considering my target audience – elderly people – and the circumstances in which they would find themselves. In order to do so, I tried to think about elderly people I know. After a certain amount of reflection I determined that elderly people do think about death quite a lot. I also considered that elderly people are slightly more religious than the mass of the population.

I therefore determined to try what was fundamentally the same approach, but with two different openings. I wrote two envelope messages. One read: 'Do you believe in life after death?' The other read: 'For everyone over 55. Inside: an important question that cannot wait . . . and some *free* advice.'

Both the mailings attempted to empathise with the prospects. Let me give you the opening of one of them:

> A free 12-page booklet, with our
> compliments, which may prove *of*
> *priceless value* to those you love.

Dear Reader,

Do you believe in life after death?

This is one of the questions which people talk about less nowadays than when we were young. Yet if you – like me – are over 55, I would be surprised if you are not more concerned than you used to be about what will happen when you pass away.

You will notice that, in accordance with my own rules, I open with the offer – although I am not totally clear about that offer.

Both these approaches proved successful, one more than the other: I wonder if you can guess which? The answer is: Life after Death did about 25 per cent better than the other message. Nevertheless, the client felt that that message was probably too insensitive for our target audience, and we pursued the less successful one. (Incidentally, the mailing also raised a record amount of money for Save the Children, apart from a lot of requests for booklets.)

Once again, with this subject as with others, we emerge with the same moral: considering the people you are about to address, what they want, and what situation they find themselves in will almost invariably prove the key to the creative approach – rather than the key which most people try to find: an ingenious or clever approach.

Nationalities and social groups

Direct marketing works in most countries, to most social groups, in both business and leisure contexts. One maxim I would like to instil in you is: **'People are more united by their similarities than divided by their differences.'**

Time after time I listen to self-important businessmen who tell me that of course businessmen are far too busy to read those long, boring letters, or play with those little stamps on mailings. Or particular nationalities claim that direct marketing won't work with their fellow countrymen.

Happily, I have had the opportunity to see my copy run in many countries, and appeal to many groups of people over the years since I first got into international direct marketing with the Bullworker. People everywhere respond to the same motivations. For the most part they respond to the same copy.

My last job at the Franklin Mint was to write a mailing package for a product (to do with baseball, incidentally) to be sold in Japan. Prior to that I wrote for Italy, Belgium, France, Australia, Holland and, of course, the UK. The same appeals worked everywhere.

There are clearly products and services likely only to work in particular countries, because of national peculiarities. For instance, one of the biggest sellers in Japan for some time now has been a cooker which will prepare your rice for you while you are out at work. In Britain and the United States, the general population do not eat rice every day. Clearly, such a product would not be appropriate. Yet other products clearly appeal to the right audiences no matter what the country. Coca Cola is perhaps the most famous example amongst consumer products. Credit and chargecards amongst financial products seem to have a pretty universal appeal, too.

The moral is to make allowance for national differences, but profit from similarities. Often you don't have to reinvent the wheel by creating entirely new copy for a market you are about to enter. A lot of people will tell you otherwise. Almost all nationalities hate to admit they are in fact similar to other races. My advice is, if it seems to make sense, at least *test* the creative work that succeeded for you in another country, even though you may simultaneously wish to try a different approach for the country you are moving into.

Another canard is that the businessman becomes a different animal when he gets in his car to go to the office. Of course he doesn't. He is a human being first, and a businessman second. If you write to him about some way of doubling his profits, he doesn't say: 'I'm too busy to read this ten-page letter.' He says: 'God, do we need extra profit. I wonder if they've got something here.' After that, it depends on how cleverly you tell your story.

This point about businessmen is not something I have just dreamed up. We have conducted research which indicates clearly that business-men respond extremely well to gimmicks; particularly things they can play with – and they are *always* happy to read news which they think is relevant.

All you have to do when addressing people is to bear in mind who they are. Don't be put off by people's desire to imagine they are either superior to, or different from others. Their motives are what matter. Indeed, if you have the right message, it will overcome even the most crass of approaches. On countless occasions, even the most aggressive, insensitive US mail order blockbuster has succeeded because it offered what people wanted. And if people want something, they want to believe they can have it.

Once again, it comes down to commonsense, no matter what the market you're appealing to. If the product makes sense, and the motivation is there, you can usually find a way of presenting that product to the appropriate audience and selling it.

Of course, sometimes it isn't always clear whether there is a market for the product you have in mind. Xerox, for instance, put a great deal of faith some while ago in a copier that could reproduce in colour. It seemed a brilliant idea. It *was* a brilliant idea. Unfortunately, as one of their top executives observed wryly afterwards: 'You have to have something to copy from.' And there simply wasn't a great deal of full colour material people wanted to copy. So the product was not the success they thought it would be.

However good the idea, whatever the nationality, whatever the social group, I believe you'll find that the principles you apply will always hold true. Curiously enough, the same thing applies when considering another question often mooted: how do you approach working in different forms or media; how do you translate ideas from one to another?

Media vary; principles don't

Most of the principles which govern success in creative work tend to apply to *all* media.

By that I mean, they apply to advertisements, door-to-door leaflets, direct mail letters, complete mailing packs, inserts, television and radio commercials and posters – everything.

This is difficult to appreciate when you first start as a writer or art director. When asked to prepare a direct mail pack for a product which has already been sold successfully through advertisements, the tyro will commonly scratch his or her head and wonder how to set about it. The answer, of course, is to *start with what has worked already* and see whether you can adapt it to the new medium. One particular approach will not always translate easily into another medium, but with a little ingenuity it often will.

If we start with what is fundamentally the simplest format – an advertisement – and look at the elements, you can then build up from there to other more complex formats.

The elements of an advertisement (and this would be true of a single-sided leaflet) are usually a headline and a picture which together attract attention; subsidiary headings and pictures, supported by copy and captions, to do most of the selling job; and then the coupon or, if it's a very small advertisement, the request to write in or ring up.

Building a good opening sequence in a simple mailing pack – envelope message, opening to letter, opening to brochure and heading to order form – is not radically unlike starting an advertisement. The difference is that once inside the mailing pack the reader can choose to turn anywhere – to the letter or the brochure or the order form. (Some research suggests they turn first to the order form to find out what the commitment is and what the price is.)

Nevertheless, in all media, you must first get the prospect to start reading, and to start reading in the right frame of mind. Or to start paying attention to the broadcast message – once again, in the right frame of mind.

Let's return to the AIDCA formula. The sequence is not rigid. Sometimes, the urge to action can come at the very beginning of the message. There are often other good reasons why it should. It may of itself compel a degree of attention. Sometimes the interest, the conviction and the desire are intermingled. But *whatever* you do you certainly have to attract attention somehow.

The only figures I have seen suggested that only 20 per cent of the readers of a newspaper even noticed the headline of the average one-eighth page advertisement – and then only a small proportion of those would carry on and read it.

In the case of a direct mail shot the most recent research I have seen – from the Post Office – suggested that over 90 per cent of mailings are opened. Seventy-five per cent are opened and read to some degree. In the US the figures are lower. Only about 70 per cent are read. And few that are read do all that well.

Virtually every telephone call is listened to, but this is the nature of the medium. And most catalogues are obviously opened, because they are either requested or, at the very least, seen as a pleasant read.

The situation is different with a television commercial: most viewers will probably notice your commercial and sit through it. The problem is, will it motivate them to *do* anything? In fact TV and radio have their own special requirements which I shall touch upon, but for much of this chapter we are talking about your major direct marketing media, and especially how to get people to *start* reading your ads, mailings, and inserts. And *keep* reading them.

Happily, we do not have to guess what most often attracts attention, because the famous copywriter and research pioneer John Caples spent many decades testing to find out.

Headlines that attract attention

In advertisements the attention-getter is almost always the headline/picture combination. It is vitally important. Yet over eight out of ten advertisements are never read beyond the headline. Therefore most headlines are clearly not good enough to make people want to read on. Ergo, not enough work was put into them.

Most people think (especially consumers, when asked their views on ads) that unusual, shocking or funny headlines work best. This is not so. The best attention-getters are headlines promising *benefits* to the consumer. (If people want to be entertained they will watch TV or go to the movies, or read a book. If *you* want to entertain people, get a job in the entertainment business, and get out of direct marketing.)

The second best headlines give *news*. People like to know new things. The third best headlines are *curiosity* headlines.

Note that I say 'headlines'. Some may say a picture is worth a thousand words. Not so in our business. A picture should complement the words or lead you into them – certainly never conflict with them. But it is almost impossible for a picture *alone* to express a buying proposition, or benefit. You need words. On the other hand, words *can* very often explain your proposition, unillustrated.

Some of the very best headlines combine the elements of news, benefit and curiosity. Thus, several fortunes were made in the 1950s and 60s from a mailing and ad for a special kind of spark plug. The headline was: *'Now, run your car without spark plugs.'*

It was a startling way of implying a benefit. I tried to write a better headline for some months, featuring the big fuel savings that the product could deliver, but my headlines never beat that unusual opening, which in any case was followed by the main benefit in a bold subhead.

We all like to be clever or original. All too often one comes out with a striking phrase and says: 'How can anyone ignore this?' I have lost count of the number of times *I* have said that. For example, some time back one of my partners wrote an ad for Dr Barnardo's with the memorable headline: 'The frightening truth about Barnardo's new adoption shop.'

I thought this brilliant. So did the writer. The frightening truth was, of course, that without enough money, the establishment would have to close down. The public was unmoved, and sent hardly any money in. Our faith in their curiosity was not justified.

When curiosity works

Clever curiosity lines rarely work in ads. But they often do well as envelope messages. Sometimes, a curiosity line can be very powerful.

Figure 9.1. This is from the team of Bill Jayme and Keikke Ratalahti. They specialise in magazine subscriptions, and probably do it better than anyone else.

The 'Damn' envelope I have illustrated is such an example. (Though it also says 'How to stop cussin' and start crowing' – a pleasing, if vague benefit.)

In the broadcast media, which are entertainment more than news-orientated, you will often find relevant and amusing curiosity is very good in attracting attention. Thus, in the 1950s, for a commercial selling hair-restorer, the opening line was: 'Did you ever see a bald sheep?'

The problem with using curiosity appeals is the same as the problem with humour. What some people find funny, others don't. The great Claude Hopkins (more about him later) used to say flatly: 'No man buys from a clown.'

In fact humour can work if it does not overshadow the message. The idea of a bald sheep is not only curious: it is funny.

If you think you do have a clever opening, it's a good idea to put in a benefit by way of an insurance policy. For example, Courtney Ferguson, formerly a writer with us, has a bizarre sense of humour which results in some pretty striking lines. Being a professional writer, she tends to restrain her wilder excesses.

Walking past her desk one day I saw two lines she had written to go on the envelope in a mailing to sell dried minced beef to caterers. One said: 'You can't send cottage pie by post.' The other said: 'How to get 2lbs of minced beef, free.' She had rejected the first as too far out. We discussed it, and ran them both, the first very large, the second quite small beneath it. The results were very gratifying. There was a clear benefit. And caterers were naturally interested in shepherd's pie anyhow.

You can't lay down hard-and-fast rules about which headlines will work and which won't – only for which are *likely* to. You could probably write a book on the subject. But since nobody has done so, the next best thing is to get a copy of a marvellous opus by Vic Schwab called *How to write a good advertisement*, which contains a list of 100 effective headlines. I keep a copy in my desk. Every time I'm really desperate, I look at this list and see if it doesn't start me thinking. It usually does.

When I first came into this business, people used to talk about 'stoppers' – headlines that would 'stop' the reader. But it's no use stopping them if you don't immediately start them, too.

A charity ran the headline during the Biafran war, 'Fresh food is flying into Biafra daily.' It showed a giant picture of a locust. It garnered hatfuls of awards, and made the writer's reputation. What a stopper.

It produced relatively little money, I am told by a member of the governing body of that charity. Who likes looking at locusts? A picture that stops you dead may not make you want to read on.

Incidentally, often the most effective headlines are not originally conceived as headlines. They are *buried* in the copy. That's because writers and art directors tend to be like car engines: they take some time to warm up. Often the first ideas they come up with are by way of revving up; the first few paragraphs of copy are just a series of circles around a problem. You will often find diamonds in your own back yard by looking through the body copy for a good headline. (For the same reason, when editing copy you will often find it pays to cut out the first two or three paragraphs almost entirely.)

Sometimes the opening to the letter in a direct mail package is really the attention-getter. The envelope may have no message on it at all. Often the quietest openings, which merely *single out* the prospect, work best.

One famous letter opening is: 'Dear Mr. Bird: If the list upon which I found your name is anything to go by . . .' Here is the soft, but very effective beginning of a successful letter I wrote for an insurance policy aimed at teachers: 'Were you aware that there is an insurance company which offers preferential terms *exclusively* to teachers and their families?'

The most *boring*, unimaginative way to single out a prospect is to say: 'As a teacher, you . . .'. Poor stuff – but very common amongst second-rate writers.

Once you have gained people's attention – what next?

Each medium may have its special demands when it comes to attracting attention, but it is when you try to create *interest in* and *desire for* your product that professionalism often shows most clearly.

Above all you must keep your reader with you.

Joe Sugarman, the US mail order wizard I mentioned earlier, has likened good copy to a 'greased chute'. All you have to do is make sure the reader will read the next sentence after the one you have just written. This is true, but easier said than done.

You must look back at what you have *already* said, and see what the person would next like to know. And – just as important – what you can deduce about them simply because they read the previous copy.

The only thing you know about the person who starts to read the body copy is that they have probably already read the headline. Thus, the opening should amplify or explain what the headline has said; *enlarge* upon it.

That's why so many proven ads begin with something like: 'Yes, it's true, you can . . .' (do whatever has been promised).

One measure of good copy is what I call the *nod factor*. You must picture your reader, and see how many times you can get him to nod in agreement. People like to have their prejudices confirmed. It keeps them reading happily.

Let's follow the sequence in the teachers' insurance package I mentioned when discussing how to open the letter copy. After the first sentence, the copy goes on to say: 'Although we choose not to spend large sums of money advertising the fact, we have been helping teachers with their investment and insurance plans for over a century now.'

Thus, the reader knows more about you, realises why he has never heard of you before and the mention of the century in business shades into *conviction*, another of our key objectives. The sentence also implies a saving, and capitalises on teachers' well-known dislike of advertising: gets a nod.

In the next paragraph of our letter we go on to say: 'Over the years, we've helped many thousands of NUT members,' and so on.

As you see, nothing in this sequence is unclear or tricky. Each point logically follows the one before.

The assumption is simply that if the reader found the last thing you said relevant and interesting, then all you have to do is follow with something that explains or elaborates (without wasted words) and carries your argument forward.

You need an ability to get inside the skin of your prospect which I find few possess. You need to be able to write the telling phrase which only comes from deep thought and understanding of both product and market. (Sometimes the phrase itself may have come from something you have heard your prospects say themselves.)

Yet, difficult as this talent may appear, I know many clients as well as agency people who have it, if they will but bring it out. All of us need to communicate in business. So imagine that's just what you're doing. Don't be 'literary'; be straightforward. Imagine you are sitting across the table from your prospect, and speak in his language. Here is the kind of expression I've found helps:

- 'When we obtained the rights to a remarkable new product from Canada I thought of you immediately.'
- 'I think that the perfect chest of drawers should have six special qualities. I wonder if my checklist agrees with what yours would be?'
- 'I'd like to tell you about a remarkable breakthrough we have just achieved, which you (as one of our customers) are the first to hear about and benefit from.

  'If you're interested, then I can tell you you're in excellent company, because already three of Britain's leading direct marketers have decided they can't pass this opportunity up.'
- 'Would you agree with me that the business decisions you make often make sense to your colleagues?'
- 'I am sure that you, like me, are often assailed by people making "limited" offers of "unique" experiences; which is why I had quite a problem when I sat down to compose this letter to you.

  'You see, I *do* have a unique experience to propose . . . one which indeed will be limited to very few people. In fact only 700 will be able to join us on our 1985 World Cruise.'

I have already referred once to the matter of sloth. Once they've had the bright idea that got people into the copy, writers tend to be particularly lazy when it comes to describing the 'nuts and bolts'. But it is in the detailed explanation, the piling-on of facts, that people become convinced that what you say is true. You must work on this. Otherwise the sale will slip away. Tell people what it is you're offering in clear and unambiguous terms. Explain why it is better than alternatives (if any). Go into detail. Use all your persuasive powers, quietly and reasonably. *Not* with the hysterical enthusiasm so often found in copy.

Here's how I started to describe a bio-feedback device which was sold extremely successfully to previous purchasers by one of our clients:

This remarkable monitor actually 'teaches' your body to relax. You're familiar no doubt with the saying 'a healthy mind in a healthy body'. But only in recent years have doctors and psychologists learned how true this saying is.

Now it is possible, by measuring the stress your body is undergoing from minute-to-minute, to *train* yourself to relax.

And this unique device does it all for you, measuring how your system is physically reacting to surrounding pressures, and then enabling you to adjust your emotional reactions so as to relax easily.

And so on. . .

Let me emphasise that *every* product – be it an insurance package or furniture – needs to be explained fully and properly. You must consider and explain every possible advantage you can offer, and forestall every possible objection.

Thus, in the letter quoted above, I went on after the passage quoted to reassure people, for I knew the claim was hard to believe.

> *Impossible*? I myself thought so until I actually placed this Monitor in the palm of my hand and used it.

Desire – or Want

I have used the word 'desire' in our formula, but you could just as easily talk about encouraging people to *want* what you are selling.

By this I do not mean the old canard put about by half-baked sociologists that we can 'create' wants that didn't exist before. There has to be an underlying need for what you are offering, otherwise it will never sell. But the way in which you remind your prospects about that need, or amplify, it is very important. It's usually done by the use of example, imagery and word pictures.

Here's a section from the 'burned letter' I wrote a number of years ago.

> As you know – no matter what politicians say – the world's economy is in a bad way. And looks like getting no better. People like yourself, whose businesses depend to some extent on the construction industry are well placed to see this, because the construction industry is very sensitive to economic change.
>
> Yet curiously, amidst this depression, some people in the wood and paper business are doing much better than others.
>
> I travel all over Europe, viewing factories such as yours. Outside some there are huge piles of unsold stock. Outside others this stock situation is less depressing. And even in these difficult times they are making headway.
>
> I am happy to say that many of these companies which continue to thrive are my customers. Which brings me to the reasons why I asked you to practise a little arson.
>
> This letter has been treated with 'Fyreprufe' paper fire retardant to prevent it flaming. We also make a wood-fire retardant which will prevent wood burning.

and so on. . .

Your reader can appreciate this. It talks about something he wants: he would like to be one of the timber merchants who are doing well. I then go on in the copy to build up conviction by explaining that because of recent fire tragedies and the need to conform to consequent new regulations, timber merchants who use a fire treatment to treat their wood will be adding value to their product – and thus more likely to sell. This copy incorporates both a word picture and relevant examples.

Here are some extracts from letters written for The Royal Viking Line who sell extremely expensive sea cruises:

'From the very moment you step on board one of our ships, you're pampered. A steward shows you to your Stateroom. We give you time to settle in . . . order Room Service . . . and relax, before inviting you to join your fellow passengers on deck for a big send off from port:

> Champagne and a live jazz band spur on
> the jubilant atmosphere. Waving crowds on the
> quayside are showered with confetti and streamers
> as the mighty ship pulls away.

There's no more exhilarating start to a holiday. And as you lean on the railing, feel the quickening sea breeze . . .'

Here's another piece of copy written for the same client, selling a cruise to the Orient. We start creating desire on the envelope, with the line: '"Like Jasmine blossom carried away by the stream . . . sail to a world of which you cannot dream." – Chinese poet Li T'ai-po.'

When we get inside, the overline to the letter runs: 'Mist shrouded hills . . . sampans silhouetted on silver rivers . . . proud pavilions of red and gold . . . rice paper screens dappled with sunlight . . . incense drifting softly through temple courtyards . . . quiet gardens of graceful willows and bubbling streams.'

For a product such as this, the ability to create images which build desire is quite clearly critical.

Incidentally, in this pack we placed a sachet of Jasmine tea which showed through the envelope, and certainly helped attract attention. People imagine gimmicks like this do not work to sophisticated clientele. They certainly do: 8 per cent of those on The Royal Viking Line prospect list have titles – Sir this; Lord that; and so on.

Perhaps one of the greatest examples ever of creating desire for something comes from a famous advertisement written by John Caples 65 years ago – 'They laughed when I sat down at the piano'.

Here are two extracts from that ad.

Then I Started to Play

Instantly a tense silence fell on the guests. The laughter died on their lips as if by magic. I played through the first few bars of Beethoven's immortal Moonlight Sonata. I heard gasps of amazement – spellbound!

As the last notes of the Moonlight Sonata died away, the room resounded with a sudden roar of applause. I found myself surrounded by excited faces. How my friends carried on! Men shook my hand – wildly congratulated me – pounded me on the back in their enthusiasm! Everybody was exclaiming with delight – plying me with rapid questions . . . 'Jack! Why didn't you tell us you could play like that?' . . . 'Where *did* you learn?' . . . 'How long have you studied?' . . . 'Who *was* your teacher?'

Now let me quote once again the copy for the hotel advertisement I picked out earlier. As I have already pointed out this advertisement positions the product very well, but it also creates interest, builds desire, instils conviction and asks for action through the offer very effectively – as well as using phrases which enable you to picture the hotel in your mind.

HOT HOME-BAKED ROLLS

Wine-laced dishes with freshly picked herbs. Scrumptious puddings with thick local cream are served in the beamed restaurant of our small Georgian Hotel. Two miles Exmoor and coast. Phone owner-chef Dick or Kay Smith, WHITE HOUSE HOTEL, Williton, Somerset TA4 4QW Tel: 0984 32306.

[Try a 4-day]
BARGAIN BREAK
& save £30 per couple

Why are word pictures so important? The reason is, of course, that good advertisements and mailings are surrogate salesmen. You must do what a salesman would do. Quite clearly, if these people could take every prospect round the hotel they would get them to taste the food, they would show them the restaurant, they would demonstrate the setting, and they would take a personal interest in these people.

For some products, the *desire* quotient may be very small, eg life insurance. Few people want to die, but most people are stirred by the mention of large sums of money – especially if they are accompanied by a picture of a happy family, able to live on in comfort because the reader took the necessary precautions.

How to build conviction

Writing copy to sell direct is the literary equivalent of having the kind of face that nobody trusts.

First of all, they know you're trying to sell them something. That alone arouses suspicion. Secondly, because you are not selling face-to-face people are often even *more* suspicious. So this section is very important. It's an area, too, much neglected by lazy writers. Here are some ways to make your copy more convincing.

1 Make sure the tone is appropriate; and don't overstate
I get intensely irritated by the kind of copy in which everything is superb, high quality, tremendous and fantastic. It belongs in a never-never land only inhabited by poor copywriters. Therefore, eschew superlatives. Don't bullshit people. Talking in a loud voice does not make people listen: it just annoys them.

Equally, this sort of copy is rarely appropriate either to communicator or audience, and thus lacks credibility. What I mean by that is, the copy must always accurately reflect the source. Eg, if you are a bank, talk like a banker; if you are selling health products, talk like a health enthusiast. Just about the only product area I can think of where the copywriter's superlatives are appropriate is that of the used-car dealer.

And the copy must not only be appropriate to the source; it must also be appropriate to the audience. What is the right way to address your prospect? Once again, most writers behave as though they're addressing a group of subnormal teenagers.

2 Be specific
It reassures people that you know what you are talking about and that they will get exactly what you have promised.

So spell out your offer (and everything else) fully. Eg don't say: 'I will send you lots of lovely knitting ideas for an incredibly low price.' Rather, say: 'I'll send you 73 knitting patterns, plus 12 free books of hints for 49p a week.'

3 If the product is at all technical, give the specifications
Some people will want to know, and those who don't will be impressed anyhow. Always include exact dimensions and weights of products.

4 If it is a compilation, like a record album or anthology, give every title
Thus you convince people that they are getting a lot for their money. And, of course, somebody, somewhere will be looking for the one you miss out, and you'll lose a sale. The one that would have made the ad a success.

5 Write in the present tense as far as possible
The words 'will' and 'can' and 'could' imply less certainty of benefit than the word 'is'.

As soon as you can after opening the copy, you must move into the present tense. Thus, you say: This product *does* this; you *feel* this; not it *will* do; or you *can* feel.

6 Make it sound easy
Don't talk about the buyer having to do anything – talk about the product doing it for them.

Thus, you do not *learn* to type – our course *has you* typing. (And, being *specific*, it has you typing in 30 days . . . and being *convincing* . . . your money back if it doesn't.)

7 Re-state your benefits before closing
This is 'make your mind up time' – so bolster their enthusiasm just before you ask for the money.

The power of emotion

About 12 years ago, I was hired by a friend to work as a consultant to his agency. He introduced me to his staff as 'Drayton Bird – but you can call him Mummy.' The joke centred around a job I had done some years previously for the old Pritchard Wood agency. They had gained the Chambers's Encyclopedia account, but knew little about direct response advertising.

However, they put their top team to work on the job. One of them is now a well known TV commercials director. The other is widely regarded as the best creative director in Britain today – quite rightly, so he can afford this story.

They laboured long and hard, and created a beautiful full page ad, which ran in the *Sunday Times* colour magazine. It had the headline: 'Do you have a bright child?' The picture showed a child looking out of the page.

The thinking was bang on target. The product was being positioned as an educational aid. But the headline must have been wrong, because the ad only attracted literally a handful of replies. It's the sort of thing that comes every now and then to remind us we are but frail mortals.

The agency called in Bird, the man who specialised in the grubby business of mail order. (Our business really *was* the poor relation in those days.) I decided the previous ad was far too *rational*. I wrote an ad with the headline: 'Mummy, Mummy, I've passed.' The picture showed a child running up a garden path, obviously having just passed an exam, with the mother waiting to embrace him. The subhead said: 'What can you do to make sure this magic moment comes true for *your* child?'

This little gem appeared in a little eight-inch double column space. It got so many replies, the salesmen couldn't cope. There is little doubt in my mind that the secret of this headline was that it *dramatised* the emotional moment when the benefit was realised; then, it said something which made the reader want to go on.

I never got the chance to find out what would have happened to my other headline: 'Daddy, what's a hormone?'

Most outstanding business thinkers realise how important emotion is. Once I spent a day with Dr Ernest Dichter, the celebrated proponent of motivational research. How he conducted his research I do not recall, but he seemed to have an intuitive understanding of people's real motivations.

'A convertible is like a mistress,' he said. And: 'People buy a car for that first 20 minutes when they drive around in it.'

A good story to remember when thinking about those inner emotional benefits is the one about the businessman who saw his friend stepping out of a brand new Rolls, looking as miserable as sin. 'What's the matter?' he asked. 'That's a beautiful car.' 'I know,' the man replied. 'But I can't *see* myself in it.'

Outstanding campaigns always find a way to exploit emotional reactions. Years ago I saw a presentation made by Leo Burnett in Chicago to the Harris Bank, an extremely conservative organisation. The team proposed the use of a cartoon lion called Hubert.

At the time this must have seemed the suggestion of a group of demented visionaries. In those days banks did ads that looked like mausoleums. In a brilliant dramatised presentation the Leo Burnett team made the point that nobody cares about a stuffy old bank – but everyone would like a trustworthy, courageous, loveable lion. The appeal was almost entirely emotional.

Hubert is still around. And now, over 20 years later we see another lion working hard for Credit Lyonnais in France, the Lloyd's Bank black horse, and in the US again, one of the most successful financial animals of all time was a creature called Wally the Walrus. For the Marine Bank, he helped to pull in $80 million in deposits in two brief direct campaigns in the early 1980s. Emotional, irrational appeals for the world's most rational business, banking.

In creating attention-getting combinations of words and pictures, I counsel you to direct much of your effort to answering the single question: 'How can I dramatise the *emotional* benefit of this product or service?'

The nuts and bolts of good creative copy

I'd like to turn to some of the issues that come up again and again when people are discussing what makes good and bad creative work. Starting with headlines.

Short headlines or long?

In the 1950s, one famous English advertising agency had a Hungarian creative director as an art director. He would produce a layout, go to a writer and say: 'I vant three vitty vords for the headline.' Beware the three-vitty-vord system. Research shows that long headlines usually do better than short. Wit is often wasted on busy prospects.

Here's a headline I wrote for Bullworker which ran unchanged for 14 years:

> Britain's heavyweight weight-lifting champion 1962/3/4 shows *how these 7 exercises will build you a power-packed body in exactly 49 seconds a day* or all your money back instantly.

It showed a picture of my mighty friend Dave Prowse (later better known as Star Wars' Darth Vader) demonstrating the exerciser. It constantly proved a 'banker' ad, until they produced a new model of the product. Even Muhammed Ali, who was used in some ads, never did better except when he had a big fight on.

Here are some other successful headlines, none less than seven words long.

> Here's an extra $50, Grace. I'm making real money now.

> We travelled 2,000 miles just to save 2c.

> To men who want to quit work some day.

> At 60 miles an hour, the loudest noise in the new Rolls-Royce Silver Shadow is the ticking of the electric clock.

> You can laugh at money worries if you follow this simple plan. (This one, over fifty years old, was recently adapted by a UK finance house. It worked.)

> The amazing facelift in a jar. Used by Hollywood stars who don't want plastic surgery.

> How to burn off body fat hour by hour.

> The lazy man's way to get rich.

> 17 ingenious (but perfectly legal) ways to avoid paying your debts.

> How to double your power to learn.

Research shows that readership of a headline drops from 100 per cent who may read the first two or three words, down to about 70 per cent who will read seven words. After that the drop is insignificant.

But we do not want 100 per cent or even 70 per cent of our readers to reply. No product can appeal to all those people at one time. We want a *small* percentage to whom we can make a *precise* offer. Precision is not often achieved briefly.

Of course, art directors love short headlines. It makes their layouts stark and dramatic. But drama is rarely what we want. Persuasion is our goal; and that takes words, not pyrotechnics.

Envelope messages

Perhaps the most common points of debate about *direct mail* are: what –
if anything – should you put on the envelope? how many pieces should
be in the package? how important are personalisation and gimmicks?

The purpose of the envelope message – if any – is not merely to get
somebody to open the envelope. Most will probably do that anyhow.
Human beings are generally too curious not to. The question is, will
they be *eager* to open the envelope: will they open that envelope before
the other envelope? In other words, will the envelope message *set them
up?*

The brilliant man who set the pattern for much of *Reader's Digest*
activities in the United States, Walter Weintz, believes that what you do
with the envelope will have more effect on success or failure than
anything else, because it will single out that message from the many
others you receive that day.

Others believe there is no need to put any message on the envelope
because that tells the reader that a commercial message is inside, and
this tempts them to relegate it to *after* other envelopes.

Frankly, I find this somewhat unconvincing: when they open the
envelope, they will find out soon enough that the message is commercial.
Therefore, why not use that envelope to create a favourable frame of
mind? (I would enter a caveat though: if a prospect has received a stream
of mailings from you with envelope messages on them, then there is no
reason why a blank one should not, by way of contrast, prove very
effective.)

That highly successful copywriter Bill Jayme told me that the envelope
message was to start telling people what the subject was, so he didn't
have to waste time doing so once they opened the envelope – he could
get on with the persuasion.

I incline very much to this point of view. First of all, if there is some
indication of what that envelope contains, of the subject it is going to
cover, those who are not interested needn't waste any further time; whereas those who *are* will move forward into the package enthusiastically.

It has to be said that Bill Jayme has a substantial advantage in this
area, because he writes very, very ingenious envelope messages. For
Psychology Today magazine: 'Do you lock the bathroom door behind you,
even when there's no one else in the house?'

Or for a holiday magazine: 'How much should you tip when you're
planning to steal the ashtray?'

My advice to you is: first to ask yourself 'would this message *deter*
people?' Then 'would it *encourage* them?' If the answers are 'No' and
'Yes', run the message.

Anything you can do on the envelope to impart urgency is worthwhile. For that reason, many mailings may *start* by asking for action
with an indication that you might miss something if you don't open the

envelope. That's why you'll sometimes see mailing envelopes bearing stamps saying: 'Offer closes in 14 days, please open now.' Or: 'Dated documents inside.'

On one mailing aimed at travellers, I put on the reverse of the envelope: 'If you are travelling within the next 30 days, open now'. A very talented French direct marketing man, Bruno Manuel, once put a message on the envelope saying: 'Do not open until Christmas'. As he rightly surmised, this had precisely the opposite effect. People couldn't resist opening.

Sometimes the type of postal indicia used can lift response. In the UK, certainly, you are allowed to design (within certain guidelines) your own postal mark on the envelope. Attractive ones seem to lift response slightly.

It's terribly difficult to predict what will and what won't work. For instance, generally speaking, a white envelope will do better than a manilla envelope; and a brightly coloured envelope will often do better than a white one. If, however, you wish your mailing to have a quasi official appearance, then it might well be that a manilla envelope will be the best approach.

What is more, human beings are very strange. One client a few years ago tested an envelope which required the customer to buy their own stamp against his usual reply-paid envelope. Believe it or not, the reply-paid did not win this test. However, six months later in the same test to the same list, the figures were reversed. This is the sort of frustrating oddity which makes strong men weep.

Personalisation and gimmicks

Consumerists speak of gimmicks – in particular sweepstakes, competitions, free gifts and heavy personalisation – as the latter day equivalent of the Bulgarian atrocities the great prime minister Mr Gladstone used to get so wound up about a century ago.

If we must look for social evils against which to pit ourselves, this sort of thing is a puny target indeed. What does it matter if last week a German mailing arrived containing two tombola tickets and a winners' list which I opened to see if I had won or not? I had, of course. I pondered for a second before deciding I was not really interested in the wine being sold, and would not respond.

Things like this are harmless artifice. If you don't like them, you don't have to pay attention to them. Just as, if you don't like obnoxious TV quiz programmes, you don't have to watch them. Why people get so excited about them is a mystery to me; I very much doubt whether ordinary people give a hoot. Some say they insult people's intelligence. Many intelligent people would never dream of visiting a fairground, whereas others (amongst whom I confess I am numbered) still get childish delight from being whirled around on the waltzer and terrified on the ferris wheel.

Appropriately, Americans refer to many of these devices as 'bells and whistles': the sort of thing that used to attract attention to the circus when it visited town. I liken them to the fanfare at the beginning of a public event: they draw attention to what is about to come.

There is a certain type of personalisation which falls into this category. When it was first tried it increased responses by as much as 50 per cent. People like to see their names. The bigger the better. So one mailer sent out an order form with the recipient's name in huge letters on it. He got hardly any responses. When he researched to find out why, he discovered that people loved the personalisation so much they were pinning the order forms up on their walls.

Often, of course, a mailing will try to make the personalisation unobtrusive, so as to look as though it really is a personal message. This is seen by the recipient as a sign that the mailer has taken the trouble to address him by name. It is really courtesy.

However, the reason why all personalisation tends to work is simple. Byron put it one way many years ago: 'How sweet it is to see thy name in print.' But, let's face it, we like to be addressed by name and have our preferences recognised. What, after all, is more gratifying than to walk into a restaurant and have the owner say: 'Good evening, Mr. Bird. I have reserved your usual table by the window.' From the highest to the lowest, we all respond to this sort of thing.

All these attention-getting gimmicks are employed because they work. Take, for instance, plastic cards with your name on them showing through the envelope. We tested this six years ago and found these cards increased response in one instance by 70 per cent. One of the card manufacturers claims that they can sometimes increase response by as much as 200 per cent.

Appropriate gimmicks often work. A few years ago, our Norwegian agency created a mailing to people to tell them that a company which they thought had gone out of business was still around, and still wanted to work with them. Inside the envelope was a little plastic frog with a spring inside. When the envelope was opened the frog popped out. The message to the recipient was: 'Hop to it! Act now.' The little gimmick dramatised the thought of hopping to it, and also the thought that the company was still around.

You might be surprised to know that the mailing was not targeted at giggling teenagers, but at financial organisations, and the subject was related to computers. It was a howling success when no less than *eight* previous mailings – all more serious – had failed.

Why gimmicks work

Many of these techniques are easily understood if you spend a little bit of time thinking about people and how they behave. For instance, *Reader's Digest* arrived at the concept of the YES/NO alternative through reflecting upon the difference between those people who were replying to their mailings and those who weren't.

There was obviously a minority of people who were really interested in what they had to offer and did order. There was the majority – maybe 90 per cent – who didn't respond. People at the Digest wondered about these non responders. There must have been many who were *willing* to respond but couldn't make their minds up. Thus was born the concept of YES/NO. The idea was to force people off the fence. And it worked. Of course, they got plenty of NOs; but they got more YESs too.

This concept was developed further by a copywriter called John Francis Tighe in America who introduced the idea of YES, NO or MAYBE. He was selling a publication and the MAYBE sticker gave you the option of saying 'Well, I'm not really sure, but send me a sample copy anyhow and I'll see what I think.' This also worked.

Equally, the sweepstake works because – who knows? – you might win. Just as, when you go to the fairground sideshow – who knows? – you might win a goldfish.

Any device which creates involvement helps. The stamps you peel off and stick on order forms work. So do little rub-offs and things that show through envelopes indicating that something interesting is happening inside. Equally, touches of humanity help, like handwritten notes in the margin.

Some forms of involvement device work for more than one reason. Take those stickers. The idea of taking the trouble to sign your name and commit yourself overtly to buying a particular product or service is much more painful (and takes more effort) than simply moving a sticker from point A to point B on an order form. This sort of psychological ploy works in every sort of market, not just amongst the hoi polloi. *Fortune* magazine, for instance, uses stickers.

How many pieces?

I used to spend a lot of time lecturing each year, particularly for the Institute of Marketing near London. At virtually every session people questioned the need for a large number of pieces in an envelope. It is as natural as it is to question whether letters should be long.

My early adviser Bernie Silver showed me a mailing package out of which tumbled eight pieces (two of them different types of order form). I couldn't believe it. When I asked him for the reason, he laughed and said: 'One piece in the envelope means one chance to make a sale. Eight pieces means eight chances. They've got to say 'no' eight times.'

This reasoning was validated for me many years later when I heard of some research conducted by one large company which learned that each piece in a mailing package is looked at for about three seconds before being discarded.

More recent research, where we filmed consumers (unbeknown to them) looking at direct mail shots revealed that they tended to spend very little time indeed on packages which only had one or two pieces in them. On the other hand, one of the pieces we tested – a mailing for Dove soap, with a large number of pieces inside it, including a sample of the product – gained their attention for as long as five minutes.

Just as interesting, perhaps, is a simple look at the finances of direct mail. I am not going to give actual figures, since they keep changing because of inflation and obviously vary from country to country. However, the point is that the principal costs in a mailing are *fixed*. There's nothing you can do about them. You have the postage – a huge element. Then there's the envelopes. The list rental. Handling charges and other unavoidable overheads.

When you add up the figures, it may cost you only 35 per cent more to send out a 'rich' full colour all-dancing, all-singing package with lots of pieces than to send out a 'poor' two-colour affair. The question you have to ask yourself is: which will do better for the investment?

Unless you are only going for an inquiry – and certainly if you are going for a serious sale – the answer is usually the rich package. You're getting more opportunities to sell for your money, once people have opened the envelope. If they're *not* interested, they won't look properly at any of the pieces. If they are, they'll spend lots of time with them.

Your objective – to sieze attention, and retain it – may not differ, but because of the ways in which people *experience* different types of communication, the way in which you actually go about this will.

Thus, a television commercial, or radio commercial can only be seen or listened to from beginning to end. They are linear communications. But a press advertisement does *not* have to be seen in any particular order. Probably the headline will be seen first, in conjunction with the illustration. After that you can't guarantee where the eye goes. This is why you should make sure the layout is such that wherever the eye lights there is something worth seeing: a caption, an interesting little picture, some quote perhaps from an authority on the subject, an appealing guarantee – anything calculated to attract and retain interest.

Pieces working together

A mailing package present the same problem on a larger scale. It may have as many pieces of paper in it as you wish, but you can't guarantee which will be looked at first, or how. One thing is certain: you'd better make sure that *every one* of those pieces of paper is planned carefully to attract attention.

If you have a singly-folded leaflet, the headline on the front and the illustration accompanying it must attract attention. But don't forget you can't *force* your reader to look at the *front* first. They may look at the back. Make sure there is something appealing there, too.

They may look at the order form first: make sure that's doing a selling job. And they will almost certainly read the letter. That, too, must do an effective job.

It stands to reason that in this business, like any other, you will learn much by watching what others do. Looking at lots of mailing packages teaches a lot. One important point to consider is how the various elements in a mailing package work in concert.

The brochure will normally describe the service and display the merchandise – it is like your shop. The accompanying letter will be the salesman, who shows you round and points out the finer aspects of what is on offer.

There may be a second letter – (a 'lift' letter as it is known) from someone more impartial, giving you friendly advice. Or, like the shop manager reassuring you, saying 'Don't worry – we'll always do what we promised, you can depend on us. Just accept our offer.'

To add conviction there may be a testimonial sheet. Or some examples of how the product has helped others. Or a newspaper clipping. Or all of these.

Remember, a mailing (or insert or door-to-door piece) can contain anything you like – it's up to you to find out what works best.

Note that a letter in a mailing package should *look* like a letter, using typewriter script. Too many times printers produce them in a printer's type. That's not what your business letters come looking like. Why should mailing letters?

One great sin to beware of: putting in messages which conflict with each other. The whole must have a cohesion and consistency. Many unsuccessful direct mail packages fail because the message on the envelope is not followed up logically once you open the package. The creative people have had another idea which they like just as much, and which they are unwilling to jettison. This is a common error to be guarded against.

Another common error is slavish adherence to the order AIDCA. The various components should be included, but need not necessarily come in precisely that order. As I've already indicated, you can ask for action on the envelope. (Though you would be very unwise if you did not start by attracting attention, and *crass* if you did not ask for action at the end.)

Creativity in action

Inserts: a hybrid

I am often asked how you approach creating an insert, as opposed to a mailing or an advertisement or, for that matter, a TV commercial. I start by looking at the context of the communication. How likely is it that anybody is going to look at it in the first place? Is it going to be really difficult to attract attention or not? And, having done so, what do you wish to do next?

How does an insert differ from a mailing? In my view, less than you might think. A mailing is a pretty intrusive medium. The majority of mailings even in a heavily-mailed country like the United States still get opened and read. The question is: with what degree of interest? It is here that your skill comes in.

An insert is not as intrusive. In an insert you will almost certainly have precisely the same overall message as you would have in a mailing for the same product – save that you would not have a letter. (That is, unless you chose to make some sort of letter part of the insert – or even make a letter the insert, which has worked very often.)

The first thing to remember, once again is that there is no guarantee that anybody is going to look at what you have fondly designated as the front of the communication as opposed to the back. Therefore, both sides must work equally well, as with a leaflet in a mailing pack. This applies whether you are talking about a two-sided insert or a folded insert. In the case of the latter, however, the messages on the outside should be designed to encourage people to look inside. They have something in common with envelope messages for mailings.

Equally, you could say that the outside of an insert can be viewed in much the same light as the headline of an advertisement. In both cases the task is to get people reading.

Think carefully about how your prospect or customer will see that communication. By doing that you will be able to visualise what you ought to do. For instance, pick up the insert. Look at it. Would you want to open it? What do you think you would do if you received something like that? Then apply the same rules as to an ad or a mailing.

I have observed elsewhere that research will tell you a great deal about how people are likely to pick up and read your communications. This is essential.

The telephone

I am concentrating here for the most part on print media: direct mail, advertising and inserts – and particularly on the major problems of getting ideas and gaining attention.

With the telephone, there is no problem gaining people's attention. When the phone rings they pick it up. Or, if it's an inbound telephone call, they have taken the initiative themselves. They are interested to hear what you are going to say anyhow.

However, the telephone is unique: it is a two-way medium. It is also very expensive. You are paying all that money for the fact that, as long as you are polite, people will listen to what you have to say. So make sure they get the right message. This means, above all, having a professional script, delivered professionally. Relying on amateurs is not likely to work. (More on this in the chapter on media.)

Telephone scripts allow for interruptions and reactions. This is an *interactive* medium, so make the most of that fact. Scripts should be divided in two. One side is the script as planned. The other is a series of pre-planned answers to questions and objections. The script will evolve as it is used, being adapted according to the reactions it receives.

My advice on telephone is to go to professionals. In the first place it is as well to get them to do the job for you, and then at the very least get them to train your own people.

Biggest telephone sins: treating people like morons; and not giving them a chance to reply. If you simply read out a script without allowing for any reaction you learn nothing. You might just as well send out a mail shot.

Catalogues: the visual reigns

Catalogues, though apparently the medium with least in common with the telephone, actually have a similarity when it comes to the creative approach.

That is, that you don't have to worry about getting attention. Usually they have either been requested or they are received with pleasure. The challenge, therefore, just as with the phone, is to get the most out of that attention you've gained – to *keep* people interested.

In one other respect, catalogues differ from most other media apart from posters. The pictures are more important than the words. However, every word must count. Trying to describe the product in the minimum number of words, every one of which must justify its place, is splendid training. It takes exceptional professionalism to do it well. Few can.

It also takes exceptional professionalism to come up with an unusual catalogue approach. Often because catalogues are thrown together as cheaply as possible, the net result is what you would expect: rubbish. But paying more, and spending more time thinking about what you ought to do is of exceptional importance. It really will pay off for you.

For instance, the Banana Republic Catalogue in the United States has been the foundation of a business which was exceptionally successful in mail order, then moved into retail, and is now going international. This was achieved by breaking most of the accepted rules for catalogues. Thus, drawings were used, rather than photographs. There was a lot of copy, developing a narrative line based upon an imaginary republic. The catalogue is entertaining, as well as selling.

In the business-to-business field, Inmac have developed a style of catalogue for computer accessories and the like with a visual approach which differentiates them very well from their competitors. But when you look at it there is nothing unusual. It is just good typography – rare enough in that field to make them stand out.

The leads me into the first of 14 suggestions for improving your catalogue.

1   Find a way to make your catalogue different
Certainly make it different visually, and try to make if different verbally,
too. Develop a *character* for it.

2   Catalogues should not be impersonal
Some of them read as though they are produced by computer. Your
catalogue should have an introductory letter to establish a relationship
between company and buyer.

3   Position is vital
Your letter, for instance, will almost certainly do better bound on to the
front cover, just revealing the merchandise beneath than looking like a
printed piece inside the front cover. Your order form – better bound in
than floating loose – should be constructed so that it is easily seen.

4   The cover is your prime selling spot
Tests show that whatever is on there will sell at least three times as well
as it it were in the body of the catalogue. So you have to have good
reason indeed not to use the cover for merchandise.

5   Space is at a premium in a catalogue
Areas given over to 'mood' shots are usually not selling. Build mood
into your overall treatment, don't just ladle it in at intervals – it's wasted
space.

6   Don't underestimate the number of items you can get on a page
Properly planned, it can accommodate more than you think. Pages with
few items usually won't make as much money as those with many – so
you must have good reason for using them.

7   Create changes of pace and interest
Put in little 'hot' spots that make people open up on certain pages – like
pages with heavier weight paper, gatefold pages and, of course, the
order-form pages. Testimonials will also add interest, especially if you
put people's faces in them.

8   Every catalogue entry should be a 'mini-ad', with its own headline

9   Your catalogue can point to what will work for you in ads or mailings
For this reason the presentation of items in the catalogue should be in
the same style as you would use for other communications.

One client of ours used to use a different style of copy, headline,
photographic treatment and even typography for his catalogue as for his
ads. He could never understand why items that did well in one medium
so rarely did well in others; nor why he got relatively poor results from

his catalogue when sent to his ad respondents. People who have responded to one style of presentation will not necessarily react well to another.

10   Photographs almost invariably do better than illustrations
They are more credible. If using illustrations, make sure they give a very detailed impression of the products.

11   Pay great attention to the order form and how it is planned
Making it easy to order, just by checking a few items and having the customer's name already filled in, will have a critical effect on results.

12   Great care must be taken to ensure that the captions (and prices) are easily related to items
It's infuriating to make people *hunt* for information.

13   Catalogue results can be boosted enormously (sometimes over 50 per cent) by the use of contests and sweepstakes

14   For reasons of finance and logistics, it usually pays to use as few photographers or illustrators as possible

Broadcast media

What you can do in broadcast media is affected clearly by the very limited time those media allow. That time is itself governed by another factor: you have to allow a sufficient period within the commercial to give details of how to respond.

Television is watched with a fair degree of attention by its audience. This is one of the reasons for its power. You don't necessarily have to do anything *particularly* startling to attract attention. (Though this doesn't mean you shouldn't try.) The challenge is, having opened the commercial, to build people's interest.

Here are three basic things to remember about TV or radio, (bearing in mind that radio is TV without pictures). Here, once again, you're trying to create pictures inside people's minds.

First, you must seek a single, simple, central idea.

Rosser Reeves in his book *Reality in Advertising* uses the expression 'there's only so much room in the box'. People can rarely take on board more than one simple idea in a commercial. You may buttress it with supporting facts, but don't try to introduce any conflicting thoughts.

For example, *Reader's Digest* has for some years used a brief commercial to tell people that a mailing is going to come through their door offering them a chance to win a sweepstake. The simple idea here was to put a former newscaster in front of the camera and let him tell people. This gave the whole thing credibility. The only time we moved away from the central shot of this newscaster was when showing the mailing coming through the door.

Again, if you look at the commercial I have illustrated for Time-Life (see pages 220–21), you will see that the simple idea is just to put a lot of scary things on the screen in a logical sequence, which demonstrate the content of the books being sold.

This brings me to the second cardinal principle: never forget that TV is a *demonstration medium*. In the case of the commercials I have mentioned above, the first commercial demonstrates the mailing arriving through your door; the second one demonstrates the content of the book. Indeed, the very first successful television commercials were made by somebody taking street corner hucksters selling food processors and similar gadgets through demonstration, and sticking a camera in front of them. It worked beautifully.

In the case of radio, demonstration is perhaps best used when selling record collections, which are clearly made for the medium.

The third thing to remember is that is you are going to be entertaining, that entertainment should derive from the sell. It should not be inappropriate. Thus, in the case of the food processors I have just mentioned, after doing straightforward pitches for the product, it was decided to try using somebody *entertaining* to demonstrate the products. The agency very wisely didn't build in entertainment for its own sake: they got a well known cookery expert, Richard Simmons, to do the commercials. He was funny, but he was talking all the time about the product.

Whereas, when *Reader's Digest* tried to run a funny commercial with speeded up film of people running to the post box to post their entries, the gimmick overcame the idea. It didn't work.

Here are some of the points likely to make your broadcasting work more effectively:

- Are you really exploiting the medium? For instance, if you're on TV, is it truly visual, or just words set to pictures? If you're on radio, is it just words or are you using the medium properly to conjure up images in people's minds?
- Is there a key visual or sound which acts as an mnemonic device to fix in the memory. Have you repeated it?
- Is the product the hero – or is the execution?
- If there's music, is it relevant or just gloss? The same applies to any visual device. Everything should be essential to making the commercial work better.
- Do you get straight to the point? You have limited time: get people involved instantly. In particular, a dramatic opening at the beginning of radio commercials to set them aside from the tapestry of sound – a loud noise, a fanfare – are obvious things. A challenging

Figure 9.2. Time Life Books 'Enchanted World'

Illustration	Video	Audio – Male voice over
	Man's hand stroking a glowing rabbit's foot.	'A rabbit's foot, carried luck ...
	Man at table knocks over salt shaker and throws pinch of salt over his left shoulder.	a pinch of salt, tossed over the shoulder ...
	Black cat in front of fire place hesitates, meows, runs out of frame	a sense of foreboding at the sight of a black cat ...
	Woman's hand mirror falling to the floor. It shatters; fluttering calendar page showing Friday 13th; knuckles knock on wood.	Are they harmless superstitions – or reminders of a darker time when the world was young, nature seemed all-powerful, and humble charms were man's best protection against unknown evil?
	'Wizard's worktable' filled with books and occult objects. Cover opens by itself, pages begin flipping quickly by. Camera moves in on werewolf illustration.	Enter The Enchanted Wood ... a spellbinding series from Time-Life Books that probes the forgotten origins of the world's strangest curiosities.
	Book visuals: Dragons; Dwarfs; Fairies and Elves; Night Creatures.	In each lavishly illustrated volume, you'll move through storybook lands where the *original* endings to the tales of childhood weren't always happy ones.
	Darkened hallway. Wind stirs curtains ... a ghostly figure moves towards you from far down the hall.	The Enchanted World takes you back to a time when restless apparitions drifted through darkened hallways ...'
	Book visuals: Ghosts.	*Female reading passage:* 'Some ghosts were nothing more than cold spots on floors or shadows in corners. Others took human form.'

Robed figure laying down Tarot cards.

Male voice over:
A time when men who called themselves sorcerers used the Tarot to prophesy the future ...

Male reading passage:
'The Hanged Man, dangling from a gallows, was a sign of life in suspension, while the Death card indicated change ...'

Male voice over:
'and a time when malevolent creatures were thought to stalk the night in search of hapless victims.'

Traveller on foot at night on shadowy path. As he passes large tree, 3 pairs of eyes watch him.

Female reading passage:
'Unwise was the wayfarer who journeyed by night ...

Book visuals: Book of Christmas, Night Creatures.

for in the shadows greedy eyes glittered, claws curled, teeth clicked.

Wizards & Witches volume stands centre screen.

Male voice over:
Begin your journey through The Enchanted World with Wizards & Witches. Examine it free for 10 days. If you keep it, other volumes will follow, one about every other month ... Spells & Bindings ... Ghosts ... and Water Spirits.

Gnarled hand with large signet ring closes open volume on table, hesitates – and knocks wooden surface.

So enter The Enchanted World ... where anything is possible, and a little luck never hurts.

statement is another, or some tricky form of delivery like somebody speaking very fast.

- Does the product or service solve a problem? If so, is it shown clearly?
- Have you made it clear this is a direct offer? Preferably at the beginning, so people know they have to take note of somewhere to reply to.

Two secret ingredients

Two ingredients for successful creative work are rare – yet perhaps most powerful of all. They are *genuine* involvement in the topic and *enthusiasm*.

You encounter these most often amongst copywriters who also happen to be the proprietors of their own businesses. My favourite example (but then I am biased) comes from my own mother. At the age of 67 she started running a charity which rescues homeless animals. I kept on telling her she ought to write to her supporters because she had spent all her money on this project and was getting desperate. So at the age of 71 she finally wrote her first piece of direct mail copy. I reproduce it here in its entirely.

Every one of these letters that went out raised £5. I sent the letter to David Ogilvy. He wrote back: 'Hire your mother.'

Why is it so good? Clearly, first of all it comes from the *heart* – the enthusiasm and urgency shine through. Secondly, she is able to give the *facts* because she is so intimately involved in what she is talking about. You can see the whole letter is peppered with details which add verisimilitude. And you can also see that her love for animals comes out in phrases like: 'for the first time, [the cats] are able to scent the fresh air and see the blue sky' – phrases that conjure up vivid pictures; pictures that move you to action.

Dear Animal Lover,

We are about to reach our second Christmas as a recognised charity. During this year and nine months we have rescued and homed over 925 cats and kittens, along with a number of dogs and puppies.

We have, with your help, been able to improve our cattery and the cats are now, for the first time, able to scent the fresh air and see the blue sky. Originally we had 8 spacious cages, two storeys high, down one side. With the help of donations and money raised by members at charity functions, we undertook the much-needed improvements.

We decided to close in August for two weeks except to the most needy cases, in order to carry out these alterations.

Firstly we built another 8 cages on the opposite side of the cattery, all with a removable perspex sneeze barrier, power point and electrically-heated bed. We then added a false ceiling for heat conservation. The rough concrete floor was covered with smooth asphalt for easy cleaning. At one end of the cattery the old garage doors were replaced by toughened patio-type doors to let in more light and these are left open when weather permits for extra ventilation. They now lead onto a high, walled-in 'adventure playground' which is escape-proof and fitted with platforms and a peep-hole.

Our second smaller cattery is next in line for up-grading.

I would like to add that except for the asphalt floor and the brickwork on the outside run, all this work was done by members and members' families.

We are now very proud of our cattery and, most important of all, it must add to the comfort of the cats while they are with us.

In March of this year we started to run an active neutering plan for the cats which come to us. Under this scheme we have neutered approximately 120 she-cats and 40 toms.

I would like to take this opportunity to thank you for your generosity for without your help we could not survive. As you will appreciate, our vets' and feeding bills are colossal and we have to struggle to keep our heads above water. Our members work hard and continuously for nearly all have another job so their time is limited.

Finally, have a wonderful Christmas and a happy and healthy New Year.

The professional – the condottiere, as it were, who is writing because he has been hired to write on somebody else's behalf – finds it difficult to summon up this degree of enthusiasm or to acquire this depth of knowledge. But it is the ability to do so which distinguishes the outstanding writer from the also-ran.

Where does this ability come from? In my view, from an emotional determination, born of pride in one's craft, to align oneself totally with the client's interests and do the very best job possible. This is an egotistical characteristic. It is the belief that one has the mysterious power to persuade other people to do what you want them to do.

Few people have it; but that does not mean to say it cannot be nurtured within you, and I am absolutely certain that a clear understanding of what you should and shouldn't do to get good creative work is utterly essential.

For that reason, the next chapter will deal with *lists* of what works and what doesn't – and why.

10

How to Make Your Creative Work Virtually *Foolproof.*

'There's no safety in numbers,
or anything else.' James Thurber

I live way out in the country in an old house.

The other day, on my way up our long, overgrown drive, I glimpsed an agile little creature less than a foot long darting into the undergrowth, then pop out its head to peep at us. It was a weasel. A cynic might describe the weasel as the patron animal of a certain type of copywriters.

The word 'weasel' in our business defines a word or expression which the reader may not even notice, but which changes the sense of what is written. Like the animal, they are rarely noticed. But they can, if ignored, do a great deal of damage.

The word *virtually*, which I used in this chapter title is an example; or the phrase 'up to'; or the word 'helps'. The latter is often used when making claims about beauty products, such as 'helps give you younger looking skin'. (Actually, even 'younger looking' is a weasel: people notice the 'younger', and don't bother too much about the 'looking'.)

Weasels work because people believe what they want to believe. That's one of the great truths of selling. However, when I read the other day about a new computer programme called 'Headliner' – described as 'thought processing software . . . a series of linked databases for ideas', which writes headlines for you, I did not want to believe it.

My brain goes numb when I hear of devices like that, but once I have penetrated the jargon and understood what they really are, I usually recover my sang-froid.

I cannot believe anyone will ever invent a machine that can produce good weasels; nor can I imagine any machine that can generate imaginative ideas – or for that matter evaluate them. And since everything we do in our business is based on getting and judging ideas, 'I am encouraged to go on', as Harold Ross of the *New Yorker* used to say.

If you have ever had to assess creative work, then you know how hard it is; almost as hard as thinking it up – but not nearly as much fun. No matter how tactful you ae, the people who had the idea will never thank you for anything short of pure adulation.

One of the reasons why many people find it hard to separate the sheep from the goats in creative work is that it's so easy to judge subjectively. Do you like the picture? Do you find the headline ingenious? Are you titillated by the snide remarks made about your competitors in the copy? All these are easy things to say 'yes' or 'no' to. Because people have no *objective* criteria, they tend to fall back on what they like – and often what they find *original*.

The reason for this is that if you spend a lot of time (as we do) looking at selling communications, you become blasé. 'Oh! Not another headline announcing a new product' . . . 'God! Not another free offer.' You've seen it all before – and you don't want to see it again.

So you look for something different. Unfortunately, there is little evidence to suggest that something different necessarily sells, as we have already learned.

In 1985 the Ogilvy Centre for Research & Development wanted to discover whether people bought more products as a result of seeing television commercials they liked. The answer was – not surprisingly – that they did.

But what kind of commercials, the research went on to inquire, did they find 'likeable'? The answer was emphatically not 'original' TV commercials. They prefer commercials which are relevant and meaningful.

So, beware the siren call of the original.

Never is this truer than in headlines. For instance, I received a while ago a mailing from Barclaycard to tell me how I could use my card to get money out of cash machines all over the world. You might imagine a sensible heading to the leaflet would be: 'How you can use your card to get cash'.

Nothing of the sort. The heading said: 'The shape of things to come'.

I do not propose to speculate by what curious process of transmogrification the writer had arrived at this headline, but it managed to obscure entirely what I wanted to know.

Of course, very often you can be as original as you like in general advertising. Your objectives may be quite other than those of raising sales. A significant proportion of people in general advertising are interested above all in gaining awards. Marketing directors want to run commercials which reflect their good taste, which their relatives and their friends at the golf club will applaud.

Unfortunately, their friends are not necessarily likely to be the same sort of people as our customers. What is greeted with squeals of delight by sophisticates of the communications industry may be greeted by those who cough up the lolly with an uninterested yawn. Worse, it can ruin your business.

Two or three years ago a UK chain of retail stores hired the photographer Richard Avedon to take some pictures around which they would create some advertisements. His work was superb – and rightly acclaimed. He took a beautiful black model and posed her in some stunning and bizarre make up. The campaign was showered with awards – and sales plummeted. The agency lost the account. The client could measure what was happening in the shops, and was not too keen on going broke.

Because direct marketing reveals what works and what doesn't (often in a way which upsets sensitive egos like mine) bitter experience has helped me formulate a pretty comprehensive idea of what works and what doesn't. I have put together a series of laundry lists, therefore, to help you create more effective work, or if you are judging work, to judge it better.

I must warn you, though, that like most failsafe methods, these lists don't guarantee success. No two creative problems are identical; every market differs slightly from every other market; but the principles that make for success are usually the same. You are far more likely to succeed by using these lists; and when you decide not to follow their advice, at any rate you will do so *knowingly*, for good reasons. That's where your commonsense comes in.

Despite what I have said already, you may still wonder whether working like this – to what is really a series of formulae – can help in something so quirky and personal as having ideas. Well, let's go back to the old definition of advertising being 'salesmanship in print'. This is all very well, but face-to-face selling allows you to do things that are impossible when you cannot actually *see* the reactions of your audience.

For instance, I was making a speech in Brisbane when suddenly the air conditioning stopped working. I was able to witness what effect this had on my audience: it put them to sleep. So I livened up the presentation.

You can't see the reaction of somebody receiving your direct mail shot or looking at your advertisement. You don't know what's going through their minds. And you can't vary your approach to fit in with their reaction. Once that mailing shot has gone out, it has gone out. Once that commercial runs, you can't change it.

The only exception is telephone selling. You can quickly evaluate the way people react to particular lines in a telephone script, and alter it accordingly. But even the phone is a very deceptive instrument. You might be talking to somebody on the telephone, and saying something you find very witty. The person on the other end may misunderstand it – being unable to see the expression on your face – and even take it as an insult. Indeed, because I have a strange sense of humour, this has happened to me more than once.

A salesman with a strong personality can break all the rules and still succeed. I remember sending a man up to Birmingham to sell £3,000 worth of fire extinguishers. He was so ill prepared he didn't even know how much they cost – and had to ring me up to find out. But his personality overcame his lack of preparedness: he came back with the order.

You can't hope for miracles like that when addressing people in print or broadcast. You must have a logical sequence of argument. One that offends nobody, convinces as many as possible, and leaves out nothing which will help you achieve your objectives. For that you do need a formula – a set of rules.

You will notice that some of the points listed here are mentioned elsewhere in the book. This is because these lists are not just to be looked at but to be *referred* to. I am trying to include everything that's relevant. In any case, even though I'm very familiar with all these points myself, I still forget them very often – so they bear repetition.

A famous copywriter was once asked how he apportioned his time. He said: 'I spend 90 per cent of my time thinking about how to approach the prospect before I even start writing. And of the remaining 10 per cent, I spend about half the time writing the envelope message and the beginning of the letter. The rest is easy.'

When you see an ad or mailing you may be struck by the compelling language, the brilliant visual, the elegant typography. All these things, if they are effective, come not simply from technique, but in the first place from how the communication has been planned in advance. The inner structure, as it were, which supports the building.

All this comes from proper preparation and careful evaluation of what you have done before you send it out.

For this reason, the first of my lists is perhaps the most important. Not only the most important, but also the most neglected, because as I have already pointed out people are often far too inclined to get on with the job before they should even start it. That's simply because writing and drawing can be much more fun than hard thinking.

Fourteen pointers before you write a word or sketch a layout

Not only should most of the work be done before you actually start writing or drawing; it is also at this point that most things could go wrong. The questions I am about to cover are those which should all be incorporated in a comprehensive brief – but rarely are.

1 What is the objective?
Gather names? Provide qualified leads? Make firm sales? Get free trials? Different objectives require different solutions.

2 What's the budget?
It's no use arranging a shoot in Tahiti if the client won't pay. And it's no use agonising for three weeks if we're only getting paid £2,000.

3 When is it wanted?
Obvious – but never lose sight of the deadline.

4 Are you clear on the positioning?
What will your message tell the prospect about your product or service? Does it fit in with your positioning? Or does it conflict?

5 Who are you selling to?
What are their hopes, fears, likes, dislikes, needs? Are they male or female? Young or old? Rich or poor?

Until you know these facts, you will not know what tone to adopt, let alone what to say. Try to visualise them, and think how they would talk, where they would live, and what they would do for a living, or for fun.

As discussed in the chapter on planning, 'who?' may well be the most important question of all in our business.

When considering your prospects, it is often worth dividing them into two types. First, the *natural* prospect. The person who is an obvious target for this product. Second, people who might be *persuaded* to buy. Beware of trying to kid yourself that what you are selling appeals to the whole wide world. This is extremely unlikely. To all intents and purposes if you have covered off these two groups, then you've done all you should do.

6 What is it? And what does it do?
You'll remember I commented in the last chapter on how often people fail to describe what is being sold accurately. This failure often begins because an accurate description has not been written down at the outset of the job. Make sure it is.

7 What need in your prospect does your product or service fulfil?
Here are nine basic human motivations. How many of them are relevant to your product or service?

People like to: make money, save money, save time and effort, help their families, feel secure, impress others, gain pleasure, improve themselves and belong to a group.

You might be surprised at how many of these motivations can justify a purchase. Consider our old friend the American Express Card. I have calculated that every one of those human needs, save perhaps self-improvement, can be met to some degree through the range of benefits offered to cardmembers.

8 What makes it so special?
Interrogate your product or service. How does it differ from alternatives? Is it better, worse, cheaper, dearer? Is there something new about it? Does it replace anything? And what does it compete with? All these factors will give you an idea of what to say . . . and, equally important, what to *avoid* saying, or to argue against. Included under this heading of what makes something special can be some peculiarity to do with the way the product was discovered, or its background.

For example, I mentioned earlier a new kind of spark plug which was sold a few years ago. One interesting thing about this spark plug was that it was discovered by a World War II test pilot. You should always keep an eye open for something topical or interesting like this.

9 What benefits are you offering?
We covered this to some degree in the previous chapter. It is a very common error to talk to prospects about the characteristics of a product rather than the benefits: what it *is* rather than what it *does*.

Thus, when I was advertising the Business Ideas Letter, I could have said in my ad: 'Gives news of how other people are making money'. That was the characteristic of the newsletter. But the *benefit* was expressed in a very successful ad that said: 'Make up to £50 a week in your spare time.'

10 What do you consider the most important benefit to be?
If you can find one that is unique, that would be ideal, since you would have no competition. Eg: calorie-coded cooking cards, introduced in the UK a few years ago, and successful in many countries.

11 Can you make a good offer?
This is very important. Often, the difference between success and failure lies in the offer, which overcomes the prospect's sloth. Here are 19 offers you can make:

- Free trial.
- Easy terms.
- Pay no interest – or less interest.
- Free gift for ordering.
- Free gift whether you keep product or not.
- Sweepstakes entry.
- No deposit.
- Nominal deposit.
- Temporary price offer.
- Buy now – pay in a few months. Eg Pay for your Christmas gifts in January.
- Sale.
- Two for one, and variations of this.
- End of stock close-out.
- Mystery gift.
- More than one gift.
- Discount or gift for quantity.
- Discount or gift for buying in a certain period.
- Double your money-back guarantee. (You must always check on the nature of the guarantee for a product or service.)
- We'll buy back from you after a certain period. (Sometimes used for investment products.)

Once you have discovered the most important benefit you offer, settled upon your positioning, determined your target audience and how best to reach them, it is the offer which will make most difference.

12 If you cannot make a good offer, can you say something of exceptional interest?

Here are some examples.

- New improved product.
- News item related to your product.
- Prices are about to rise. Buy now. (An extremely powerful motivator.)
- We don't know how long we can hold this offer open . . . prices *may* rise.
- Lots of powerful testimonials. Once, when unable to say anything else about a slimming product, I just filled a page full of testimonials. It worked exceptionally well.
- We're repeating this offer because it was such a smash hit last time.
- Limited opportunity for a certain number of people.
- Specially imported from somewhere else where it was a great success. (More convincing than you might think: remember Krona Margarine? It became a best seller largely because commercials told how it had been a sensation in Australia – a land famous for its *butter*.)

All the offers, or 'non-offers' mentioned in the last two points are particularly relevant when planning follow-up mailings to enquirers or past customers. This is important to remember. There is more potential profit lying in inquiry lists and customer files than most companies imagine.

13 Proofs and testimonials

The whole area of conviction is so important, as we have already discovered, that any information calculated to give the product or service credibility is of extreme importance.

14 Sacred cows

It is not at all infrequent for an agency to come up with what it thinks is a splendid approach to a particular problem, only to be informed by the client that the company doesn't believe in doing that sort of thing. One frequent area is that of making specific comparisons with other companies. Some organisations love the idea of attacking their competition. Some consider it most ungentlemanly. As I have already indicated, I believe it all depends on how you go about it.

However, if the company has any constraints of this nature, the agency should be told about them in advance. This will save a lot of trouble.

Planning your creative treatment

Back in 1957 when I came into the advertising business, the people who wrote and the people who drew were segregated. Generally I would write my copy and then it would be taken along to the studio, where somebody would put pictures to it. It was rare for us to spend much time talking about what we wanted to do. We worked in isolation.

In direct marketing agencies this segregation was given added force by the fact that copy has always been regarded in our business as more important than art. More recently, it has been realised that two people talking together and exchanging ideas can often be more fruitful than each working in isolation. Indeed, it has now reached the stage where agencies frequently wish to hire a team rather than an individual. I think this is just as rigid as approaching the matter the other way.

Whether you are a team, or a lonely individual, here is a list of points to refer to as you work towards a good creative treatment.

1 Your safest opening (though not necessarily your best) is your prime benefit and offer
On the envelope of a mailing. At the beginning of your letter. At the start of your brochure. At the commencement of your commercial. On the phone, too, once you have told the prospect who you are and what you are talking about, the benefit and offer are normally the first things you talk about. (Assuming your prospect has agreed to listen to you.)

2 Tricky, clever openings rarely work
Remember, the average ad is seen for perhaps two seconds, and each piece in a mailing package may be picked up and scanned briefly before the prospect decides to read or not. An *instant* statement, *instantly* comprehensible, is most likely to work.

Thus, one of the most effective headlines ever written in the insurance business is: 'Cash if you die. Cash if you don't'. Nothing clever about that, but it certainly got to the point.

But don't forget that teasers – as long as they are relevant – often work well on envelopes. As do broken messages, like the first half of a recipe, to which you can only find the conclusion by opening the envelope.

3 Seek a dramatic central idea; preferably one that works in words and pictures
'Unless your campaign contains a big idea, it will pass like a ship in the night,' said David Ogilvy. I have already quoted one such idea in the point above. Another was produced by my Belgian colleagues, when they put a stopwatch in a mailing to dramatise their intention of delivering the product quickly.

If you can have an idea which is both visual and written, perfect! And if that word-picture combination *demonstrates* – as the stopwatch did – even better (see point 5). Finding a strong idea is vital. That's why you shouldn't just settle for the first one you come across. Seek plenty of alternatives. Work hard!

4 Is it the right length?
When asked how long copy should be, one of my Indian colleagues says: 'How much string do you need to wrap a parcel?'

The length should fit the objective. If your objective is easy to achieve, you probably won't need to say much. If the product is cheap, the same will be true. If, on the other hand, you wish to sell a very expensive product or convey a complicated proposition then use the necessary amount of words – but no more.

5 Can you give a test drive?
When preparing your work, remember what I said earlier: what would a salesman do? A salesman would try to demonstrate the product. Good communications do the same thing, either in words or in pictures or both. Sometimes a direct mail pack can *literally* demonstrate the product – as in the burnt letter featured in the last chapter. Nothing convinces more than an involving demonstration.

6 If your name is well known, feature it strongly
As I have pointed out to you, this could double your response. But make sure it *is* well known. Most people can only remember about three brands in a product category, until they are prompted. Even then they can usually only remember about seven.

For this reason, if your company is not well known, you will often find it pays to lead your letters with your benefit (your 'headline') and put your letterhead at the *base* of the page.

7 In mailings, give great thought to the envelope
Remember the shape, the texture, the colour can all influence response. When wondering whether you should have a message on the envelope, remember that *normally* the answer is 'yes'. And don't forget that texture, colour, shape and brand names can all be envelope 'messages'.

Remember, the offer, or a hint of it, should usually go on the envelope, together with an indication that people must reply quickly.

Don't forget that envelopes have fronts and backs and insides. If there's a window envelope, there's a space behind that. That should be used also.

Some mailers use the entire inside of the envelope to put testimonials on. I have also seen it used as an additional order form.

8 The letter is the key element in direct mail, the most personal part of the communication
The letter comments, amplifies, makes more human, 'sells' the facts in the other material.

People expect to receive a letter. They *like* getting letters. If you can't afford a costly mailing, then leave out the brochure *not* the letter. (On one occasion an American insurance company left a beautiful horoscope brochure out of a birthday mailing to clients by accident. Sales jumped 25 per cent.)

You can get the best of both worlds by illustrating your letter – but make sure it's still in the letter 'convention' by using a typewritten script.

Eleven uncreative (but tested) ways to make your layout work harder

We have now arrived at the point where copywriter and art director bring their individual talents and the techniques they have mastered to express your message as powerfully as possible.

I have managed to pursue my own career so far without being able to draw anything except a cartoon sketch of my dog. Thus, I may seem little-qualified to comment on what makes good or bad art direction. But I am heartened by the fact that a great many art directors I know (amongst them some of the best I have worked with) aren't too impressive when it comes to draughtsmanship. The reason for this is that it is visual *ideas* and *good design* which matter most.

Unfortunately, just as the majority of copywriters direct a turgid stream of predictable cliches at their unfortunate readers, so do the majority of art directors hanker after self-defeating layout formats. If you look through any publication, you will see that over half the ads fly in the face of tested principles of visual comprehension. Or, to put it in another way, they are difficult to take in and difficult to read.

God knows, it's hard enough trying to entice people into paying attention to your message without making them struggle to wade through it.

Accordingly, here are some *facts* about what makes for easy visual comprehension. These statements are not based upon opinion, but upon research into what works and what doesn't. In particular, I would like to acknowledge the work of Colin Wheildon of New South Wales University. For two years he conducted research into the effect of layout upon comprehension. He worked with 224 subjects to discover what they found easy to read and comprehend, and what they didn't.

I don't suggest you follow these guidelines slavishly. But why ignore them unless you have to?

First, here are some ways to make life easier for the reader to take in your message:

1 Easy-to-read typefaces
Most daily newspapers are set in serif type, in caps and lower case. The type will be roman, and most of it will be set in black on white rather

than reversed out. Most of the body will be in upper and lower case, not capitals. This is because these things are all easy to read. And that is because:

- The serifs – or little feet – at the bottom of letters line up to keep the eye moving horizonally along the line of type, rather than straying below to the next line. That's why if you wish to use sans-serif faces, you should have heavy leading between each line.
- The eye recognises shapes more than letters and a word in capitals has less shape than the word in caps and lower case.
- The eye finds it tiring to read reversed out type in any great volume. Reversing out of copy has been known to *halve* response.

    The eye does *not* find it difficult to read serif italic type, by the way.

    Let me emphasise, this is not a plea for the wholesale banishment of sans-serif faces, capitals or reversing out. I am merely suggesting you use these in moderation.

Wheildon found that on an A4 page sans-serif type reduced comprehension by 67 per cent. Imagine losing two-thirds of your readers – and your sales!

2 Clear contrast
Just as reversed out type is difficult to read, type set over tints or textures or colours, so that it does not stand out clearly, is even more difficult to read.

Equally, very small type is not a good idea: lots of people (including this writer) can't read it very easily. Indeed, around one person in ten has eyesight which is less than perfect. And when you consider that the difference between success and failure for an ad may well be 10 per cent, that's worth thinking about.

3 Don't change typefaces unnecessarily
Constant changes in typeface are ugly. If they happen to be in a headline, they are also confusing: your eye doesn't like constantly having to readjust.

4 Narrow measure
You will note in your newspaper or magazine that the words are split up into narrow columns. That's because the eye likes to travel down the centre of a column if it can, rather than having to go back and forth all the time.

If possible, don't set to a measure wider than about 50 characters. (You may ask why this book isn't set that way. Well, frankly, I don't know.

5 Long unbroken blocks of type are hard to read

Big blocks of type are daunting. To the reader they look like great trudges through the desert. Moreover, when the eye first looks at a layout, it tends to skip around like a butterfly before settling at one place.

For that reason, you should break up your copy with lots of crossheads, subheads, and changes of width. This makes it interesting to look at. It also enables the reader to learn the essence of your message from the subsidiary headings, which should make it interesting enough for him or her to want to start reading the body copy.

To encourage readers to do this, it's often a good idea to have an explanatory subhead after the headline leading into the copy. A 'dropped' – ie oversized – initial capital letter also encourages readership.

6 Try to justify your columns

Comprehension goes down if the edges of columns, either left or right, are unjustified – that is to say, ragged.

7 Huge headings are stupid

Art directors tend to do layouts and then pin them up on the wall somewhere in order to review them. But people do not read these things from the other side of the room. Nor do they have arms ten feet long. Large headings are a waste of space and a waste of time.

8 A headline should be a headline, not a baseline

Sometimes people design clever layouts where the headline is actually underneath the body copy. They turn them into baselines. You will not be surprised to hear that all this does is stop people from reading the copy at all. Wheildon found that readership was reduced substantially as a result of this practice.

9 Don't mislead the reader's eye

Illustrative elements which point out of the layout – like people's feet, or the direction in which they look – lead the reader's eye out of the advertisement. Also, illustrations which block off a column halfway up the page will often discourage the reader from travelling further down. The reader may be tempted simply to move straight to the top of the next column, thus omitting the section *beneath* the illustration.

10 Make sure the coupon is easy to cut out

Don't maroon it in the middle of a page so that people have to make four cuts to get it out. And don't give it a fancy shape. The origami school of coupon cutting has never flourished.

I once saw an advertisement prepared by a very well known agency in which the coupon was designed in the shape of the product. Ninety per cent of respondents had gone to the trouble of cutting out this bizarre shaped coupon. I wondered how many couldn't be bothered. (And for God's sake don't print your coupon on a funny colour on which it's impossible to read the respondent's name and address. More common than you might imagine.)

11 Lay out your letters

In the same way that advertisements should be laid out to be interesting to the eye, so should letters, with the obvious difference that you are using typewriter face (which, again, should always be the serif face for ease of reading).

So, in your letters, use indents at the beginning of each paragraph, indent whole sections and use numbered points or asterisks, just as you should in long-copy advertisements and brochures.

The use of second colour, 'handwritten' notes in the margins, underlinings and the *occasional* word in capitals can all add variety and interest for eye and brain.

... and two qualifications

I seem to lay down so many rules, that I realise I am in danger of being seen as an old curmudgeon. That's why I am at pains from time to time to emphasise that I am certainly not always right.

When considering layout and typography one has to say that views certainly vary. A traditional one – that typography is an art or science to help you communicate better – has been questioned. This questioning arises from one of two ways of thinking; and sometimes both. These ways of thinking are:

- That the typography itself by its appearance (usually bizarre, novel or even downright ugly) signals to the potential reader something about the nature of the product or merchandise or communication. Thus, for instance, on launching a publication designed to appeal to young, unconventional people (or at any rate people wishing to conform to a different convention) magazines have deliberately formulated a typographical style which flies in the face of just about every fundamental typographical given. A classic example of this in the UK is the magazine *The Face*. Here, typographical styles – sans serifs, reverse outs, all sorts of eclectic design features – have been used to signal the anti-establishment nature of the magazine. It certainly seems to work. The typography in effect is saying: 'Do you like to be different? Do you like to break the rules? Then join us!' Of course, the fact that most of the people who read *The Face* have established their own new form of non-conformist conformity is neither here nor there.

One of the consequences of this form of typography is of course that to read a publication like this you have to make a real effort. Which leads us to the second theory of the new typography:

- You should be required to make a deliberate effort to penetrate the message. This extra effort means that the reader is more likely to take it in and relate to it more effectively.

Candidly, I have no research to support either of these theses. Nevertheless, I believe there is a certain logic behind them. And I certainly believe you should be aware of them. In any case, I think it is quite possible to combine unconventional approaches with legibility.

Thirteen attention-grabbers

Just as there are proven rules which make replying easier, there are many facts known about what tends to attract attention. Here are twelve to remember:

1 'Busy' layouts often seem to pull better than 'neat' ones
In one split-run test on catalogue pages a 'busy' layout out-pulled a neat one by 14 per cent. So it would appear that those little flashes and panels that art directors loathe add interest. Where you can introduce them without making the layout look like a dog's dinner, why not do so?

2 Vary shapes, sizes and colours
Just as the eye is bored with regular shapes, people lose interest if all the elements in a mailing package are the same size and the same colour, or if all the mailings in a sequence are to the same format.

Vary your colours, vary your shapes, vary your sizes in individual communications and sequences. Try a huge typewriter face, or a giant order form – or a Lilliputian letter.

Experiment!

3 Of all illustrative techniques, the cartoon attracts most attention
However, see my comment below about photographs before you put cartoons in all your ads.

4 One large picture attracts more attention than lots of small ones

5 A picture of somebody staring out of the page at you attracts attention
People look at people: and men look at men more than at women – and vice versa.

6 Colour will attract attention
But it is only appropriate where the product itself demands colour to convey its appeal. In a series of tests we conducted for one client colour was *not* cost-effective in four cases out of five.

7 Putting something odd into a picture will attract attention
One famous campaign which did this was David Ogilvy's for Hathaway shirts, in which the model always wore a black eye-patch.

8 Too many extraneous props divert attention
So, make sure that the product is hero. This is particularly important in TV commercials. Make sure your *actor* is not more interesting than his *pitch*.

Even in an ordinary ad you can get some surprising results from using eye-catching props. I recall a campaign twenty-five years ago for a type of curtain material in which a cute Teddy Bear was used as a prop. More people wanted to know where to get the bear than where to get the product.

9 Extreme close-ups of a product attract attention
But make sure the close-up is not *so* close that you cannot identify the product.

10 Be careful where you put your headline
Tests with an eye camera revealed that the eye tends to settle naturally around the middle of the page. So don't put your headline at the top of the space, above the picture. Put it below. In a series of four tests, we found that response went up by between 27 per cent and 105 per cent in the latter case.

11 Use tables and graphs when conveying complex information
Tables definitely increase response where relevant. In an insurance mailing, response increased when the size of the benefit table was doubled.

12 It pays to use layout styles that make coupons look 'valuable'
Use the sort of visual devices that you see on currency.

13 But will they believe what they see?
Point 12 is an instance where a visual signal makes your message more convincing. Often, even if people are attracted by what they see, and assuming they find it easy to take in, they still may not believe what you have to say. Effective art direction can do much to add conviction.

- Photographs are more convincing than drawn illustrations. I learned many years ago that a photograph can sometimes increase response by over 50 per cent.

This is hardly surprising when you think about it, yet frequently people use illustrative techniques for no reason other than personal preference. Short of sending people a sample, nothing can be more convincing than photography.

- 'Before and after' pictures are very persuasive. Seek opportunities to use them. People believe what they want to believe – and a before and after is a wonderful way to dramatise it. So much so that on more than one occasion I have seen before and after *drawings* – clearly not realistic – work very effectively.

- Positive 'reward' pictures tend to work better than negative 'problem' pictures. This is not surprising when you consider that people like rewards more than threats. A classic instance of this is insurance advertising; telling people about the dreadful things that will happen to their family if they die is not as effective as displaying the large sum of money which will be their family's reward.

  The only product area where negative approaches seem to work is in pharmaceutical products and the like. For instance, advertisements with themes revolving around the words: 'Oh, my aching back!'

- Don't use illustrations that do nothing. That may sound a strange thing to say, but if you look through many advertisements the product is merely *shown* when, with a little effort it could have been *demonstrated*.

  I have touched upon the importance of demonstrations in TV. But it is equally true that anything which demonstrates the product, either still or moving, is a good idea.

- A consistent visual tone is vital. Very early on in this book we talked about the importance of positioning. This positioning must be respected in everything you do, everything you say – and that includes the 'look' of the things you do. Otherwise people get confused – and you start to lose conviction.

  Why should this be? Imagine if each time you saw a salesman he had a totally different appearance. One day wearing a sober suit. The next appearing in jeans and T-shirt. One day speaking quietly and sincerely. The next day bubbling with superlatives.

  Either approach might work well, depending on what he was selling. But alternating between the two is confusing and diminishes conviction.

- Break down the product or service visually. Show the fine details of the way it is finished, or put in panels which show different aspects of a service or product.

  You can show the fine stitching on a suit. Or illustrate in a series of shots precisely how a customer's query is dealt with. Or show the various points in a kitchen where craftsmanship is superior.

All these things convince people they are getting good value for money, and that you have taken trouble to provide it.

- Showing the faces of people who give testimonials, and reproducing those testimonials in facsimile, adds credibility. You should also put in their signatures if possible, and – if their statements are used in headings – put quote marks around them. This increases response.

Tricks and techniques that keep people reading

Earlier in this century a man called Rudolph Flesch devoted a great deal of time to discovering what makes for easier reading. Many of the hints that follow come from him.

Here are seven writer's tricks that keep people reading.

1 Use short sentences. They are easier to read and understand
The easiest sentence to read is eight words. The average length of sentence for easy reading is 16 words. Any sentence longer than 32 words tends to be hard to read.

2 Use short paragraphs
Make sure each paragraph contains just one thought, if possible. People don't read copy with great attention. Advertising communications are driftwood on the surface of life.

Try to make sure that the first paragraph in any piece is short – preferably only one sentence long. This is particularly important if the piece itself is very long. That first short sentence makes it easier to get into.

3 Count the number of times the word 'you' is used in your copy
There is a direct relationship, Flesch discovered, between effective selling and the use of that word. Talk about your prospect, not yourself. Certainly the word 'you' should occur at least two to three times as often as any reference to 'I' or 'we'.

4 Use guile to keep people reading
End a column or page half-way through a sentence so people have to keep going. Eg.: 'This week we are offering a special discount of . . . Next page, please.' (Always be polite enough to ask people to keep reading.)

5 Use 'carrier' words and phrases at the ends and beginnings of sentences and paragraphs
Once you have got people reading, you want to keep them moving. So anything you can do to signal that some added, interesting information

is coming up is a good idea. Good tricks include: ending and beginning paragraphs with questions, so that the reader clearly has to read on to find out the answers. Other tricks include starting sentences and paragraphs with words like 'Also . . .', 'Moreover . . .', 'For instance . . .', 'What is more . . .', 'And . . .'.

The secret is to read through what you have written and as you come to the break between paragraphs, ask yourself if anything tempts people to keep reading.

6 Don't use pompous Latinisations
Use short, Anglo-Saxon based words. When you use 'posh' words – the kind you would not use in your ordinary conversation – you become false. You also become obscure.

When writing, you should try to be yourself.

7 Don't use three words where one will do
'Now' is much better than 'At this point in time'.

Nobody has time to meander through your copy. They are more concerned about their dog being ill, or the wife playing around with the man next door, or the rent being due.

A digression here. Jerry della Femina, author of the best book I have read about what it feels like to work in advertising (*From those wonderful folk who gave you Pearl Harbor*) described his idea of the perfect ad. It goes:

Have you a dollar and have you piles? Send us your dollar and we'll cure your piles. Or keep your dollar and keep your piles.

This is a wonderful example of simple, effective language, apart from being funny.

One very important point about writing. It is very much easier to over-write and then cut than to under-write and then expand. Why this should be I do not know, but it is.

Charity advertising: a special case

In reviewing charity advertising, you must remember that it has its own peculiar demands. And it has its own particular problems.

People are usually tempted to dramatise the *miseries* of the particular situation. They're even tempted to be clever – I gave the instance earlier on of fresh food flying into Biafra daily. I also quoted the Dr Barnardo's case of the frightening truth about the new adoption shops.

I can think of others equally unsuccessful: 'Colin will be eight years old for the rest of his life' – referring to a retarded child. And: 'How Snow White and the 57 dwarfs helped Martin talk' – an involved story about a pantomime.

The secret of successful charity advertising starts with the realisation that in this area, perhaps more than any other, emotion is all important. People give from their hearts, not their heads. Thus, a headline I wrote a few years ago: 'How much would you pay to give a lost little girl a start in life?' did very well. Other headlines that have done well include: 'Won't you play Santa to a lonely little girl?', 'This Christmas help make a blind man see. £10.' Or: 'For £7.64 you can buy her safe water for life'.

Therefore, here are some guidelines to follow when doing charity advertising:

1 Ask for a specific sum

Thus, for Save the Children: 'Won't you give £10 to save 10 children's lives?' Asking people to give generously is simply not enough. Talking about deadly perils is not enough either. You must tell people how much money is needed as well as how much you hope they will give. Eg: 'It costs £2,500 every three months to provide drugs.' Or: '2,000 doses of antibiotic cost just £42.'

2 Rule of threes

Successful headlines often contain three elements. For instance, in the headline I quoted above for Save the Children, we have:

- a problem (children's lives need to be saved);
- a solution the reader can supply, and thus feel good (you can save the children's lives);
- something which makes it sound easy (£10 is not a lot of money).

3 Come right out with it

Don't be cowardly about asking for money. Always ask people for more than you think they are likely to give. They won't feel insulted – on the contrary. And you will probably raise the average value per donation.

4 Be personal

People give to people – individual people – not causes. That is why it is a good idea to feature a particular person in the advertisement.

5 Sound the alarm

Emergencies are always the best source of revenue. If you can make a situation sound like an emergency, do so. If there is an emergency, then for God's sake shout from the rooftops.

6 Christmas spirit

Christmas is the time when people give most. At that time *always* include the word 'Christmas' in your headlines. It focuses people's minds.

7 Be precise
You must tell people what their money will do, and how much money is necessary. For instance, UK tax rates have recently gone down. Good news for everyone – except the charities. Because charities can claim back from the Government the tax that the donor would have had to pay. Thus, where previously the top rate of tax was 60 per cent, now it is 40 per cent. Ergo: a drop in revenue for charities.

But a mailing I saw to donors from one charity explained this problem but did not *quantify* it. It was not precise. It didn't say how much money this charity was actually likely to lose as a result of this change in the law. This is a fatal error.

8 Suggest an amount
Actually put in the coupon, or the order form, a set of specific sums, starting with the highest sum and going down to the lowest, that people can give – plus a box with a blank so that people can give any other sum they choose.

9 Be amateur
People like charities to use their money wisely. That's why you should mention how little money is wasted on administration; and why charity ads very often work better if they are set by the newspaper, and look cheap.

What to watch for in broadcast

The things that go wrong in broadcast tend to be simple. Many of them stem from the fact that time is limited. People who are used to writing direct mail, or long copy, find it exceptionally difficult to accommodate themselves to the needs of broadcast.

That's why my first point – though apparently a very obvious one – is extremely important.

1 Don't over-write
A good thing to remember is that the number of words you can get into a commercial is normally no more than three times the number of seconds.

2 Don't cheat
Because people like to cram as much as they can into a commercial, they almost invariably cheat when reading it out in order to time it. They

gabble, and they don't allow for the silences that will occur in that commercial. Don't do this sort of thing.

3 *How long should it be?*
Have you just arbitrarily selected a particular commercial length, or are you suiting the length to the objective? For instance, if all you want is a simple inquiry about something, you may be able to do it in under ten seconds. If you think you're going to sell something to somebody, then you're very unlikely to be able to do it in under 90 seconds.

4 *Poor presentation*
Explaining to people who don't understand the medium what a commercial is going to look like is quite a problem. Traditionally storyboards have been used. These are a series of frames, each with an appropriate description of the action and the script under them. Most people find this hard to take in. Other alternatives have been to go to 'animatics' – stills which a camera roams over to give an illusion of action, accompanied by a soundtrack. That's quite easy to understand but very expensive.

In the early stages of presenting commercials, I counsel you to do so by *describing* them, merely showing one or two key visuals. Trying to go through a series of ten to twelve frames, explaining what's going on in each frame and also what the script is, is very difficult indeed.

5 *Don't sell too literally*
In the need to convey the wonders of the brilliant commercial you have just dreamed up, you may be tempted to produce very detailed visuals, or to write down very detailed treatments. (A treatment is a description of the commercial in words, without the actual script.)

Making things too detailed can often lead to a problem. When the commercial is finally produced, the client may say: 'But in the third frame you presented originally, you had a large rock on the right hand side – where is the rock now?'

6 *Choosing the production company*
The choice of production – and in particular director – is crucial. Pricing can vary phenomenally. But your judgement should not be on price alone: it should start with looking at a show reel and assessing whether a particular director can, in your view, do a good job for you. Then think about price.

7 *Missing out on key stages*
Once you have recovered from the thrill of dreaming up your epic, you may be tempted to skip out boring but essential details that have to be gone through as this dream becomes reality. You must make sure you're

present at every key stage, without actually getting in the way.

It is particularly tempting to absent oneself from pre-production discussions. But working out how long it's going to take to produce your commercial, and what's going to be needed is very important.

8 Don't be daunted

There's such a mystique about the broadcast media that sometimes people are reluctant to say to the director: 'This isn't what I had in mind.' The director himself may be tempted to pose as an expert, not merely on directing, but on copywriting. Don't let this happen. I can promise you that if things go wrong, you'll carry the can before the director does. Make sure your original vision is kept to.

9 Pay attention to editing

Editing sounds a very technical business. It isn't. Spending time watching while somebody edits a commercial, making sure you get what you want and you don't get what you don't (without trying to be bossy) is essential. Many great directors have started out as editors. You can't be any good at this job unless you pay attention to editing.

10 Approach it step by step

Because of the mystique I have already referred to, and because you may not be familiar with the making of commercials, the whole process will at first sight seem terribly complicated.

It isn't really. It simply has to be approached with the same care as you would approach anything else. It's just that you have a different set of things to worry about.

Personally, my overwhelming feeling about broadcast is first, that it can be an extremely tedious process (on the set, as far as I can make out the only person who ever has any fun is the director). Second, despite this it's a tremendous challenge. What is more, I am quite convinced it is going to become an increasingly important area in our business.

Five things to re-check

Broadcast may have its own demands, but it is not *all* that different from any other medium. What you're trying to do is the same. You're trying to attract attention and lead people through to a sale.

However, here are five things I would look out for with particular attention in reviewing your broadcast ideas.

1 What's the idea? Is it *really* a big idea?
2 Is the *technique* stronger than the content? Are you relying upon dancing and singing rather than the strength of the concept?
3 If you switched the sound off, would the pictures communicate the idea? And vice versa? Neither of these things is essential – but they sure help.

4 Are you using 'supers' – words over the screen which communicate the benefits? These can be very powerful.
5 Do the scenes flow logically one after another? If they don't, you're in trouble.

A simple way to find out whether this is the case is to get somebody in off the street and ask them whether they understand what the commercial is all about. It sounds obvious – but very few people think of doing it.

Now that you think it's perfect have you forgotten anything?

For the most part our communications are rather like aeroplanes. Whether it's a commercial, a mailing shot or an advertisement, once it's gone out, that's it. You can't call in three million pieces of paper because you have just had a good idea. You can't stop the printing presses to change your headlines.

So it's utterly important that after you think you've finished creating or perfecting your message, you check once again to make sure you haven't missed something out. This admonition is not just to the writer and the art director; it is addressed with particular force to those of you with orderly minds – the account handler and the client. Writers and art directors often get carried away. And as a colleague of mine in India, Mani Ayer, once observed: 'The obvious is always overlooked.'

Here are areas I think you should pay particular attention to – especially when you think you've done everything. (You won't be surprised to see that I have mentioned some of them before.)

1 Have you included every convincing reason for responding?
Go back to your planning stage and make sure it's all included. (But don't forget that if you are only going for an inquiry, you don't have to tell the full story ... just enough to get your prospect keenly interested.)

2 Is there anything you've taken for granted?
Your guarantee, your money-back offer, even the fact that you are selling direct.

These things may be boring to you through familiarity but they are important to your sale. That's perhaps why a common omission is that of describing and showing the product properly.

3 Have you built in maximum credibility?
Your prospect cannot see you or all the trouble you take to deliver the perfect product.

So ensure that you have made full use of testimonials, third-party opinion, independent research. In products where the claims are hard to believe, emphasis given to money-back offers (even the simple words 'or all your money back instantly' prominently placed) can make a great deal of difference.

4 Do your pictures show what your words say?
Research shows that many advertisements are found confusing simply because the pictures illustrate some phrase in the headline, rather than the benefit of the product. One of my favourite examples was an advertisement for a copier where the headline (a stupid one in any case) suggested that it was 'ahead of the field'. The illustration actually showed a field – with a field mouse.

5 Is it all logical?
Re-check that the package is consistent. Don't have three or four ideas which are slightly contradictory (even if each is good, they may counteract each other). Make sure you are following one theme. And, equally, make sure that in each piece there is a logical flow. Write a phrase describing each paragraph, and see if the sequence makes sense.

6 Are you going all out for telephone calls?
They will form a substantial proportion of your replies in all possibility. Feature and illustrate the phone heavily.

7 Have you paid sufficient attention to the ordering mechanism?
Repeatedly tests show that:

- The more time you give to the ordering instructions in a commercial, the more response you get.
- The more size and prominence you devote to the coupon, the more replies you get.
- The larger the order form in a mailing, the greater the response.

On occasion I have spent literally hours writing and rewriting an order form to get it right. It is well worth spending such time to ensure that the instructions on how to order are full, clear and easy to understand. Ask somebody unconnected with the job to read through the order form, and find out whether they understand what to do.

Ensure that the address is in more than one place in the advertisement or mailing pack. (I have heard that it pays to put it on *every* piece of a mailing pack.)

Finally, remember that people often put the order form or coupon aside to be sent off later – then forget. For that reason, it's important to restate the benefits and offer in full there.

8 Have you built in a sufficient sense of urgency?
Can you in some way mention the time factor right at the beginning –
even on the envelope? Have you given people reason to act: time
incentives, gifts for speedy action, or threats of imminent price rises?

You'll be surprised what even the simplest gift does. As I was
rewriting this paragraph I read a letter from an academic publisher who
revealed that to his great surprise a simple pocket calculator costing him
£2 had increased his orders by 20 per cent, for a book costing £50.

9 Are you getting as much as you can out of the piece?
I am not proposing that you cram everything to the limit. But look
through your layout to see you have wasted no space unnecessarily.
Weigh your mailing pack: maybe you can include some extra telling
element without going over the postal limit.

10 Have you edited and polished sufficiently?
Write with fury; but correct with care. Look at your layout sternly and
settle for nothing less than the very best you can do. The finished article
will always reflect the work you put into it.

11 Don't be proud
Show what you have created to others. Try it out on them. You are not a
genius. For instance:

- Get someone to read it aloud: does it *sound* good?
- Check it with someone who's not too bright – or even someone who
  doesn't like you. They will give you a fairly honest opinion.

All truly professional creative people accept criticisms – even if they
don't welcome them too much. Remember what Napoleon said: 'There
is somebody who knows more than anybody . . . and that is everybody.'

While I was working on this book I read an article about the humorist
S J Perelman. He was a great perfectionist. When somebody asked him
how many drafts he went through to create a piece, he replied 'Thirty-
seven'. I am afraid I am not as perfectionist as him. Ten is usually
enough for me. Probably if I tried harder I would be a better writer.

It may be that you, dear reader, are one of those rare human beings
who can produce perfect work every time. Or you you may find it
demeaning to subject your work to a mechanical process like a list of dos
and don'ts.

All I can say is that I have found it *does* pay to subject your work to the
kind of analysis I have outlined on the previous pages. Though I must
emphasise that *first* you must let your fancy fly free. Be generous with
your thinking. Try everything from the straightforward to the crazy.

I believe you will find these checklists not only concentrate your mind and give direction to your work: they will actually *help* you get ideas.

There's an old saying I'm particularly fond of. It is: 'Search the world and steal the best.' Well, after 30 years in this business, the lists above cover just about all I've learned, and all I've stolen. Be my guest. There is no honour amongst thieves – especially when it comes to ideas. I hope my list helps you.

One word of warning. Everything I have said has proved true for someone. Most of it will prove true for you. But not *all* of it. And not always.

11

How to Test – and Evaluate Your Results

'One must be a God to be able to tell
successes from failures without
making a mistake.'

    Anton Chekhov

'To find a Prince, you have to kiss an
awful lot of frogs.'
    Seen on a lapel badge at the time of the
    wedding between Prince Charles and
    Lady Diana Spencer.

Earlier I gave you the results of a series of tests for a company called Comp-U-Card, which operates a home shopping service.

As you saw, the best combination of variables gave you 58 times more return for your money than the worst. As we've discussed, this ability to test what you are about to do and thus deploy your marketing investment more effectively makes great appeal to intelligent marketers. Particularly because it is almost impossible to foresee what will work and what won't. I learned this the hard way.

In 1968, my partner and I bought the Business Ideas Letter. One of the first ideas I had was to mail 50,000 people who had previously inquired about the publication but had not yet decided to subscribe. I had reviewed the previous publisher's promotions and decided he had missed this obvious opportunity. I was also buoyed up by the confidence born of almost complete ignorance which convinced me he knew far less about direct mail than I did. (He is now a multi millionaire. I am not.)

My partner and I concocted a mailing so splendid and so much better than anything previously done that we decided to dispense with testing and send out to the complete inquiry list. True, it was a little close to Christmas to mail. On the other hand, the mailing was so good that it couldn't fail. So we went ahead.

It was an expensive mailing, because it included a copy of the newsletter itself – a ploy which many publishers have since been kind enough to inform me is almost invariably a mistake. Few publications can live up to the claims your promotional material can make for them.

In terms of consequences, it was *the* most expensive mailing I have ever sent out in my life. It proved a complete disaster and cost us so much money that it took a year for our business to recover from it.

This inspired piece of commercial nonsense shows why you should *always* test if you can. A 50,000 mailing is a mere bagatelle to a large company. But it is enough to ruin a small one. And time after time I have learned that no matter how much experience one may have, it is almost impossible to foretell the results of anything. One reason is that we marketers lead very different lives and have very different interests to most of our customers. We find it hard to put ourselves in their shoes and predict how they will think or how they will react.

In the case of the tests we conducted for Comp-U-Card, several results came as a complete surprise to me. First of all, the most cost-effective membership price we tested was not the lowest (£12.50 a year) but the highest (£20 a year). And despite the fact that Comp-U-Card is a telephone shopping service, the telephone did not prove as effective a response medium as returning a reply-paid card. Moreover, offering the option of phone *or* post did not work as well as post alone. I was also a little surprised to discover who were the best prospects for this service. You might imagine that the people most eager to save money would be those who have the least to spare. On the contrary, it was affluent professionals who proved our best prospects.

The American publication *Direct Marketing*, regularly asks readers to predict the results of split-run tests. After over 30 years in this business I get almost as many wrong as I get right. I doubt if you would do better.

The moral is: *test*, don't *assume*.

Testing: the first duty

It was the fact that one could test which drew me to the direct marketing business. The opportunity to *know* rather than *guess*.

I suggested at the start of this book that once you have isolated your prospect or customer as an individual, two activities will govern your success: testing and building a continuing relationship with your customers.

Both are important, but you will never get as far as starting a relationship if you can't recruit the customer at the right price. Moreover, once customers are recruited, they will never prove as profitable to you as they might unless you test your communications to make sure they bring in the maximum return for you.

So testing is your *first duty* as a direct marketer. Apart from anything else, it will ensure you don't lose money – and that is what you have to concern yourself about first.

A friend of mine once worked on the Buick account in Detroit. I asked him why their advertising was always such boastful piffle. He explained: 'Every year the agency works flat out for months, producing hundreds of ideas. All the layouts are pinned up on a wall. The client comes in and chooses the ones he likes. Usually those are the ones that make him feel good about his company.'

Judging by the fact that much General Motors advertising remains boastful to this day, I imagine they still go about it in much the same way. But there is no need to produce your advertising like that. There is no need to spend days speculating about how the public will respond (or even whether the client will like it or not), if you *test*.

Claude Hopkins

The man who said the final word on testing – over 60 years ago – was Claude Hopkins. I have mentioned him a number of times already in this book because anybody in the business of marketing ought to know who he was. Sadly, many people don't. Let me tell you a little of his story here.

If the advertising business has ever produced a full blown genius, Claude Hopkins may have been the man. Certainly his employer must have thought so: he was being paid \$168,000 a year (plus bonus) back in the 1900s – and in those days you paid no tax. By the end of his career in the 1920s, he was allowed to fill in his own salary cheque. John O'Toole, a former chief executive of Foote, Cone & Belding – the lineal successor of Hopkins' agency, Lord & Thomas – commented that Hopkins was cheap at the price, despite his enormous salary.

Hopkins helped build Lord & Thomas into the largest agency in the world. He wrote a short book entitled *Scientific Advertising* in 1924. In some ways it remains the best book ever written on the subject – and the briefest.

Hopkins learned his trade in the mail order business, then applied what he had learned to general advertising. Although he was a copywriter, he did not restrict himself to writing copy, or even advertising. Thus, for example, he resuscitated the business of the Bex Bissell carpet sweeper company when he suggested to them that instead of having a wooden handle on their sweepers, they offer consumers a choice of colours.

For a suet company he had the splendid wheeze of baking the world's largest cake and placing it in the window of a Chicago department store.

He introduced putting 'buried' offers in the body copy of his advertisements so that he could measure which were most read. He also started putting coupons in advertisements that people could take to the retailer to redeem. His thinking was behind many of the techniques now taken for granted (or sometimes neglected).

He was the man behind the success of famous brands like Schlitz beer, Pepsodent, Chevrolet, and many others. Shrewdly, he used to take shares in the companies he wrote advertisements for and as a result became extremely wealthy.

The school for advertising

Hopkins recommended mail order as the school from which one must graduate before hoping to succeed. (He also said he shifted to general advertising because it was easier to make money in.)

'There, false theories melt like snowflakes in the sun,' he observed of mail order, and conclusively: 'Almost any question can be answered, cheaply, quickly and finally by a test campaign. Go to the court of last resort – the buyers of your product.'

I am going to devote *two* chapters to testing, because I am astonished how little people know about it, appalled at how little they value it and alarmed that many who are starting in direct marketing neglect testing almost entirely.

I started this chapter with the story of my own blunder because it shows that even people who ought to know better (and I had read Hopkins long before that mailing) make silly mistakes.

In my experience, you can almost always tell the difference between a really professional direct marketer and an amateur by how much testing they do. When asked to define the perfect client in three words at a conference in 1980 I said without hesitation: 'Willingness to test.'

But willingness to test is not enough. If you don't know how to test, and how to read results, you can get into a great deal of trouble. A little learning, they say, is a dangerous thing. In our business it can be downright catastrophic.

A former partner of mine, Brian Thomas, was once taking over a seminar on direct mail for the Institute of Marketing. He was handed the previous lecturer's notes as a reference. He read them carefully. One section he read several times, because he could not believe what it said.

'If you have two letters and you want to know which will do better, you must conduct a test,' said these notes. 'Take a hundred copies of each and mail them out to your list. The one that does better is the one to go ahead with.'

This is such a parody of the truth that it verges on the criminal. Indeed, if you were to act on it all the time, you would be committing commercial suicide. When I deal (very briefly!) with statistics, you will see why. But if the man who gave the advice (a respected consultant, by the way) knew anything about the mathematics of testing, he would never have committed such a crass error. For such a test to be at all reliable, you would have to be anticipating a response of over 40 per cent to your letters. An occurrence as rare as sunstroke in Manchester.

Dangerous Rules

If people would only test more, they would never say or believe the things they do. In our business it is so easy to end a discussion with a fine generalisation, or to take it for granted that because someone else has said it, then it must be true.

This is one of the dangers of the rules beloved of many direct marketing experts. What may work for someone else with their product may not work for you.

To take the subject I'm about to discuss: paper-set ads (those set by the newspapers themselves) may work very well for charities or language courses, but I'd be amazed if they worked for expensive collectibles. Equally, many direct marketers assume that a premium will always increase response. One company offering mortgages found that free offers *reduced* reponse. One magazine tested three premia and all three lowered response.

Another cherished belief amongst many experts is that an envelope message will always increase response. Not if it's a stupid one. One of my clients tested a blank envelope against a singularly inane one produced by our agency, and it did 25 per cent better.

You have to consider the *context* carefully when you start to apply rules. Thus, in the cases I have just cited, cheap offers which do not reflect the quality of a magazine will depress response. Silly envelope messages will put people off rather than encourage them to start reading. So you must test. The knowledge you gain will make your marketing more effective than your competitors' and your knowledge greater even than that of some of the experts.

In his direct marketing book, Ed Nash, to take one example, states that your message must look different from its environment. 'The first law of layout is to be noticed.'

Ed Nash claims to be the 'Master Strategist' of direct marketing, yet the exact reverse of his first law of layout is, in my experience, often true. I have found time and again, not just with charity advertising, but with record advertising and consumer durable advertising that, on the contrary, a very good principle of layout is to blend into your environment.

Richard V Benson, whom many regard as the pre-eminent direct marketing consultant in the United States, expresses the view that an editorial ad will increase readership by between 500 per cent and 600 per cent. I do not know whether this is true or not; but I do know that when we started running editorial-style ads (see page 260) for our retail client Magnet, people came into the stores and commented on what 'good write-ups' we were getting. This was despite the fact that all these advertisements are clearly headed, at the insistence of the publications, by the word 'Advertisement'.

In the magazine *British Reader* a Young & Rubicam creative director suggested in 1987 that consumers are becoming so sophisticated they are no longer 'fooled' by editorial layouts. And indeed that being constantly exposed to advertising layout formats has made the readers prefer them. His is an opinion, and an interesting one. My views are based upon experience and testing.

Claude Hopkins, as so often, said it all first: 'Some advocate large type and big headlines. Yet they do not admire salesmen who talk in loud voices.' 'Others look for something queer and unusual. They want ads distinctive in style or illustration. Would you want that in a salesman?'

'Do nothing to merely interest, amuse or attract. That is not your province. Do only that which wins the people you are after in the cheapest possible way.'

But does that mean that *all* your ads should melt into the background by aping the editorial style? Does it mean that I am right, and others are wrong? No: it means you must test, and find out what works for *you*, and *your* product.

Thirteen ways you can learn by testing

It does not matter what media you are in, or how much you spend; you can test, observe your results, and learn from them. Some methods are

New "Low Emissivity" double glazing works 52% better

Tests show "Magnashield" retains more heat — works as well as triple glazing yet costs little more than ordinary double glazing

by OWEN MATHER

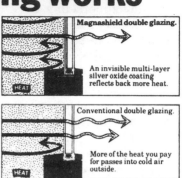

Magnashield double glazing.

An invisible multi-layer silver oxide coating reflects back more heat.

Conventional double glazing.

More of the heat you pay for passes into cold air outside.

YOU can now buy a new kind of double glazing which works as well as the triple glazing that fights the cold in freezing Scandinavian winters.

The secret? A multi-layer coating containing silver oxide between the two panes of glass. This coating is so thin you can't see it, but gives the glazing what scientists call *low emissivity.*

It lets out less of the heat you pay for, yet allows the sun's rays through the glazing, and traps the warmth for longer inside your home.

Scientific tests conducted on a typical 3-bedroomed house prove low emissivity "Magnashield" performs 52.46% better than ordinary double glazing.

Slash your fuel bills

"Magnashield" costs only a fraction more than ordinary double glazing. Yet tests indicate the difference in cost between "Magnashield" and ordinary double glazing could be paid back over as little as 9 months.

"The price is low because we make it ourselves and sell it direct," says Magnet Southerns Chairman, Tom Duxbury. *"This is a big advance on ordinary double glazing — we believe it will cut fuel bills by an extra 15%. It cost us £7.0 million to build a facility. But since it's better, we thought we should offer it to our customers."*

"Magnashield" is only available through Magnet Southerns stores.

You are unlikely to see this new kind of double glazing elsewhere. That's because the manufacturing plant to produce it is very costly. So a company wanting to make it needs a huge volume of sales. Each week many thousands of double glazed patio doors and windows are sold through Magnet Southerns stores. That's why the company could afford the investment.

Free brochure tells more

If you'd like to know more about "Magnashield," visit your nearest Magnet Southerns store. At the same time you can pick up a **free** copy of their 116 page, full colour brochure.

This brochure tells you not only of "Magnashield" but other Magnet Southerns' exclusive products. They are Britain's biggest manufacturers of doors and have a wide range of their own craftsman-made kitchens. Many customers particularly like their free computerised kitchen and bedroom planning service.

Virtually everything you buy at Magnet Southerns is made by their own craftsmen and sold direct to you. This keeps the quality up and prices down. Check for yourself. Come into a Magnet Southerns store.

There are 250 stores throughout the country where you can see "Magnashield" window units and doors for yourself.

Figure 11.1. Magnet 'editorial' advertisement

far more statistically reliable than others. But *all* are better than just using your own judgement.

1. The A/B split

Many publications are printed on cylinders with each cylinder printing more than one copy of a given page on it. So it is possible for a cylinder to carry different advertisements on the same page of a publication.

Thus, you can have the publication printed so that one half of the copies have one piece of copy, and the other half a different one. This is what an A/B split is.

In some cases you can have a four-way split. But the reason why these splits are so valuable is that the copies of the publication bearing the advertisements you wish to test come off the presses alternately in the case of an A/B split, or in sequence in the case of a four-way split.

In this way you get very close to statistical perfection. There can be no geographical or other bias, and each newsagent is delivered a pile of papers with alternate examples of the advertisements you are testing.

Newspapers normally charge you for arranging a split run, but when you realise that one ad may be two or three times as effective as another, this is a small price to pay.

It was through split-run tests that we found out some fascinating (and valuable) information about Dr Barnardo's, the child care charity.

My friend Harold Sumption knows more about charity advertising than anyone I have ever met. He told me: 'People don't like the idea of charities squandering their donations on expensive advertising. They like to feel everything is done on a shoestring, by voluntary workers. The best ads look as though they were put together late at night by a group of dedicated amateurs on somebody's kitchen table.'

I had also learned that the Linguaphone company found their paper-set ads outpulled trade set ads by about 25 per cent. Moreover, years previously, I had tested paper-set editorial style ads for washing machines. They had consistently done better than ads that looked like ads. (And the newspaper will typeset your ad *free*, whereas trade setting is very expensive.)

However, when we started work on Barnardo's our creative director, John Watson, and his art director, Chris Albert, hated the idea of having our ads look ugly.

Accordingly, we compromised. We ran ads trade-set in a typeface which implied cheapness, because it looked rather like a typewriter face. But in the end we arranged some split-run tests. The paper-set ads outpulled the trade set ones by between 60 per cent and 250 per cent.

2. Split-run inserts

The weakness of the A/B split is that in most publications you can only test two things at a time – occasionally four. But the ability to *insert* material which you have had preprinted yourself into publications gives you considerably greater flexibility.

What is more, since the insert pulls greater numbers of replies than advertisements do, you don't need as many copies of an insert to get a statistically reliable response level. I shall explain why in more detail later. But several benefits result.

In the first place, you can usually afford to test several publications at the same time, thus finding out which media are likely to do best for you. In the second place you can test a variety of different creative approaches. So you can acquire a great deal of knowledge very quickly.

The drawbacks of the insert are that the initial print cost will almost certainly be greater than most ads, so you must balance this expense against the benefits.

Time, too, is an important factor. It can be infuriating to wait for a magazine carrying your insert to publish; and then to have to wait again until a sufficient percentage of the results are in before you project.

You must, therefore, beware of making hasty decisions on the basis of early insert results. A few years ago, when testing a series of inserts for a knitting-card club, we made a costly error. In the early run of responses, one of these inserts was doing very well. Copy deadlines were looming, so we prepared an ad based on this insert. As further results came in, it turned out the early winner was not in fact by any means the best insert. Another one did much better. But by the time we learned we were wrong, it was too late to do anything.

So, although the insert may be a more flexible medium for testing, a daily newspaper split-run gives you a shorter copy date with results that come in much sooner than with a monthly or weekly magazine. In a fast moving world, that can be important.

3. Split-run mailings

This is the third major test bed for your business, and in some ways the most valuable.

That is because there is a wide range of outside lists available for you to test and you also have your own database which can be segmented down according to any number of variables. In this way you can test new lists, new approaches, and the effect of particular approaches upon particular segments.

This latter is particularly important. For instance, in the United States our agency tested a service which helped the business customer arrange his finances better. Response was good when targeted generally to business people. Then, the creative approaches were varied to approach each profession with a special appeal. Responses increased dramatically. The only exception was when mailing accountants. Predictably, they didn't see any need for advice on the subject on which they consider themselves experts. It was thus possible to eliminate them from the activity and save some money, whilst increasing revenue from the other segments.

Fundamentally, you can divide mailing tests into tests of new *lists* and tests of new *approaches*. But you must remember two things.

- Never test a new list with new copy unless you are also testing it with your existing, proven package – or 'banker'. If you ignore this, you will never know whether it was the new list or the new copy that worked.
- By the same token, when you test new copy make sure it is tested against your 'banker'. You can't rely on comparing what your 'banker' did last time out and what a new piece of copy does this time out. The timing can make a lot of difference (as you saw in the Comp-U-Card test, where it doubled response).

  What I am really saying here is: don't test two variables simultaneously. You will rightly reply that this is obvious, but I can tell you that otherwise very bright people do this quite frequently. For this reason, I shall be restating the point in a different way in the next chapter. It is extremely important.

4 Geographical splits

Most publications don't offer A/B split facilities, but they often publish different geographical editions. This enables you to test many ads simultaneously in different parts of the country.

The problem is, of course, that different areas respond very differently, so you have to allow for that when testing.

You can do this in two ways.

- Break down your customer file and response records by geographical areas. Monitor the results. You can then relate your own historical experience of geographical variations to the number of replies coming in from the various regional editions of the publication.

  Don't forget though, that you have to allow for the *relative* circulation in each geographical area of the particular publication you are using. This can also cause misleading bias because it may differ from the geographical bias amongst your own customers or the population at large.
- If you *rotate* your copy region by region, so that each piece of copy appears in each region, you can then make allowances for such biases.

  Thus, first you run ad A in the north, and ad B in the south on week one. Then you do it the other way round on week two. Add the results of the two tests together and you have a fair reading. Rotating more than once will make this more reliable.

  However, bearing in mind that you should be always looking for big differences, not small ones, worthwhile results should emerge quite clearly.

5 Telescope testing

If you have statistical inclinations, you may already have worked out another, very valuable form of test: valuable because it enables you to learn faster.

This is a test in one publication using both a geographical split and an A/B split simultaneously. For example, if you test ads X and Y on an A/B basis in the southern editions, whilst splitting X and Z in the north, you should learn which of the three ads is best.

To learn more, you then take the winning ad and use it as a control against two more ads, in the same way.

Note that you must have one ad in *both* geographical areas, as a control. And use your common sense; make sure that none of the appeals has an obvious geographical bias which could distort the results.

This technique is obviously even more valuable with publications which have many geographical editions.

6 Your own database

We have already established that the customers you seek will be similar in character to the ones you already have. That's why your own database – apart from being the most accessible test medium – is probably the most valuable one. Apart from anything else, your customers are almost invariably the most responsive group of people you can reach, so you are far less likely to lose money with them.

As your knowledge grows, you will constantly be able to compare the response you get from your own customer file and that which you get on the same offer when made to other lists, or in other outside media. In this way, once you have tested an offer to your list you can project roughly what it is likely to do elsewhere.

Unquestionably the cheapest way to test a new offer is to try it as a 'bounce back'. That is, an insert in a despatch parcel when sending out merchandise. There's no postage; the people receiving it are the hottest of buyers. This is the very best time to catch them: you will get a very high response. This means small numbers of inserts will suffice. Sometimes, you can put together a modest leaflet that allows you to test several possible offers simultaneously.

In the same way, an insert placed in one of your regular communications to your customers – a statement for instance – is also a very cheap and effective test medium.

In all these cases you can often use existing printed inserts and save money. Many forget this and waste money needlessly.

Once again, I must nag you with another warning. Make sure you express your offers to your list in the same way you plan to express them when going outside. It's no use using one headline and illustration to your list, and then being amazed that it doesn't pull well outside with a new headline and illustration. That's a *new* test. Obvious – but all too often ignored.

7 An ad catalogue

Another way of reaching your customers to find out what might work outside – because what works in your catalogue should do well with the similar people you seek. However this form of testing which is indictive rather than decisive.

The catalogue is a medium with its own peculiarities. A product which works in a catalogue may not work on its own. It seems that, sometimes, products do well only in propinquity with others: they benefit from being one of a crowd.

However, although what works in a catalogue doesn't *always* work elsewhere, very often it does. And certainly, if you find something is *doing* extremely well in a catalogue, it ought to work elsewhere.

The test will be the more valid if you create a catalogue made up of quasi-advertisements, which have a presentation as identical as possible to your advertising format.

Some companies simply have catalogues which consist of reproductions of all their advertisements. This is a very, very inexpensive way of putting together a catalogue. It will also make it easier for you to insert a new product in the accepted format within your catalogue.

I must say, however, that this is not normally the best format for a catalogue. Catalogues, as a rule, tend to do better when there are several items on a page. Often a great many. This format makes it more difficult to test the validity of such products when run solus. Nevertheless, if you have a catalogue, then it is foolish not to use it as a test medium. (And if you don't have *some* sort of catalogue, that is probably foolish, too.)

8 Questionnaire

The questionnaire, in my view, is the Cinderella of direct marketing. A humble, drab, unexciting drudge which has now become transformed into the key to many direct marketing activities.

You will already have concluded that the business of direct marketing revolves around acquiring knowledge about customers and prospects and then deploying it effectively. What better way to acquire knowledge than simply to ask your customers and prospects? Sophisticated direct marketers have known this for years. One of my clients has a sequence of over twenty tests, the first of which is a questionnaire, before launching any product.

You cannot normally base your final marketing decisions on the responses to a questionnaire. Like the responses to a catalogue they merely indicate what might happen. But in the early stages they are of enormous value in setting you off on the right track. As I suggested in Chapter Four, to find out what you ought to sell, start by asking your existing customers. You will learn a great deal.

Constructing a questionnaire mailing requires a knowledge of research, for it must be a combination of research document and mail shot. Too many are seduced into selling at the same time and thus erode the validity of the responses.

To your own list, a well written letter with a questionnaire can pull a 50 per cent or higher response – depending on the closeness of the relationship between you and your customers. But you *must* emphasise that you are asking them to give you advice that will help you serve them better in the future.

Properly written, such questionnaires do not even require inducements to be completed, though many companies offer a modest gift. One, for instance, adopts the ingenious and worthy ploy of making a gift to charity in return for each response.

This whole subject of the series of mailings you can employ to pre-test your product or service calls for lengthy treatment beyond the scope of this book. However, it is well worth your attention because it is the key to a *systematic* approach to selling which will virtually eliminate the possibility of any large-scale loss.

Parenthetically, I would say that were you to employ even *half* the techniques I have recommended in this chapter so far, you would be working more scientifically than the majority of today's established direct marketers.

Hardly surprisingly then, some of the smarter 'new' direct marketers have started using the questionnaire to fine effect. One ingenious use of the technique was made by my colleagues in the United States who initiated a great 'debate' on that matter of consuming interest to all Americans: chocolates. Was a new product a *cookie* or a *candy*? This was the burning question respondents were asked to vote upon. A very simple form of questionnaire, but nevertheless taking advantage of the fact that people like to answer questions.

This is not testing, but it is interesting as a way of suggesting that you think very carefully about the potential of the questionnaire.

9. Radio and TV

In Britain these two media are little used by direct marketers, which is a great shame. Commercial radio in particular came late to Britain and is relatively underdeveloped. The quality of radio commercials in this country is generally low.

TV, on the other hand, where creatively many people feel that British advertising is better than any in the world, is a frustrating medium for the direct marketer. The channels are limited in number, the time available each hour is (wisely) limited by law, so it is difficult to obtain the two prerequisites needed for much effective direct marketing: long time-slots and unsociable hours. However, as I observed in Chapter

Seven, this is changing as cable and satellite TV channels appear.

As test media, both TV and radio have a great advantage: speed of response. Their great disadvantage is that translating what works on television or radio into print is difficult.

Nevertheless, radio in particular is an ideal test medium. The production costs are low. The tape of a commercial can be altered so that you can easily and inexpensively insert or delete particular phrases. And one thing we have learned in this business is that particular phrases can make a phenomenal difference. Moreover, there are many small radio stations that charge relatively little for time.

Because of its low cost, even though it may not be potentially the most profitable medium for a particular offer, I think radio has a lot going for it. You may make little, but you won't lose much. And you could learn a lot fast.

One thing you should never forget is that the object of a test is to *learn*, not to make a profit. A test that loses you money today may yet tell you enough to make you a fortune tomorrow. Too many people try to test *and* make money. That is nice when it happens (which is quite often) but it is not the primary object of the exercise and is a short-sighted approach.

The astronomical cost of TV makes testing a very costly business indeed. Nevertheless, an inexpensive video-taped commercial shown at off-peak would prove an economic test.

You cannot conduct a true split-run test on TV and radio. You can, however, arrange geographical splits (particularly useful in conjunction with regional issues of the TV papers). And you can alternate commercials and achieve much the same effect, using different phone numbers or addresses, or referring to different advertisements in the commercials.

The US direct marketing man Lester Wunderman has the credit for inventing one particular technique known as the 'Gold Box' which helps in testing. On the TV commercial, mention is made of a box in the advertisement which – if you tick it – will entitle you to a free gift when sending in your order. No mention is made of this in the ad so that it is possible to measure how many of the people who saw the commercial were motivated to reply to the ad: how much 'uplift' the commercial gave.

10 Small ad tests

The small advertisement is a much under-utilised test medium, and yet it can be immensely valuable. Most of the old-time advertising pioneers like John Caples learned their first rules from small ads.

The only difference between a small ad and a large one is size. Every element that a large ad can have, a small one can have. A headline to attract attention, with maybe a small picture to illustrate it. Copy to make you want to buy. Mention of a premium. And a demand for action, with possibly even a coupon if the ad is above a certain size.

You can't split-run small ads (most media won't allow for splits on sizes smaller than 20cm double column). But you can *alternate* them day after day for a couple of weeks to get a reading. This also applies to classifieds – the most cost-effective spaces of all.

11 Shrinking your ads

You may have a number of large ads you want to test. But you could well be appalled at the cost of full-scale tests. Once again, think about small ads.

Shrink your large ads, retaining the same elements. You already know that a quarter page can be twice as cost-effective as a full page; you already know that the headline is by far the most important element in the ad. So all you have to do is retain the significant factors you think the large ads have, and test them smaller.

Many people are reluctant to run a smaller ad. They rue the fact that it won't make as much money. *I* rejoice that it can't *lose* as much money. So should you.

12 The telephone

What a valuable tool this is, for testing *and* research!

Obviously, it is very easy to split-run appeals on the phone. What is more, good telephone people will be able to tell you, within *hours* very often, which appeals are hitting the mark.

Moreover, if you want to find out about how people reacted to your products or your mailing, getting on the phone to them is the fastest way. (And very salutory it is, too, when your readers say with one universal voice: 'What mailing?' Humility is a fine quality to engender in copywriters.)

Frankly, I am astonished at how little use is made of the telephone in our industry. I can see no good reason why, after a mailing has gone out (particularly if it hasn't done well) people do not instantly get on the telephone and ask: *why*?

Within a very short period of time you'll be able to find out. Though you must be very careful to let people tell you their real opinions, not what you wish to hear.

Deduction

There is one more way of finding things out from looking at your results. It is called deduction or – in this book – commonsense.

When we were evaluating the first-year results for the Dr Barnardo appeals, we had a wide variety of ads and media to compare. Looking at the figures, a bright media planner working with us observed a significant difference in the results for ads which had coupons in them, and those that didn't. Generally speaking, ads *with* coupons will pull about 20 per cent to 25 per cent more than ads without. In this case, consistently, ads with *no* coupons were doing better than ads with. The margin was so great (over 50 per cent) that we decided thenceforth to take out the coupons.

Once again, we had learned that what works for some clients does not work for others. Why? I think it was because the coupon acted, for the reader, like the donation box of a charity worker who is collecting on the street. If you don't want to give, you cross the road to avoid it – you miser, you!

Following from this, we set up some split-run tests to see if taking the name Barnardo's in the ads and setting it small, instead of as a display logo would get us better results. It did not. From this I deduced that people are happy to read about the good work Barnardo's does; but put off by that rattling collector's box. However, once they've read they do give, thank God.

There is an important postcript to this story which illuminates yet another instance where I was wrong about something. Upon reading the results of the tests of coupon versus no coupon, I immediately instructed everybody to eliminate all coupons from Barnardo's advertising.

I was forced very quickly to rescind this direction, when somebody more intelligent than I pointed out that one of the objects of the advertising was to recruit names and addresses. Eliminating the coupon was discouraging people from doing this. So the coupons were reinstated.

A fair test?

People read test results, or even set up tests, in a way that suits their own predilections.

The subject of coupons reminds me of a story I heard about Joe Sugarman of JS & A in the US. You may recall that his ads don't carry them. This always surprised me until I realised that his market is a very special one, dealing for the most part with gadgets and superfluities for the fairly wealthy American. Things like language translating machines and other electronic marvels.

I recall him saying at the European Direct Marketing Symposium at Montreux in 1979 that his best medium is *The Wall Street Journal*. This means that virtually everybody he sells to has a telephone and a credit card, so they buy by using the two.

However, he was challenged upon one occasion about the dropping of the coupon. He replied to the challenge by setting up a test. He ran one ad with a coupon and no phone number; and one with a phone number and no coupon.

If this story is true, it was a pointless test. The real question is, as you will already have realised, what happens when you run a coupon *and* a phone number as against a phone number and address alone. (As a matter of interest, the coupon, because it signals there is a direct offer, tends to boost response if it is boldly outlined or made bigger. Even a dotted line around an ad will boost response. A simple flash stating 'This is a direct offer' helped one company to increase their responses. Moreover, the coupon itself will increase readership – but that is another subject dealt with elsewhere.)

To revert to my original point in this section about using judgement – or commonsense – in evaluating tests, you may imagine that the best way to test whether coupons did or did not help Barnardo's would have been to use split-run tests. The problem was that we were not *expecting* the result that occurred and it was against all our previous experience – against the 'rules'. We would never have considered testing it in the first place.

It is worth bringing out one other issue in connection with coupons. In a split-run, if one ad has a coupon and another doesn't, then the ad without the coupon has more space for the copy. This means it could be made more effective by using the additional space – so the split itself is invalid: it doesn't compare like with like.

The only way to do this is to pay the publication to run a piece of ordinary news copy in the space that would have been occupied by the coupon. This would be extremely expensive – even if the newspaper could be persuaded to co-operate. In the case of Barnardo's, the results were so overwhelmingly decisive that this was not a problem. However, this issue can crop up in other ways.

On one occasion we wished to discover for a client whether we could squeeze a full-page ad which ran across five columns into four columns. We arranged to run a column of editorial copy (which we wrote ourselves) down the fifth column, and conducted the split.

The results were quite clear: there was no difference between the four columns and the five columns. Once again, we had to look carefully at the results before deciding what to do next. In practice, we discovered that the rates we were able to obtain for full pages by careful media negotiation meant it was not worth bothering with the smaller space – even though in theory it might be more economic.

What I am saying is: first get your results, then evaluate them – very carefully. This is the subject I am about to go into.

A true and proper record

I have been left speechless more than once by the way in which otherwise sophisticated companies keep (or fail to keep) their advertising records. One famous computer company could do practically anything, it seemed, except tell you what the results were. One big publisher had no record of results at all.

Once the excitement of running the ad is over, people are often quite happy to leave it to the office girl to keep the record of what happened. If the results are bad, everyone wants to forget. If the results are good, why waste time working out just how good they were? So another year of potential knowledge is lost.

Yet keeping records is no great affair. Most mail order companies have a system. You can work one out quite simply. It merely needs to record *everything* about the particular communication and *everything* about the results.

It has to be a true and proper record. It doesn't matter whether you keep it on paper or on computer: accuracy and detail are what count.

- A copy of the mailing, insert, ad or details of the commercial.
- Details of when and where it appeared, or was mailed.
- How it was posted, and how people were asked to reply. Reply-paid, stamped, first class, second class, no stamp, telephone, Freephone, and so forth.
- Weather and any political or heavy news events or holiday period that might have affected results.
- Position of ad. Whether it backed on to another coupon. The same consideration applies to inserts: how many other inserts did it go out with? What was the environment?
- Results day by day and cumulatively.
- Conversion rates day by day and cumulatively.
- Anything else your commonsense tells you is relevant. When you see a result which seems to you bizarre or unexpected, take a closer look. Take a good look at the publication and all the other circumstances surrounding that particular result. You may find something you had not bargained for – like a competitor's ad or mailing on the same day.

Your results are the most valuable thing in your office apart from your mailing list. They are your map of where you have been, and your compass to where you should go. *Don't* leave them to the office dogsbody. Keep an eye on them constantly.

Follow up conversions and customer behaviour

You will find results exert a hypnotic effect on you, like racehorse form guides for gamblers. So although you must study them, don't waste time poring over them in the hope that they will look any better. They never do.

However, a word to the wise. You must return to your results regularly, because what may at first sight appear to be happening could be misleading. For instance, advertisement A may be producing twice as many inquiries as advertisement B, and three times as many inquiries as advertisement C.

When you come later to analyse the conversion into *sales*, you may discover that in fact advertisements B and C are converting much better than advertisement A. You may then conclude that advertisement B is your best bet.

The wise businessman will then review the value of those sales over a period of time. It may then emerge that advertisement C is in fact the most effective of all the advertisements you tested to start with because it produces sales of a far greater *average value*, or customers who tend to *spend more* over a period.

Does this sound to you like a scenario I have dreamed up to make a point? Well, it may: but I can tell you it is taken from an actual case history given to me by the general manager of one of our offices.

This leads on, of course, to the next question – how *soon* do you know enough to be able to act upon your results?

How soon can you tell?

People unfamiliar with our business expect all the replies to come in immediately. They don't. One spends frustrating days (or even weeks) trying to guess what the eventual results will be. However, there is a certain point with most response figures when sufficient numbers are in for you to be able to make a judgement of what the eventual total will be.

You will find that every medium is different, but *all* media have a response pattern. That is, after a certain period, a certain percentage of your replies will normally have come in. And you can be sure that by and large this pattern does not vary much from ad to ad or from mailing to mailing.

The only variation I have noticed is that the most successful 'pullers' seem to do better than average. They will have a longer period during which they pull, reach a higher peak, and keep near that peak for longer. The flops do worse than the usual pattern.

The problem is that every business appears to have slightly different figures on this, just as every medium does. You will have to find out what is true for you. However, the basic principle is that the more immediate the nature of the medium, the quicker the responses.

Obviously, on the phone they are instant. In broadcast media, after a week you'll have had the overwhelming majority of your replies. The daily paper may produce a third of its response after a week. For a weekly, it may take a fortnight to reach that point. For a monthly it may take three weeks – and so on.

In the same way, your direct mail responses will come in faster or more slowly depending on whether you mailed first class or second, and whether you had a first class or second class reply vehicle. You could have half your replies in after a fortnight – or only a fifth. Catalogue orders are even slower. They take months to come in.

To add another piece of uncertainty, orders come in more slowly than enquiries (a decision to enquire is obviously easier to make). And the results of unsuccessful ads or mailings seem to reach a peak sooner, and tail off faster.

Every case different

If all this sounds as though I can't tell you what's likely to happen, you're right. Every case is different.

In addition, whilst your postal service may be very keen to develop direct mail, they could well have great problems in maintaining the quality of the service. So day to day results may be very erratic.

The important thing to remember is that the overall response pattern does not tend to change. You can rely on it, except when major news events depress response fortuitously.

The other important thing to remember is **the results must be read carefully**.

Let me give you another example. It comes from one of the world's most famous companies, and I won't embarrass them by naming any names. This just goes to show how easily you can make mistakes.

When they came to see us, we asked if they had tested personalisation. 'Yes,' they replied. 'It doesn't work for us.' We were surprised. We asked what the results were. 'It cost us an extra 15 per cent. And it only pulled an extra 15 per cent.'

They had never taken the next step: 15 per cent extra response brought in infinitely more in money value than the 15 per cent added mailing costs. In the intervening period they had lost a fortune in potential revenue.

As a child, I was an appalling mathematician. This business has made me quite a passable one. But to get a true understanding of this vital subject, I would suggest you read someone who knows far more than I do. Julian Simon's book: *How to start and operate a mail order business*, gives a splendid exposition of this, and all the other mathematical aspects of this business.

His book (unlike many other worthy volumes on this business) makes a very complex business fairly easy to understand; though it can never be everyone's idea of a ripping read.

Nothing is foolproof

It was the British Prime Minister Disraeli who said: 'There are three kinds of lies. Lies. Damned lies. And statistics.'

Sadly, statistics are all we have to go on when evaluating our test results. Even more sadly, they aren't foolproof. There's no guarantee that the results of your test will be duplicated when, in the case of a mailing, you project your test on to larger numbers; or in the case of an ad, you re-run it in the same medium.

This is not just because other factors (like changes in the weather, or the news, or public interest) may change. It is because testing – oddly enough – is just like gambling. It is a matter of *probability*, not *certainty*.

However, the degree of probability is such that you can predict what is going to happen with a high level of confidence.

Thus, when you play roulette, each new spin of the wheel has no relationship to the last: it is as though every time, the wheel is being spun for the first time. This means that, although you may have had an odd number fifty times on the run, there is no logical reason why the next spin will come up even. However, there is a very high degree of *probability* that it will, and probability is what we are concerned with.

So, with ads and mailings, you want to know what *degree* of certainty you can act on. This is determined by the number of test packages that go out in a mailing and the ratio between that number and the expected level or response. Or, in the case of an ad or insert, the number of replies that come in.

- In the case of a mailing, the greater the number mailed, and the higher the response rate, the greater the probability that such a response will be duplicated on a second mailing to the same list. Both these factors apply. The result one can most rely on is a high percentage response to a large mailing. The least reliable result would be a low response to a small list.
- In the case of an advertisement, the same principle applies. A small number of responses to a publication with a low circulation is not to be relied on; and vice versa.

There are special probability tables featured in some of the books I have mentioned in the bibliography (eg the Bob Stone and Ed Nash books) which tell you how much you can rely on the results you get, and the sizes of sample you need. Most people like to be 95 per cent certain that the result they got will repeat itself on another occasion. These tables tell you to within what percentage variation such a repeated result is likely.

For example, suppose you are anticipating a 20 per cent response to your mailing. If you mail out 16,972 pieces, the result should be 95 per cent certain of being accurate to within 0.25 per cent either way. Nineteen times out of 20, it should fall within 1.75 per cent to 2.25 per cent.

The moral is that you must always take care your sample size is large enough. Even then, there will be rare occasions when the results aren't to be trusted. This is why experienced mailers never just conduct one test and then 'roll out' in the millions. I'll say more on this below.

What if you are split-testing an advertisement, or an insert? Then, the criterion is the number of replies to each half of a two-way split. The more replies you get, the more you can rely on the difference between the two halves of the response.

Thus, if you only get 100 replies in total, the result is not to be trusted unless there is a difference of more than 20 per cent between the two ads. Whereas if you get 500 replies in total, then a 10 per cent difference should be reliable. So if one ad pulls 275 replies, and the other only 225, you can be 95 per cent sure that it is better.

But *don't* conclude that it is exactly 20 per cent better. We are talking about probabilities, not certainties. To get a clear idea of the difference, you would have to retest several times.

Small numbers demand repeats

People ask me: 'What do we do about direct mail testing in our market? The lists are very small. To get one of your statistically valid test results we'd have to split up the entire mailing list.'

The answer is that if you have, say, a list of 10,000 names then remember, first of all, you are looking for tests which are likely to yield big differences – 30 per cent or more. Accordingly, take a small sample of 1,000 and split it into two and mail it. Then repeat the same process ith the same test and the same numbers. Then repeat it again. The result you get on the first test will not be statistically valid, but it should reveal which mailing is actually better than the other.

The second mailing will give you a closer insight into the difference, and the third a further confirmation. You could draw the analogy with the way that artillery fires 'ranging shots' in order to bracket a target.

The idea of repetition is a sound one in any case. Nobody with any commonsense will spend a fortune just on the basis of one test. Ours is a business for cautious people.

Suppose you have a quarter of a million names. Take a small sample to start with – say 5,000 pieces – and see what happens. Then, run a second-flight test with a larger sample of 50,000 before you go the whole hog.

Where you have segments of a list to test, some more responsive than others, you will obviously test the *best* segments first: the better buyers, more recent buyers, more frequent buyers.

I think you will find this pragmatic approach safest and more practical. But your initial test results (and quantity mailed) should be reviewed and determined in conjunction with the mysterious tables I referred to above.

Frankly, I find the whole thing rather like alchemy or examining the entrails of chickens for portents. And I still can't understand why it always seems that however well the test does, the roll-out is never quite as good.

What testing achieved for one client

Three hundred years ago, George Savile, Marquis of Halifax wrote: 'Hope is generally a wrong guide, though it is very good company along the way.'

Too many people run their companies on hope, when they should be testing. But a willingness – no, an *enthusiasm* – for testing can achieve great things.

When we first set up in business as Trenear-Harvey, Bird & Watson, we tested two mailings. They determined for us what business we should be in. Then we tried testing telephone follow-ups. We found they got us in to see nearly every single person we wrote to; and nearly 50 per cent gave us work. We tried mailing *without* telephone follow-up. It got us a 3 per cent response. Ads didn't pay well either.

But our first telephone follow-ups gave us a client who stayed with us until we resigned the account eight years later. They came to see us at our accommodation address. They were not interested in how splendid our offices were. They just wanted to test us. They gave us two packages to work on.

Neither came out on top when tested. But both did well enough to convince the client that they had found a new source of creative ideas. They gave us more tests. And more again.

Eventually, we handled virtually all their business. Our work for them ran all over the world. More importantly, in the late 1970s, over a period of five inflationary years, this company's cost of recruiting new customers was virtually unaffected by inflation. In effect, this was a halving of the real cost; a result only possible because of a continual test programme. Every idea worth trying that we put up, this client tried. That gave us more of a chance, and them more of a chance.

If you rely on testing, you don't have to worry about creative flair, or guesswork. Your customers *will* tell you.

In the next chapter, we'll look at some of the things you can test and some of the things you might learn.

12

Testing Versus Research – and Other Matters

'The golden rule is that there are no golden rules.'
George Bernard Shaw

'Always challenge dogma.'
Leonard Freeman

By now, I hope, you will have been persuaded of the virtues of testing. But these virtues should not blind you to the value of research.

I get rather irritated at the lack of imagination shown by many direct marketers. If you tell them a PS generally increases response, they immediately assume *every* letter in *every* mailing should bear such a message. If you point out that reversed-out type is more difficult to read than black and white, they assume you must *never* use reversed type. And, once converted to the joys of testing, many – as is common with converts – become equally dogmatic: 'There's no need to do any research; testing tells us all we need to know.'

This is silly. Testing usually tells you what works and what doesn't – but rarely *why*. You have to deduce. You cannot be sure. Research, on the other hand, will give you strong indications as to how people are likely to react, and why.

If you put people in laboratory conditions you can see how they look at things and read them. You can find out whether your work is easy for them to *follow* and – in a mailing – what order they read pieces in. (After opening the envelope they tend to turn first to the order form to see what they are in for.) Research, too, will tell you whether they *understand* what you're trying to say.

On one occasion we changed the sequence of pages in a mailing because we discovered that prospects were not reading them in the way we thought they would. On another, we learned that – contrary to what consumers *say* – they will spend five or even ten times as much time on a detailed, multiple-piece mailing package as they will on a short letter and order form such as they always claim they prefer.

By conducting *post hoc* research you can often find out why some people didn't reply, why some did, and what kind of people they were. In one case, for a client making a financial offer, we tested two alternative mailings. Both pulled very well, with almost identical results. Each was successful: but why?

Research revealed that one mailing appealed greatly to people with organised, tidy minds and of a conventional disposition. The other appealed to more adventurous and unconventional types. So we could use *both* approaches – and get a better eventual result.

Let me emphasise, though, that you must be careful when assessing research results. You can only base your views on what people actually do, rather on what they say they do. Thus, repeatedly, consumers and businessmen with one universal voice say they don't read long letters. In my experience and that of every colleague I have spoken to all over the world, nine times out of ten a long letter will substantially outpull a short one. In fact if you are going for anything other than a very unqualified inquiry, this tends to be true. (Of course, the lower cost of a short letter may make it more profitable – but that is a different subject.)

Another research red herring is free gifts and sweepstakes. Once again, people deny they are influenced by these things – yet in practice they usually are. So don't expect research to tell you how people will behave. You can, though, learn quite a lot about their *motivations* and even *how* they behave.

In short, as the general said: 'Time spent on reconnaisance is seldom wasted.'

Tests that gained an account

The subject of long letters and sweepstakes brings me to a true story about *Reader's Digest* which is amongst the most determined and committed testers of all. For my own part I am very glad this is the case. For it was as a result of tests ten years ago that Trenear Harvey, Bird & Watson, gained the *Reader's Digest* account.

When we set out in business, we wrote to *Reader's Digest*, amongst others, offering our services. The marketing director replied politely, indicating that the company had a large internal creative department, and hardly needed us.

However, a year later they called us in and asked us to present our work. Afterwards, we were invited to prepare some work for an encyclopaedia. They gave us samples of the pages and a descriptive brochure to work from.

This was probably the most challenging project we had yet been offered. If we could get a chance to work for *Reader's Digest* it would indeed be a feather in our caps. Quite apart from anything else, the company as a rule never used outside agencies to work on their merchandise.

Fired with enthusiasm, we went away and worked on the mailing package. We brought it back on the due date, and waited for them to comment.

A week passed. Then another. Then they called us back. The job had been just a test. The encyclopaedia did not exist; it had been *invented* for the occasion to see how we (and four other companies, including what was then the world's biggest agency, J Walter Thompson) would fare. They congratulated us and told us they thought ours was the best stab at the project. My partner and I looked at each other. I knew he was thinking what I was thinking – 'We've done it – we've got the *Digest*. Champagne all round tonight.'

We were brought swiftly down to earth. The marketing director, Richard Hewett, explained that now they would like us to do a *real* test. They had had mixed results selling off the page in the past. They wanted us to prepare an ad for a split-run test against their own ad prepared in-house.

This, then, was the moment when we had to deliver the goods. Could we do better than the *Digest's* own superb creative department which knew the business backwards?

We worked feverishly on our ad, and it was accepted as it stood. ('No point in getting you in if we don't take your advice', observed the client.) Then it went into test in an A/B split in the *Sun* newspaper. Before it ran, we had a chance to see the ad the *Digest* had prepared. It was a bold, hard-hitting ad. I thought we had no chance.

In the event, our ad outpulled theirs substantially. Which goes to show that after all these years in the business, I still can't be sure – a pretty good argument for testing.

When the results came in, we *did* break out the champagne. Especially when Victor Ross, the *eminence grise* of the publication, wrote us a letter of congratulations.

Another test

But we still didn't have the business. We had to prepare *another* ad for *another* product, and do *another* split-run. Sometimes this business reminds me of the Greek myth of Sisyphus, who spent eternity rolling a huge boulder up a mountain.

Once again, we saw the *Digest's* ad before the split-run took place. Once again, everyone in our eleven-man (and woman) agency voted on which would win. Once again, I thought *they* would. And once again, I was wrong – thank goodness.

This time, we did get the business. J Walter Thompson were so interested that their managing director came to see whether we might make a suitable acquisition. It consoled me somewhat that he was no better at guessing split-run results than I, because we put him to the test in our conference room.

The truth is that *only* testing can give you the answer – and to this day, *Reader's Digest* still keep testing their ads against ours.

Two laws of testing

Obviously, if you wish, you can test anything at all. Twenty-five years ago in the first flush of enthusiasm I used to test obsessively.

I recall testing the headline: 'This fully automatic washing machine can be yours for the price of a twin tub'. I put the word 'New' in front of the headline, and results went up. Then I tried the word 'Now'. There was no difference. Then I tried 'Look'. Still no change.

I was fiddling with the headline; not really changing anything of substance. You must go for *big* results in testing.

When I tried a radical change, and wrote: 'This fully automatic washing machine can be in your home within seven days', I found a new approach. An approach no *better* than the other one . . . but *different*. We were able to rotate the ads and get more life out of our media schedule and thus, more sales over the period.

From this experience, I drew a lesson; a lesson which leads us to the two great laws of testing. These are:

1 Only test a *meaningful* factor.
2 Test *one* or test *all*.

Let's look at these two laws in a little detail.

First of all, if you don't test meaningful factors, you risk learning nothing valuable.

What do I mean by meaningful? To answer that, you must use common sense. A delegate at one of the courses I used to teach, asked me whether we had ever tested the effect different *styles* of handwriting would have in a mailing package, where we had added facsimile handwritten notes on the letter.

I thought this was a fairly irrelevant question; and my suspicions of the questioner's intelligence quickened when he pursued the matter at boring length.

Commonsense tells you the thing you have to test is the effect of handwriting itself – is its personal nature likely to increase your results? Obviously, you want to make sure the writing is legible, similar in style (if possible) to the signer of the letter, and that if it is a male writing it should look like a male – and vice versa.

Commonsense should tell you not to test different words that mean the same thing (as I tried to in my washing machine headlines.) Commonsense should tell you to test *real* differences.

For example, in my washing machine ad, we tested putting a baby next to the machine. Results increased. Then we tested putting a baby and parents against the baby alone. Enquiries *doubled*, to my amazement. We repeated the test, with the same results.

We could never have known what results might eventuate. I expected the baby on its own to do better, because I had read that babies increase response. I was wrong. But the test *was* about something meaningful. This is how you get big results.

Apart from looking for big results, you should not waste your tests. That is why I say: 'Test one or test all.' Testing *one* means just taking one element in your ad or mailing and altering it.

If you change more than one element, then whatever the result may be, you'll never know what caused it. Possibly some of the changes you made were helpful, and others deleterious. But the changes might counteract each other. You might even have a situation where a new package or ad appeared to make no real difference to the results, although amongst the changes you made one might *on its own* have improved response dramatically.

Testing *all* means taking the communication and changing it root and branch: adopting a totally new approach in the hope of a big break-through. The moral, I think, is: little changes, little differences; and vice versa.

I have spent more time than I care to contemplate sitting in smoke-filled rooms speculating why one package worked and another failed. It can't happen if you follow the rules.

When to test what

When should you test one factor; and when should you test all?

Many people whose judgement I respect believe that given the choice between testing one and testing all – because obviously there is a limit to the number of things you can test at any one time – testing a completely new package is the better alternative. However, although this radical route may give great gains, it can also fall flat on its face because you are eliminating all the tested elements you know work.

If you are only going to test one element, then make sure it is a really important one. A completely changed offer. A much larger envelope. A different type of paper.

Let me give you an example of a case where changing the offer made a great deal of difference.

Eight years ago, for the first time we managed to attract an insurance company to our little agency. The client said he wanted a new approach to his mailings. The new package I wrote was a great disappointment to him. The approach seemed very similar; the content almost identical. 'I came to you looking for a new approach', he said to me. 'You charged me handsomely and all I have is something that's much the same.'

He was quite right. The only major change we made was to alter the first month's terms on his offer, so that people got a month free, where previously they had to pay £1. And we featured this offer on the envelope, which had been blank. The style of presentation and writing was different, but otherwise the content was very similar.

It seemed to me the biggest *single* change we could make was to alter the offer. And it was common sense – from numerous previous tests – that the offer would do better if featured on the envelope. There was no need to test that.

Our new package increased response by over 60 per cent.

Once again though, there are many occasions when after you have sent out a mailing you can review it and, based upon experience, make changes which you are pretty sure are likely to lift response. These things may not call for radical change, but cumulatively they may make a great deal of difference. They can make a package which *looks* quite similar, but is substantially different. It obviously makes sense.

My suggestion is that each season some of your tests should be improvements to your proven banker, and others totally new *ideas*. Both are necessary.

A British company in the clothing business which had consistently, year after year, tested small but significant changes to their 'banker' suddenly found their results were falling off. No matter what they did to their successful mailing they didn't seem to be able to come up with the improved responses they needed.

They found themselves in this position because they had previously neglected to try really radical tests. They had a very uncomfortable couple of seasons.

Startling results

Somebody once observed that one of the joys of travel is never knowing what you will find around the corner. So it is with testing.

Before giving you some practical advice on what you ought to test, let me give you some examples of the startling things that can happen.

A great friend of mine and a long-time mail order businessman used to run an ad for night-driving glasses. His original headline was 'End blinding headlight glare'. After a while, the ad began to tire, so he changed it. He added one word: 'Instantly'. Results jumped 20 per cent.

After another year or so, the new headline began to tire. So he added two more words, to make his headline: 'End blinding headlight glare instantly – for good'. Once again, results went up about 20 per cent.

So you see, even a word or phrase can make a difference. Often, the difference between profit and loss. A good reason for testing copy constantly.

In a series of tests for a mail shot selling garden compost, the following were some of the fascinating results that occurred:

- The name was changed from Cumba to Humush: sales went up 24 per cent.
- The mailing address was changed to a local one for each area (in the same county). A 22 per cent increase was recorded.
- A premium was offered for a quantity order. Twenty-seven per cent more sales came in. When the premium was offered for quantity as long as the order came in within 24 days, sales leapt up 23 per cent.
- When the premium was changed from a trowel to secateurs, 13 per cent in sales were added. And when the premium was guaranteed, an 8 per cent increase came in.
- Perhaps the most striking results occurred when copy was put on the envelope. 'Humush for better gardens' is hardly the most imaginative line I can recall; but it pushed sales up a good 32 per cent. Almost as remarkable, when premium copy was put on the

envelope, an extra 27 per cent in orders came in. (I am in Ernest Palfrey's debt for this interesting information.)

Why test results don't 'add up'

If you review a great many individual test results you might conclude that by adding together a series of ten such tests it's quite possible to increase the effectiveness of a given communication by many hundreds of per cent. This would be wonderful if it were so, but unfortunately it isn't – as a statistician would tell you.

What happens is that individual tests when put together in one package in this way cannibalise each other, as it were. Thus, if you take an ad or mailing and make three changes, each of which *individually* increases response by, say, 20 per cent, 30 per cent and 50 per cent you do *not* get a 100 per cent uplift in response. The total uplift will be much lower. It is extremely important, therefore, that you test your new package with all the changes against the old one and check what actually happens before you start getting excited.

Some impressive results are possible when you test the *position* of a particular item within a mailing. My former partner Brian Thomas found that when an incentive in a catalogue mailing was presented as a wraparound on the cover, as compared with a loose leaflet, response jumped over 25 per cent.

On another occasion he was amazed to get 11 times as many 'Member-get-a-member' names without offering a free gift as had previously been possible with one.

Why should this have made such a great difference? Quite simply because Brian decided to feature that offer on the flap of the envelope the respondent had to use to send in the order – and he was writing to agents who used to send in orders practically every month. As a result, they could hardly ignore the message.

Throughout this book you will notice that changes which may *appear* extremely small when described, can make substantial differences. In order to understand why this is so you should always look at the packages or advertisements in question. What sounds like a small change can be quite significant – as in the example I have just quoted. For instance, an Italian mailer changed the background colour of a mailing for a collectible from maroon to grey. Response leapt by 50 per cent. The reason for this apparently trivial change having such a large effect was simply that it made the copy much more legible.

But the thing I would most like to impress upon you is that many changes cost very little – sometimes nothing. The important thing is that you decide to test, and you think carefully *what* to test. Which brings me to my next subject.

Nine key areas for testing

1 The product

David Ogilvy, in his 'old testament' vein, once observed that 'the gifted product is mightier than the gifted pen'.

As we have seen, it helps to have a gifted offer too. But changing your product will have more effect than anything else. That stands to reason. After all your product or service *is* your business. Sometimes, though, you can change your product without changing your entire business Here are two examples.

For many years I was involved in the swimming pool business, as marketing adviser, copywriter, or advertising agency. It's an interesting challenge, selling pools in the UK. Rather like selling central heating in Zaire.

My patient and persevering client Steve Liu of Azure Pools found about seven years ago that things were really getting too tough for comfort. So we had a thoughtful lunch. How could he get more leads? I put it to him that the only way would be to get a better product. Something that no one else in the UK market had. He agreed, and said he was working on it. Meantime, what could we do?

I asked him why he thought people bought swimming pools. He talked about status, and investment, and health. I suggested it was because people wanted to *swim*, which was *so* obvious it was easy to forget.

Accordingly, I asked him whether the pool would cost all that much more if it were a few feet longer – but narrower. 'Not a lot', he replied. 'It's the excavation and the labour that costs the money.' So I wrote an ad that said: 'Four Extra Feet of Swimming Pool, FREE'. That did the trick for a couple of seasons: just changing the product so we could make an offer.

By that time, Steve had arranged to import a new pool from the US, made of a different kind of plastic, which gave him a unique story to tell. That did even better, because it was a genuinely improved product.

Here's another example.

When my late partner Martin Topley and I were running the Business Ideas Letter, we were looking for a way to make it more appealing to prospective subscribers.

'Man is a gregarious animal', the saying goes. People love to belong to things. Could we create something more than the publication that people could relate to? Something that would give it added value. We started the Institute of Small Business, which offered free advice to would-be entrepreneurs. And we found – as many have done before and since – that a good way to make your service or product more appealing is to start a club.

Frankly, we stumbled on the idea almost by accident. But we wrought better than we know; for I see today – over 20 years later – that all the promotional material sent out by the present publisher sells membership of the Institute, not subscriptions to the publication.

Why not look at *your* product and see how it can be altered to offer better value?

2 Your offer

Here's an interesting area. It's quite amazing how much difference changes in offer make. My first experience of this was, by coincidence, also with the Business Ideas Letter.

Instead of asking people to pay their subscriptions immediately, we suggested they send us a post-dated banker's order, so they could try the publication for three months without risk.

Results doubled. The same offer worked for our client Comp-U-Card.

On the other hand, when a US charitable foundation tried selling membership by offering a free three-month trial, it didn't work. One more reason *always* to test. Just because it works for one product or service, it doesn't mean it will work for all. Or, as they say: different strokes for different folks.

The number of offers you can test is limited only by the power of your imagination.

I have already quoted the late Joe Karbo – a most exceptional copywriter – whose offer was: 'I'm so sure you'll like my book *Lazy Man's Way to get Rich* that I won't cash your cheque for 30 days.' The ads are still running after nearly 20 years.

Other offers include: 'If you don't like this pipe, smash it, and send back the pieces.' Or, 'If you don't like this book, rip off the cover and send it back for a full refund.' Or 'Double your money back if not delighted.'

In short, before you test any creative execution, look to test your offer, because it could pay big dividends for you.

3 Price

Many years ago I worked for the late Mickey Barnes, a most astute marketing man who rose to become the head of the famous SH Benson agency – only to preside over its demise.

He once said to me: '*Price* is creative.'

This always struck me as loose use of language; but what is certainly true is that price can have more effect on results than practically any other factor. For that reason it is also probably true that more testing is conducted based on price variations and price offers than anything else.

In the UK, it is illegal to run two advertisements simultaneously offering different prices – or if not illegal, frowned on by the newspapers, and thus impossible.

Why this should be is not clear to me. My neighbour and I shop differently. By buying at different times or in different shops we can buy the same branded products at different prices. However, there it is: you cannot conduct split-runs on price in the press.

But you can run split *mailing* tests on price. And price is a subjective thing. What you consider a proper price may not seem so to your customers. Sometimes, your price may seem too high to them; but more often than you might imagine, it can actually seem too low. In the case of Comp-U-Card which I cited, the highest price did best.

You can often charge a very high price where the product you are offering has no direct competitor. For example, the Franklin Mint and similar companies are constantly producing unique products. It is very difficult for a consumer to put a value on these. They are worth what people are prepared to pay for them.

I recall years ago talking to a shrewd mail order operator who was selling many imported US items in France, but almost always at a much higher price than in the US. I asked him the reason for his policy. He replied: 'Drayton, if it isn't expensive, how can it be any good?'

So: don't just pick a price that seems right to you. Let your customers decide. Try three or four prices, and see which makes you most profit. Remember, too, that a higher price can always be slashed. It's not always so easy to raise a lower one – particularly as that low price has set a value in your customer's mind (and vice versa).

4 Discounting: what works?

Under the heading of price we must consider the possibility of *discounting*. This can have radical effects on response. Some time ago I took part in a day-seminar on split-run testing. I learned a lot, and made some new friends including Tony Arau, the head of Arau Associates. Like so many successful people in our business he's a former *Reader's Digest* man.

He showed a series of results relating to price offers. When one organisation slashed its membership price by 33 per cent, responses jumped from 0.65 per cent to 1.20 per cent, more than offsetting the loss of revenue on individual memberships. However, when he tried a half-price offer, it was not cost-effective.

So test different discounts and test how you express those discounts.

Here are several ways of saying the same thing. They will all get a different response. Because what is important is not what you *say* – it is what people *hear*.

- Save 50 per cent
- 50 per cent off
- Save £11
- Half price
- Buy one, get one FREE
- Two for £22

You might like to know that the 'Buy one, get one FREE' formulation appears to be the most successful, according to a friend of mine who has conducted tests on this.

You can profitably spend many happy hours working out all the many permutations of price offer that are possible. A sort of commercial crossword. Obviously, these permutations depend on the nature of what you are selling. Thus, a year's newsletter subscription can be expressed in many ways. £50 a year. Less than £1 a week. Under £2 an issue if it comes out fortnightly. Or, perhaps, 14p a day.

In one case, we tested whether you ought to include the post and packing charge in the price of a mail order product: eg £47 *plus* £2 postage and packing versus: £49 *including* postage and packing.

The change did make a significant difference to response. But this depended upon the price level. Thus, if the addition of postage and packing were to bring the price above the £50 mark, then almost certainly quoting the price plus postage and packing will do better – eg £49 plus £2 postage and packing.

This is simply a matter of common sense: psychologically £50 is clearly breaking a price barrier. Indeed, the first time I got involved in this question was when I proposed to a client that instead of charging £67 for a product he charge £69 – since to the public it would make very little difference. This certainly proved to be the case, and increased his profit margin substantially.

5 Incentives

A relevant premium rarely fails to pull added response above its cost. By relevant, I mean something likely to be of interest to your prospect.

And, as we saw earlier, it should be related to some action. Early buying. Buying in quantity. Giving another person's name. Never give something for nothing.

One of our clients offers two mystery gifts to encourage lapsed agents to rejoin the clan: each for a different purpose. One is a gift for replying; one for replying quickly. Fingerhut Corporation in the US used to offer four gifts to their prospects, and for all I know may now offer five, if they find it pays.

Incentives can be offered in steps. So much for buying £10 worth of a product. Something more for buying £20 worth, and so on. You can vary the incentive according to the level of a customer's loyalty, or the nature of their interest in your product, or their demographic or geographic circumstances. Thus, a country dweller could be offered a different incentive to a town dweller; a gardener something different to an angler.

As we learned above, *changing* the premium can affect results quite dramatically, too. So test that as well. But of all the incentives I have seen produce great results, the sweepstake seems to be most effective – though it is not legal in all countries.

I confess I cannot understand why sweepstakes do so well, not being of a gambling nature myself (life is chancy enough already). However, the fact is that they can increase responses dramatically when prominently featured.

So try a sweepstake, and don't be too worried about the fact that you may think your own particular customers are too sophisticated to react to this sort of nonsense. Lots of ordinary people play the football pools each week. But lots of very rich people go to casinos in Monte Carlo, London and Las Vegas. Gambling is a universal source of amusement. What you have to do is try a *sophisticated* sweepstake.

In recent years *The Times* has managed to raise circulation substantially by offering what to all intents and purposes is little more than a simple gamble. The trick is that they call it 'Portfolio' and relate it to share prices.

A word of warning, though. Incentives of this kind are not likely to produce the same level of quality in your respondents as a straightforward product sell.

It stands to reason that someone who has been induced to buy as a result of being attracted by big prizes in the sweepstake is less interested in the product itself. (Remember, for a sweepstake, in most countries your customer cannot be asked to buy anything or do anything: that is illegal. However, people always imagine that the buyer stands a better chance than the non-buyer.)

The thing to remember about sweepstakes is that if people are brought in by this sort of device, then they are likely to be responsive to the same sort of thing in the future.

Contests are also a good incentive, with the advantage that people who enter a contest must buy something, and must exercise some 'skill or judgement' – however minimal – in entering. I suspect the quality of contest entrants is marginally higher than that of sweepstakes buyers, since some effort is required.

What about prize structure? I have always understood that the best structure is one where there is a very spectacular major prize, and lots of very small ones. In this way, you combine the large promise with the chance of as many people winning as possible. (Incidentally, the best prizes seem to be *things*, not money, for they dramatize the offer. But people tend usually to take the money in the event of winning.)

Latterly, I have been told that the best structure is just to have one big prize and no little ones. But this is a technical subject I am not competent to pronounce on. Test it and find out.

The most spectacular example I can recall of a prize offer getting results was when, for the first time in the UK, Leisure Arts ran a mailing in which 'you have *already* won a prize' was the draw.

It was worth offering a prize to all, because, as Lenny Joseph their UK boss once told me: 'We got 50 per cent response.'

6 Time and number closes

In my experience men fear to lose as much as they hope to gain. That is perhaps why offers which encourage you to act now lest you miss an opportunity are extremely effective.

Many of these offers can be made in conjunction with the price. You can offer a price advantage if the customer orders by a certain time. You can offer the opportunity to avoid a price rise: an exceptionally powerful incentive.

On one occasion, for instance, one of my clients – Solarbo – was selling bedrooms and kitchens which people had to put together themselves. At that time, the government had just increased the rate of value added tax. We offered to pay the extra VAT for the customer if the order came in within 30 days, with full cash payment.

Eighteen thousand letters went out. Orders worth £78,000 came in; with a nice boost for the company's cash flow, since usually many of their sales were on credit.

Another way of motivating people is simply to say that you only have a certain number of the item in stock. This is unquestionably effective. Almost as effective is to set an arbitrary date by which applications or orders must be received. *Anything* which helps to move people out of their lethargy is worthwhile.

7 Your logistics

There are many physical things you can and should test. For example, in the area of media there are a number of significant test opportunities.

For three years the Metropolitan Opera Guild in New York tested television to recruit subscribers. They discovered that not only was television a very expensive way of producing results (for instance it cost $20,000 to produce an inexpensive commerical, with Placido Domingo appearing for nothing) but that the calibre of subscribers was not as high.

Direct mail, obviously, can tell a complete and convincing story; the TV operation as compared to direct mail produced a renewal rate from subscribers of 25 per cent as opposed to 75 per cent. One comment made was that responses on television tend to be more impulsive than those made through direct mail.

But quite apart from testing new media themselves there are a number of other things you can do.

- Test your media *timing*. Most people get their best results in January and February. But your product or service may be different.
- And what about days of the week? For years, I imagined that after Sunday, Saturday was the best day. The reason for this is that a long time ago, when the newspapers couldn't sell space on Saturdays, they inaugurated the Saturday bargain page.

This page became associated with mail order offers, and, in my mind was *the* mail order advertising day. Of course, on Saturday one could also usually negotiate discounts, which was a sweetener.

In fact in the UK Tuesday is the best day for most people, followed by Wednesday, Thursday and Monday, then Friday then Saturday. But for you, it may be different. In fact, one client of ours selling to DIY buyers and small tradesmen *does* find Saturday the best day.

- Consider size of space. Are you better off having a larger space or two small ones scattered through the publication? Or one small one, flagging a larger one? You'll never know till you try. And don't forget, just because the figures indicate that small spaces are more cost-effective, this may not be the case for you. Your product may be of such consuming interest to people that the impact of a large space will more than pay for itself.
- How about taking your ad and trying it in the form of an insert in a magazine? Normally, it will pull far more than an ad – maybe three to five times as much.
- Or, if you're running inserts already, try changing their format. An L-shaped insert with the reply-paid card on the foot of the 'L' often works as much as 50 per cent better than an oblong one. And a bound-in insert tends to do better than a loose one, as I believe I have already mentioned.

One of the interesting things about this direct marketing business is that there are so *many* things to try, and you learn so much as you go.

- How about your ad's position? I cover this in my section on the media. This is critical. And certainly you should pay great attention to it. Moreover, the effect of position will vary according to your company and your product. One of our clients finds that his left-hand-page ads tend to do badly. Another finds that the right or left hand makes no difference at all. Why don't you find out what works for you?
- Then there's the vast number of things you can do with catalogues. Every catalogue has its own personality. But where you place items in a catalogue has a radical effect on sales.

Where is the order form? Is it laid out easily enough? Have you tried putting extra blank space in it that people can fill in to give you more orders? Some people find this increases sales automatically.

- What about your mailings? Are you testing enough new lists each season? Are you testing new formats?
- Are you testing the growing opportunities for inserting in other people's packages? Cecil Hoge, in his *'Mail Order Moonlighting'* recommends this as the cheapest (and most cost-effective) way of getting started in business.

● And are you inserting enough material in your own fulfilment packs. Have you tested the optimum number of pieces? Have you tried simply filling up envelopes right to the postal limit?

So you see, in mere mechanical areas – nothing much to do with 'creativity' – there are huge test opportunities. Don't neglect them.

8 Creative

Sometimes it ain't what you say, it's the way that you say it. And this brings us to the subject of creative tests. Here, by definition, the possibilities are almost limitless, for what we are simply talking about is getting new ideas, or adapting old ones.

What's particularly valuable about creative changes (and particularly copy changes) is that not only can they produce the most surprising results, but often they cost little or nothing to make.

A few years ago, our agency was asked to work on the sale of a new business publication. The only change (other than the copy) that we suggested was that the price be raised by 20 per cent, so as to enable us to offer an incentive to the subscribers if they would join within a certain period. The product was not altered; the ad appeared in exactly the same media.

The response was *20 times greater* than the previous mailing. The only additional cost was our fee.

As you will already have guessed, the previous ad was not exactly a great work of persuasion. But that is not the point I am making. I am sure many other people in our industry will have similar stories to tell, where the creative content alone was changed, at little cost, with remarkable improvements.

9 Tricks

Some of the most worthwhile tests fall rather between two stools. They are not quite creative; they are not simply mechanical. They involve thinking about techniques which of themselves attract attention. Tricks.

For example there are the yes/no stamps in all their various forms. People have found that having such stamps printed in gold can increase response. Others have tried not just stamps, but envelopes, one for your 'Yes'; the other for your 'No' (the one you want people to use obviously being a pleasing affair; the other a nasty dun-coloured mess.) There are yes/no vouchers, too. All these things tend to work.

Then there is personalisation in all its various manifestations; cut-outs in envelopes; pop-ups. Or trying a miniature type-face on a miniature letter; or a giant type-face on a giant letter.

The actual *feel* of a package can make quite a difference. A friend of mine tells me that for a giant publishing house they decided to test simply making their insert slightly larger than other people's inserts, and using a heavier weight of paper. He believes that as a result their responses went up 20 per cent.

On another occasion, a paper company, Svecia Antiqua, arranged for a series of tests to be conducted to determine what effect using a different texture of stock has on responses. The answer was that in a series of tests, a textured stock improved results by: 15 per cent, 25 per cent, 32 per cent, 61 per cent and 92 per cent.

On a number of occasions simply changing the colour of an envelope has dramatically improved responses. In my experience, by as much as 20 per cent.

How much should you test? And when?

Testing is the *kernel* of direct marketing. The truth is that every major direct marketing business that succeeds does so largely by testing – or a run of quite exceptional luck. Luck is not something to base a business on; if I were you I would try the safer route.

If, at the beginning of each season you were to see the number of tests scheduled by a major mail order company, you might be quite surprised. It could easily fill a sheet of A3 paper, typed quite closely. And these are *successful* companies with *successful* products. They know that testing is in some ways more important when you are doing well than when you are doing badly.

Complacency is a poor basis for long-term success. Yet I have often heard people reject a proposed test on the grounds that they were 'doing very well, thank you.' This is poor thinking. For it is precisely when you *are* successful that you should worry about possible competition.

That's why you must have a body of knowledge built up from testing which will beat that competition when it comes. Anyone can copy your idea. But nobody can steal your knowledge.

Perhaps you recall the story of the victorious generals in ancient Rome who were allowed to ride in triumph through the streets of the city. Behind them in the victor's chariot a man was stationed. His job was to whisper at intervals: 'Remember, thou art human.'

No matter how well you are doing, the day will come when – perhaps for no reason you can fathom – your results suddenly slump. Your control mailing stops pulling. Your winning ad tires. That's when you'll be glad you've tested some alternatives.

When you are in trouble, it's natural to test. You have to, in order to succeed. But each year, no matter how well you are doing, you are wise to schedule a good 10 per cent of your budget to testing. More if you can afford it.

Often, it's a good idea to schedule tests for the off-season. In the summer you can get cheaper ad rates, for example. And having done your tests, you're ready to take advantage of the results when the best time of year comes round.

The best companies never stop testing.

Your test programme can be compared in many ways with the industrial investment programme of a great nation. Britain and the United States invest only a puny percentage of their gross national product in new plant and equipment each year, whereas Japan invests many times as much. We all know who's doing best today.

A famous case-history

I started this chapter by telling the story of how we became involved with *Reader's Digest*. Let me end it by re-printing a speech made by Tony Arau for a Florida Direct Marketing Day a while back. This story, too, is about *Reader's Digest*. I think it is both amusing and educational. I hope you do too.

Tony's title for his speech was 'The world's most successful direct mail piece – and how it grew'.

The object of the mailing was to get new readers for the *Digest* by offering a reduced-rate introductory subscription. The market was American families with telephones in selected census tract areas.

150 million pennies

Probably the most famous direct mailing piece ever created was the highly successful "Two Penny" mailing used by *Reader's Digest* in the 1950s.

It was so successful that at the peak of its use it required so many pennies that conventional suppliers and banks couldn't supply the *Digest's* needs (some 150 million pennies a year), so the *Digest* became the first private customer in the history of the US Mint.

But the famous penny mailing did not spring into being, full-blown all at one stroke of genius. And its history is instructive for everyone who plays a role in the creation of direct mail.

'If thou has two pennies . . .'

Back in the early 1950s, the *Digest's* circulation director, Frank Herbert, wrote what remains today one of the simplest but most brilliant direct mail letters of all time. It was known at the *Digest* as 'The Persian Poet' letter, and it began like this:

"Dear Reader:
    An ancient Persian poet once wrote, 'if thou hast two pennies, spend one for bread, and with the other buy hyacinths for thy soul."

The letter then went on and, obviously, suggested the *Reader's Digest* as a modern sort of hyacinth for one's spirit, proposing a short trial subscription as a way to discover the pleasures of the *Digest* for oneself.

It was first mailed in a plain, white nine inch envelope; inside was a simple order card (with the *Digest's* Pegasus logo faintly imprinted in the background); the letter was run in black and red on both sides of a single sheet; a small four-page, four-colour brochure was enclosed.

Since it was a typical *Digest* "Send no money" offer, the order card had a business reply back.

Worked for several years

The letter worked for several years, undergoing minor modifications from time to time. At one point, the copy line "If thou hast two pennies ..." was added to the envelope in an oriental sort of type.

When the *Digest's* new book club began at around that time, the Persian Poet letter was successfully adapted for condensed book promotions, too.

Reader's Digest has always been rather paranoid about revealing results of its various promotional efforts (and, within reason, properly so) so actual figures cannot be used here.

But using a scale of ten to 100 for comparisons, the original Persian Poet letter scored about 35. By adding copy to the outer envelope, sprucing up the order card and the like, response was eventually boosted to a 45 level.

Response slipped

But then, after several major mailings, response began to slip. It had drifted back to somewhere around the 40 level when Frank Herbert retired from the *Digest* and a young *Digest* copywriter named Walter Weintz found himself promoted to circulation director.

Weintz promptly began a series of vigorous copy tests to find a way to either strengthen or replace the fading Persian Poet mailing.

Results were generally disappointing until he tried a remarkably ugly, sort of gold coloured plastic 'Savings Token' – really the first of the *Digest's* famous "gimmick" mailings.

This brought response back to the 45 level, then up to the 50 level by using the token in combination with the Poet copy.

But Weintz felt that he had still not achieved the major new piece he was searching for. And then he thought of pennies.

Horrified management

Although the thought of mailing two pennies, twice a year, to nearly every American household with a telephone horrified *Digest* management, Weintz was given the go ahead (the *Digest* is probably the greatest direct mail testing laboratory in the world).

The early penny tests took three basic approaches.

The first contained two pennies, tied directly to the Persian Poet copy concept (keep one penny to buy 'bread', send the other back to buy 'hyacinths for the soul', the *Reader's Digest*).

A pocket was provided on the order card for return of the penny, and a business reply envelope was enclosed to carry the order card and penny, but the offer was the same, basic introductory subscription 'trial' offer.

Response jumped

Results were dramatic. On our scale of ten to 100, response immediately jumped to somewhere around the 60 mark.

A version was also tried using a single penny (hoping to save $10 per thousand in the mail cost) – the copy modified to a simple 'here's your penny for hyacinths' approach. It did not do as well, pulling something like 50 on our scale.

Then the two-penny version was tried with a brand new offer, something of the order of 12 issues for $1.98, we'll bill you later for $2.00, and you keep the enclosed 2c as your 'change' in advance.

The basic copy and outer envelope were still a variation on the Persian Poet. But response jumped to something of the order of 75.

The *Digest* had its big breakthrough.

Later, the envelope copy was changed to a simple 'Here's your change', with the two pennies showing through a window beneath the copy, and response inched up another five or so.

Poet retired

Eventually, a version was tried using completely new straightforward copy, without any references to Persian Poets – and response went up another five or thereabouts. The Persian Poet, after several years of yeoman duty, had finally been retired.

The new two-penny mailing was successfully adapted for the *Digest's* Condensed Book Club ('Your first book for only 8c – just send us a dime for convenience, and keep the enclosed 2c change, in advance'). And it was even used for a couple of the *Digest's* one-shot book promotions.

Over the years, numerous attempts were made to improve on the basic two penny piece. One, resurrecting the Persian Poet copy, was tested with two real Persian pennies (actually, they were bronze Lebanese piastres). Another, based on the philosophy that if 2c is good 5c should be about twice as good, actually included a nickel 'change' in advance.

Both were comparative disasters. In fact, if anyone would like to start a coin collection featuring Lebanese piastres, the *Reader's Digest* can probably provide several thousand cheap.

Staying power

But good copy and good promotional concepts sometimes have an astonishing staying power.

When the *Digest* bought the RCA Victor Record Club, the first successful new promotional piece was a variation on the basic two-penny offer.

Several years later, *Life* magazine put together a very successful piece which used its own variation – a single penny, showing through a window, with the copy line "Here's your change . . . and here's your chance . . . to see life . . . to see the world . . . to eyewitness great events". And many other mailers have over the years used the penny technique in any of a number of different ways.

Historical footnote: Because the pennies cost more to return than they were worth, the *Digest* attempted to have the Post Office simply destroy undelivered mail. And because some people who didn't want to subscribe to the *Digest* felt uneasy about keeping the two pennies, the *Digest* ran a copy line urging people to keep the pennies, please, not to return them, even if they didn't want to take advantage of the *Digest's* offer.

But the Post Office informed the *Digest* that they could not legally destroy or dispose of the nixies containing pennies – the *Digest* had to pay to have its undeliverable mail returned. And many people insisted on sending their pennies back.

So the *Digest* was stuck with a growing warehouseful of penny mailings – mailings that cost about 4c each to open and salvage the pennies from. It became both a problem and a mild embarrassment.

Then Al Cole, General Manager of the *Digest* and president of the Boys Clubs of America, made his major contribution to the penny game.

He knew the local Mt Kisco Boys Club was struggling to raise money to build a new club building, so he made the kids a deal: if they'd open the mail, shuck the pennies off the cards and separate them into two piles, the Boys Club could keep one pile and return the other to the *Digest* to be reused.

At the time, a staggering total of something like 50 million pennies was involved. And the Boys Club of Mt Kisco got its new club house.

Not bad for a cheap little 2c mailing piece.**'**

A footnote to this story: The *Reader's Digest* is *still* using coins – not to mention stamps for the cost of your response – in their mailings. And it still works. Because contrary to what some believe, human behaviour changes very little over the years – if at all.

13

How to Choose Your Agency – and When to Do Without One

'Those who counsel do not pay.'
  Flemish proverb

A while ago I saw an article by a Mr Ragu Chellan, in *The Times of India*, on the subject of choosing a computer. I have never met Mr Chellan, but I thought he gave a most apposite analogy; one which applies just as well to choosing an agency – or for that matter a mailing house or printer.

Deciding to buy a computer is like deciding to get married – the Indian way. You look at a variety of models, you compare attributes, you make a mental checklist of the points you like and the points you don't like, you ask friends and family about the prospective spouse and you try to imagine the situation a few years ahead.

The writer goes on to point out that the first question is not how to buy, but *why*? Once again, remarkably appropriate whether you are considering an advertising agency or a mailing house. What precisely do you want to achieve?

There are circumstances under which I wouldn't recommend an agency at all. The same may apply to using a mailing house. If you have a small operation which you are building from the ground floor up, you may decide to start by fulfilling this function yourself.

In considering any supplier it is certainly wise to review the range of options. Don't do a deal with the first kind face you meet. Don't just go and see one agency – have a look at several.

Certainly ask around. Consult friends, colleagues. Look through the trade press. Visit seminars and conferences to check out the available talent. I am astounded how few people do these things. Indeed, I sometimes think people make significant decisions about suppliers with less care than they would in choosing a new car. Some, because they are excessively grand, do not deign to take the basic step of going round and having a look at the premises of the people they are proposing to do business with. They deal with the whole thing as though they were hiring a chauffeur-driven limousine.

Very few bother to do the obvious: ask for a list of current clients and go and talk to some of them. Perhaps they are too shy.

One other point Mr Chellan made impressed me particularly. 'Try to imagine the situation a few years ahead.' When you choose an agency or any other supplier, then you must envisage what the future situation is likely to be. If it's a small agency, are they going to be able to cope with your business as it grows? If they're large, and you intend to stay small, will you retain their interest? Do they have sufficient talent in depth – bright young people – to be able to handle your business over a period of time?

One consideration, of course, which applies to brides and to companies is perhaps the most important of all. Do you actually *like* the people you meet? Do you think you could develop a good relationship with them – a friendly one? You should certainly spend enough time with them to get some impression of what sort of people they are. And not just on a business basis, but if possible socially, too.

Agency or not?

Choosing an agency reminds me of a statement made by a French nineteenth century wit, Count Montrond: 'Beware first impressions; they are almost invariably good.' Agency people tend to be fairly articulate and often very charming, and are hardly inclined to wax lyrical about their failures when you come to call.

So many factors may be involved in the final decision that it can prove something of a lottery. Here are my thoughts on the matter, having sat on both sides of the fence.

First, there are certain situations in which I do not think it is a particularly good idea to have an advertising agency. This is especially true at the moment when there is a great shortage of talent. In London, for instance, I consider there are only four or five good direct marketing agencies and another three or four in the rest of the country. In the US there is a much wider choice, but in less developed markets choice is even narrower. Try shopping around for a really good agency in Australia or New Zealand for example. In some cases you may find you are educating the agency as much as they are helping you.

Moreover, certain businesses are so complex and work-intensive that you can only understand the problems and produce the promotional material economically inside. This is typically the case with a large publishing organisation with many products selling to small, specialised markets.

Sometimes, too, your budget may be too small to make it profitable for a good agency. Yet although your business may not be large, your problems are just as important to you as a large company's – and, for the agency, just as demanding. Under those circumstances it's certainly no use dealing with a large agency. They have high overheads. They can't afford to employ top talent on your business. You might be able to locate a good *small* agency – but such gems are rare. What is more, unless your business is going to grow with them, they may prove short-term partners.

Under such circumstances, do it yourself: because you are the only one who cares enough. Do it entirely on your own or in conjunction with a freelance, but don't waste time with an agency. (You may be wondering what is a large budget and what is a small one. Unfortunately, there is no simple answer to this; it depends on the market. A million dollars a year may be a huge budget in Denmark. In New York it would be very small. When looking at an agency the best thing to do is to find out how large their average account is. If you are going to be a little fish in a big pool you should beware.)

Unfortunately, agencies themselves are not always that shrewd about selecting their clients. They are often so excited by the idea of getting any business that they will take on all accounts, no matter what size.

A few years ago a small client came to us because he was not satisfied with the service he was getting from a competitor. Had we been wise, we would have reflected that our competitor is a man who normally services his clients very well and declined the business. Foolishly, fired by the thought of taking the business away from our rival, we took it on. We soon learned we could no more afford to service it properly than our competitor. In the process, we lost money and so did our client because we had barely begun to understand his business before we mutually agreed to call it a day.

You will already have gathered, I hope, that I think agencies are far from faultless. And in the particular area of taking on either more business than they can handle, or the sort of business they should not try to handle, they are often particularly foolish. The question therefore arises: should you deal with the whole thing in-house?

Why stay in-house?

One of the most consistently successful direct marketers in the world, *Reader's Digest*, plans and creates its mailings in-house. A powerful argument in favour of the in-house operation.

In 1987, a survey of 12 advertisers by Ad Business Reports in America outlined their reasons for having in-house advertising units. They were:

- More control of the process.
- Greater confidentiality.
- More access to company people, products and customers.
- Better knowledge of product or service.
- Direct contact between writer and merchandiser.
- Less likelihood of information being misinterpreted as it is passed along.
- More involvement.
- Greater speed and flexibility. Eg one company took 100 photos, and set up two 16-page catalogues in 15 days for a trade show.
- Creativity which is as good – maybe better.

I hold no particular brief for either in-house or advertising-agency route – I have worked as an agent, and I have run an in-house advertising department in the past.

Unquestionably you can get greater flexibility in-house. One US in-house advertising unit receives sales figures five times a day. Particularly in the retail business it is important to be able to make changes quickly. The market is very volatile. Something as simple as the weather can affect what is happening.

In addition to the benefits cited above, economies can be made. For instance, you need no account executives to mediate between client and agency.

I believe the major drawback of the in-house operation is that it is *introverted*: it is difficult for fresh thinking to emerge. That is where the relatively objective – if less well informed – agency's contribution can be beneficial.

The argument that creativity is as good, often better, is one I find hard to accept. I can think of very little in-house creative work of very high calibre. This is because in-house operations tend to pay less money and attract a lower grade of talent. The challenge and variety of work in the agencies appeal more to young people.

Us and them

The average marketing man's wife, if asked to define her idea of hell, would probably reply: 'A night out with my husband and a group of his colleagues.' Whenever two or three marketing people gather together, they talk nothing but shop. The agency world in particular is a most inward looking one.

This navel-gazing attitude comes out nowhere more strongly than in the average agency's presentation. They stand up, thrilled to bits to have the opportunity to talk interminably about themselves, their philosophy, their theories, their staff, their agency's history . . . and so on.

This agency weakness of talking about 'us' when the conversation should be about 'them' is very prevalent, and should be stamped out to the profit of all.

When client and prospective agency meet, the conversation should always centre around the client's particular needs. Thus both parties are more likely to find satisfaction. The client will get a good idea of the way the agency approaches a problem. The agency will be able to display its prowess. Drivel will be minimised.

Whenever a prospective client comes to see us just because he's 'looking around', my heart sinks. It gives you nothing to get your teeth into.

Apart from their views on your problem, the thing you want to know about an agency is how they have dealt with others' accounts. For this reason, a presentation of case histories is usually worthwhile. (I would *insist* on them.)

Don't let the display be confined to vague befores and afters: 'Before it was like this; now it's like this, and didn't we do well.' Ask *why* changes were made. Look for the thinking more than the general impression. Try to get some facts about results.

Learning what they did for others could prove more useful than wondering what they might do for you – or even speculative work, which I come to next. In addition, if I were choosing an agency, I would also ask if anyone there has worked as a client or has general business experience. If nobody at your agency has ever actually had to face the kind of decisions you face, their advice can only be based on abstract theory bolstered by what they have seen happen to other clients. Is that enough?

Speculative presentations

When Dr Barnardo's came to see my old agency, THB&W, they told us they had been looking at agencies for eight months, and had a shortlist of five, who were putting up speculative work for nothing. Would we like to join them?

We declined with thanks. How could we possibly understand their organisation and activities in a couple of weeks?

Generally speaking I do not think you should request any speculative work unless the agency understands your business very well. On the other hand, I see no reason why a client should not give the agency a full brief on some problem which concerns him, and get the agency to react with suggestions as to the course he might consider. This allows the agency to demonstrate its thinking ability, and gives you a fair insight into its calibre without the ruinous costs of a full-scale creative endeavour.

Where speculative creative work calls for more than a cursory skirmish, it ought to be paid for. If it costs nothing, what is it worth? In any case, why should my existing clients subsidise free work for you when they are paying me to work for them? We only do serious work for nothing if we have idle hands at the time, or where an existing client requests it. Our normal policy is to demand a rejection fee if we don't get the business.

One must be honest, however, and admit that the thought of a fat, lucrative account or one with enormous potential erodes one's views on this. Nevertheless, the practice is wasteful; in the end, clients as a group pay for it one way or another.

One way to assess an agency is to pay them to create something you can test against the existing material. If you do this, it's a good idea to give the agency more than one test opportunity. A single test is like deciding a World Cup result on one penalty kick.

Organisation and procedure

Many agencies are partial to complex organisation charts. What you really want to know is precisely how they *handle* business. Ask them to show you how a job goes through from start to finish. Try and get an insight into their views on marketing *strategy*, too. Tactical direct marketing is all very well, but only good strategic thinking will build your business.

One thing you may find very confusing when meeting or dealing with agencies is the titles they deploy in such large numbers. Thus, you may well be taken aback when some beardless youth is presented to you as an *art director*.

It started back in the 1920s. Albert Lasker, then head of Lord & Thomas, the world's biggest advertising agency, noticed his people were not winning as much new business as usual. He found a simple solution. He called his account executives in and informed them that as from that moment they were all vice presidents. This had the desired effect: prospective clients thought they were dealing with important chaps and business started pouring in again.

This nifty little idea has been repeated over the years: there is a sort of inflationary spiral on titles. 'Director' in an agency often means little or nothing today.

For instance, when I came into the business 30 years ago an art director was very important. He was in charge of the visual output of the agency. Nowadays an art director is just about anybody with some slight visual facility (one of my colleagues denies even this is true). His job is to work with a copywriter to develop creative ideas that sell your product or service.

Indeed, don't be overly impressed with anybody presented to you as a 'director' in an advertising agency without checking what they direct. Thus, you may meet an account director. This does not mean he is on the board of the company. It merely means he directs the handling of a particular client's business, or maybe several clients' businesses.

Above him there may well be a real live board director. Don't be too impressed by that either: one London advertising agency has a staff of 160 and 23 board directors. How much say do you imagine they could have in running the business? Not a lot.

If you're introduced to a man who is described as a creative director, you should try to find out how many creative directors the agency has. A few years ago there just used to be one. Now some agencies have several. They will all report to some supremo who may well be described as an *executive* creative director.

It's all harmless fun really; titles in advertising agencies are used in the same way that the American army distributes medals. Apart from being popular, they don't cost as much as wage rises. But because of this love of titles, it is probably wise for you to ask your agency for a simple chart which shows you who does what.

Who will actually work on my account?

One common complaint is that when pitching for the business the agency quite naturally puts up its best possible team – which may not always be the one that will finally be working on your account. So you buy a Rolls-Royce and end up driving an old banger.

Some clients react by insisting on meeting the team that will be handling their account right at the beginning. This is a fair request; but – as in so many things – a little commonsense must be brought to bear. The agency may not know who they will eventually assign, because they don't yet know your business. In any case, they would be crazy to hire people before they have gained your account.

When a new client with a new set of problems comes into the agency, the best possible thing the agency can do is to put its best brains on to the account. You would be mad to object.

Equally, once the agency has grasped your needs it can quite reasonably turn the account over to other personnel. Knowing what I have learned about agency finance, if the top people worked all the time on your business, then the agency would go broke.

What you should ensure is that your business always has the interest of the people at the top; and that at least one of them is *personally* concerned about it. The minute you are disturbed about something, speak to that person. Don't sit in your office quietly festering.

Remember, the agency principals are just as anxious as you for your success. If they don't appear to be, then something is wrong. Either with the agency, or you.

The Brief

The quality of the *thinking* that the agency delivers to you in a presentation will depend almost entirely upon the quality of the brief you give them. I am going to cover this subject in the next chapter from another perspective. At this point however, let me simply say that unless you have given the agency a detailed, complete briefing on what it is you wish to achieve, and how you are thinking of going about it, then the presentation will never be as good as it might be.

I cannot know *enough* about what it is you plan to do, how you run your business, what problems and opportunities you see. I cannot spend too much time meeting your sales people, your colleagues who understand how you operate. I am delighted to talk to your customers and find out why they buy whatever it is you sell. Every scrap of information you can give to me is worthwhile.

Unhappily, some clients seem to regard a presentation as an opportunity to find out whether the agency can *guess* what it is they want. It may give a wonderful feeling of power, and even a few moments of entertainment. But it is an almost complete waste of time.

The same sort of clients like to sit in godlike judgement on the agency, reviewing their puny efforts. This is also a waste of time. Discussion as between equals will get you *much* further.

A clear point of view is vital

The best agencies have a clear personality which derives from the people who run them, who choose kindred spirits to work for them, and also have a point of view about what constitutes good work.

When you have a clear view about the business, then you can explain it to your clients and to your co-workers. Everything can be assessed in the light of that view. When new clients come to see you they know what it is they have come for.

Without such a clear view, you are rudderless, with no idea of where you wish to go, and no idea of how to get there. I think this is important – if only for the selfish reason that I like to know what I am selling to people.

Agencies are difficult to evaluate in any case. At least if the agency consistently approaches problems with certain criteria in mind and goes about things in a certain way, the client has a feeling for the *kind* of agency he has chosen. This is easier than choosing agencies simply because they seem to be nice chaps and you like the look of their work, or even because they have lots of people working for them and offices all over the world.

Because there is a grave shortage of high calibre creative people, many agencies are forced to use freelancers. They have no choice. Nevertheless, I think having to go outside to whatever freelancer is available at the time means the agency is unlikely to produce a consistent body of work: a recognisable product.

The only alternative is to do what we have done: train your own people in the fond hope that if you are nice to them they will stay with you. It seems to work.

Presenting ideas

The point at which the agency starts to present the creative work is the moment when the client sits up (after his somnolent period during the media presentation).

Many agencies skate gaily over this period, relying on well-finished roughs and bright colours to get them through. And many clients will depart satisfied with the amount of work evidenced.

But finished roughs are not ideas. They are just executions. And the fact that the agency creative department has produced 20 of them will not make them any better than if they had come up with one brilliant idea on the back of an envelope.

The agency must be able to explain how and why they came up with a particular proposal. That is really what presentations are all about.

Some think they consist of elaborate charts and witty lines. Being a bit of a wag myself I do enjoy making a presentation a lighthearted affair. But all you really need to hear is why the agency arrived at a particular solution. If the agency cannot tell, then the proposal is merely whistling in the dark. Throw it out and start again.

Far too often, the agency team does not include the people who did the thinking – the hairy art director and nervous writer round the corner. They may not have been invited to bring their uncouth personae to the meeting. They may be shy (a lot of creative people are better at expressing themselves on paper than in person).

My advice is to coax them out of retreat, offer them a drink (most creative people react to this like horses to carrots) and ask them what they had in mind.

You may even establish that they don't exist: the work was done freelance outside. This in itself begs the question as to how the agency can express its approach to direct marketing when using people they don't control – see above.

One more point: waffle is endemic in presentations. Some clients judge thinking by the thickness of the report produced. All agencies know this. Good thinking is better thinking if someone has to compress it. Get your agency to write a brief executive summary. It will make them concentrate, and save you time.

Figures, and large claims

Practically everyone would like to know how well an agency is going to do for them in advance. At some point a client will ask: 'How many per cent do you think this will pull?' No agency likes to disappoint a client, and there is a natural tendency to come up with a figure, if only to satisfy the beast.

Professional clients and agencies both know that results are to some degree in the lap of the gods. Too many factors can influence them. And, if the product is a new one, there is no real basis for comparing with previous experience. So, as a client, beware large claims about results. As an agent, don't make them.

What an agent should be able to explain is what he is doing to make your mailing or ad work better. Has he put in a better incentive? Or a new way of personalising the package? Or a new format?

In short, don't settle for promises. What you want is *ideas*.

Entertainment

When I was young, my parents had a restaurant. My idea of a perfect job was one where I could go to fine restaurants every day. I cannot say that the reality lives up to my dreams, but in my present job we do a lot of entertaining.

Entertaining will never gain or keep business – or if it will, the business isn't worth having. Never entertain a client to say 'please'. Entertain to say 'thank you'. Or just for fun.

Never award or gain accounts through bribery. What can come through corruption can go the same way, and both parties have given hostages to fortune.

Playing the field

There is a longstanding tradition in our industry whereby clients quite happily put out work to several different agencies, as though they were all freelancers, or printers. This is dying out but is still quite common.

A building society talked to my partner, Rod Wright, a while ago about the possibility of us working for them. At the conclusion of the presentation the building society said: 'What we plan to do in fact is to try out a number of agencies over a couple of years, and then settle on one we like.'

My partner was tempted (but restrained himself, being a tactful sort of fellow) to reply: 'Well, we plan to try a number of building societies in the same way and see how *we* get along.'

The fact is that very few clients like the idea of agencies dealing with their competitors, but feel they themselves are immune from such strictures. This is arrogant twaddle. It is not only arrogant twaddle – it is a silly way to go about things.

I am not saying it is a bad idea to give out the odd project to start with before choosing an agency, but to carry on in the same way over a period of time is sheer folly. The reason is quite simple. You end with having a lack of consistency in your communications, no continuing relationship with any given supplier who is dedicated to you – and probably, in my view, very poor stuff. I don't see how you can maintain your positioning successfully if you are constantly dealing with different people.

Just as it's unsettling to an agency if a client is constantly hobnobbing with other agencies or seeing their presentations, you are unlikely to get the best possible work from an agency if you are also dealing with other agencies on the same business.

Our agency has worked for two organisations that we do not care whether we ever deal with again. They both have a rich variety of faults, but they share this one of dealing with several agencies at the same time.

A variation on this particular approach is peculiar with some clients: to keep on threatening the agency, overtly, or implicitly by seeing other agencies' presentations when they have no real intention of moving. They do this because they believe it keeps the agency 'on their toes'. I can tell you this is not the case. It simply makes the agency hate you.

The truth of the matter is that the analogy with marriage is most appropriate. Why should I work caringly for you if you are not faithful to me? More importantly, how can I possibly master all the complexities of your business if you only give me *some* of the problems you have? (Of course, large organisations have many divisions. Different divisions often, quite rightly, deal with different agencies.)

It goes without saying that just as clients should stick to agencies, agencies should not speak to clients competing with their existing roster unless they are thinking of changing the client.

One reason why people jump around from one supplier to another is economic: they can negotiate each time for the best possible price. I think this may be shortsighted. Mr Chellan whom I quoted earlier makes an interesting observation: 'Buying the cheapest may be the costliest decision you ever take.' This leads me very neatly on to the subject of money.

How much you should pay

At one time when prospective clients came to see us, I used to dread the moment when the question came up: 'How much do you charge?' I used to reply lamely: 'Well, it all depends – we don't have any standard arrangement with our clients, because they all ask us to do different things.'

Let me consider three basic ways of charging which I have found work for one type of client or another.

1 Charging by the hour
It is possible to charge by the hour with a different rate of charge for each person working on the account. It is wise in advance for the agency to give the client, once his requirements have been carefully discussed, a rough estimate of how much it is expected these fees will work out at per month. It is also extremely wise to have an agreement *in advance* that the fee structure will be reviewed regularly: probably fairly quickly after the opening of the agreement, say three months. The reason for this is simple: when a client becomes engaged in direct marketing, very often he suddenly discovers more areas of his business where it can be applied. What looked like a sensible estimate to start with becomes ludicrously unprofitable.

2 Commission plus relevant fees
Where a client is spending a lot of money in the media, it is perfectly possible to work on commission. There will always be hard bargaining about this. I will only say that when a lot of money is being spent, 15 per cent commission is sometimes a high figure, but I have never seen an account really well handled by an agency on less than 10 per cent. In order to make a profit the agency cuts corners. Some advertisers (particularly in the retail field) offer their agencies a much

lower rate of commission. It tends to show in the quality of the work. In short, if you pay peanuts, you get monkeys.

Often, in addition to any commissionable revenue from the media the agency will be preparing mailings, and helping in other areas such as database building. If the budget is a very large one indeed, then these activities can sometimes be covered by the commission. If not, an additional fee should be negotiated in advance, based upon hourly rates.

3 An agreed monthly fee

In some ways this is the method I myself prefer. The agency and client estimate in advance how much work is going to be required, and the agency quotes a figure. Once again this figure can and should be reviewed regularly. But it does give the agency the certainty of knowing what its revenue is likely to be over a period. This in turn enables the agency to plan better for your business. Consequently you should get the best possible deal on this basis, because most agencies are prepared to sacrifice a little bit of revenue for extra security.

Few look very deeply into the charges and the basis for these charges. If one company is charging more than another company – why?

For instance, our own agency provides a very wide range of services, and consequently charges premium rates. When we deal with you, you are able to call upon the facilities, for instance, of a research department – something few direct agencies offer. We also have a fully recognised media department which plans your media for you. Smaller direct marketing agencies do not have their own media department and rely upon an outside broker.

Therefore, if you think research is not important to you, or you don't need the sort of agency that is building up a wide library of material to call upon, then you would probably not be advised to deal with our agency. Conversely, if you are dealing with our agency then you are wise to make the best possible use of the many facilities available to you.

There is an analogy with going on holiday. If all you are going to do is get up every morning at seven o'clock, go touring and not return until late at night, you hardly need an hotel with a very good restaurant. You won't be eating there.

When you are negotiating with your agency you might reflect upon one simple fact. That is that very few agency people – even the principals – get rich. Many clients do.

For this reason, you should not begrudge your agency a decent profit. Indeed, it might be a good idea to model yourself upon enlightened companies such as Marks & Spencer and some of the Japanese corporations who actually go to a great deal of trouble – even to the point of reorganising their suppliers' businesses, in one famous case – to make sure their suppliers earn a good living.

Payment by results

Does this work? In my experience; no. It seems a wonderful idea, and in theory it is. But in practice very few clients are willing to let the agency guide them.

We have tried this on one or two occasions, but it has never really worked. Whatever they might say, I have never come across a client who was both willing to work on a results basis and also willing to allow the agency to control all the factors that would govern those results.

Nevertheless, clients are increasingly looking at this sort of approach. Some large companies have recently started proposing *bonuses* to their agencies in a reaction against the worldwide trend to cutting agency income. For instance, General Foods, in the United States has decided that it will compensate its agencies based upon performance. The company will pay 14.3 per cent commission for average work, 16.3 per cent for outstanding work, and 13.3 per cent for work judged unsatisfactory. The previous rate was 14.3 per cent.

'Satisfaction' is defined as how well particular brands sell. I think this approach is wholly laudable, and I hope it works. Everything we know about individuals shows that companies that offer high incentives get better performance from their staff. I am sure the same thing should apply to clients and agencies.

I look forward with pleasure to the first client who can come and show me how it can be operated effectively in our own business.

Money and talent

As I have suggested previously, being a general advertising agent may in some ways be easier than being one who specialises in direct marketing.

Results are less subject to scrutiny, and the client's business is not nearly so dependent on the effectiveness of his advertising. On the other hand, for just those reasons a conventional client can change his advertising agency simply because he feels like it – and they often do.

Creating a full-scale mailing package is just as hard as creating a TV commercial (having done both in my time, I would say it is usually harder). Yet a TV campaign may net the agency commission on many millions of pounds of expenditure, whilst few mailing packages will command more than a few thousand pounds in fees.

As the weight of promotional expenditure shifts more and more towards direct marketing – which it is doing and will continue to do – then clients will find themselves paying increasingly higher fees. Indeed, since 1977 it is my impression that the fee paid for a mailing pack by a client to an agency has increased many-fold. Yet I still do not think clients are paying enough. It shows in the fact that (in my experience at any rate) people work longer hours and harder in direct marketing agencies than they do in general agencies. It shows in the fact that much of the material put out by direct marketing agencies is of a very poor calibre indeed. Only money – and the talent that money will attract – will change this situation.

If as a client you try to get first-class work for second-class money, you will end up paying in other ways. Nobody can afford to have top-class talent working on your account for a £2,000 mailing package unless that talent is churning out the work as fast as the words and pictures come to mind.

Try to understand the process

Hardly any clients bother to do something I would have thought absolutely essential. That is, go to the agency and ask to be shown round and have the whole process of putting together your communications explained to you *in detail*.

What is the procedure when you have a complaint? What is the after-sales service like, so to speak? Who precisely are you going to deal with? Take my advice. Find out in advance. Who is responsible for which aspects of your direct marketing?

I would make it my business to spend a couple of days at the agency.

The more I think about this, the more it astonishes me. In all my years in the business I cannot recall *any* client at a reasonably senior level spending any considerable length of time with the agency – apart from during outside conferences.

It's crazy really. You might be about to spend millions of pounds with these people yet you never bother to learn about the intricacies of their business. You never understand as well as you might do why things go wrong when they go wrong – which they always do – and, often just as helpful, who to congratulate when they go right.

I am moved to say that this is probably the most important single piece of advice I can give to you as a client. You will get to know the people in the agency. You will forge relationships with them. They will come to know, and respect you – if you deserve it. They will like you, too. They will *certainly* appreciate you taking the trouble.

It is revealing that the only client who has done anything like this in my recent experience was one who did not come himself but sent a junior (and extremely stupid) minion to spend time with the agency, who was quite incapable of learning anything whatsoever from the experience. He thought sending someone was a good idea. But not good enough to choose someone important.

Which brings us to the next issue: once you've spent all this time finding the right agency, how do you keep that agency and build a good relationship with them?

14

Client and Agency: the Unequal Partnership

'O world! world! world! thus is the poor agent despised.'
  Shakespeare

The impossible dream

There are two words which are misused greatly by agencies talking to their clients. One of them is 'strategy' – usually applied to some minor subterfuge. The other is 'partnership' – referring to a legendary status, a dreamed-of nirvana of equality between client and agency.

In my years in the business I have very rarely come across anything even approaching this. The reason is simple, and is encapsulated in the Flemish proverb quoted at the head of the previous chapter.

Yet not only agencies refer to this partnership, but also their clients. Even clients who are notorious bullies pretend they treat their agencies as equals.

Personally I much prefer the straightforward attitude of one of my clients who objected violently when a long article appeared in an advertising publication on the subject of his choice of agency. 'Why so much fuss about my choice of a new supplier?' he asked.

He was quite right. The agency *is* just a supplier. And curiously enough this particular client, despite an attitude which some might see as rather feudal, extends more of a true sense of equality to us than others who pay lip-service to the dream of partnership.

Whether you consider you are in partnership with your agency or not, a mutually respectful relationship between both parties is well worth working for, particularly if your business is actually based upon direct marketing. Under those circumstances your communications will compose your entire marketing activity. So getting on well with those entrusted with preparing, placing or sending them out is critical. In fact, most intelligent clients take a lot of trouble to keep their agencies happy; whilst *all* agencies, since it is their bread and butter, try to keep their clients happy.

In fact, when my partners and I set up Trenear-Harvey, Bird & Watson in 1977 we always swore we would never deal with any client unless one of the partners liked him, and we all believed the account was worthwhile. If any one of the partners thought any client was behaving like a pig, then we agreed he could resign the account without consulting the others.

In the event this never happened – though we came pretty close to it more than once.

Unfortunately, I have to confess, *liking* a client tends to have a direct relationship to the amount of money he or she has to expend. A client who spends little money and is a pain in the arse is easily despatched. On the other hand, where a client is spending many millions of pounds, the decision is not so easy. One is inclined to search very hard for redeeming features – usually successfully.

Ensuring a stable relationship

If choosing a new agency is difficult, keeping the relationship in good repair is possibly even more so. Yet it is important that this repair is maintained.

Some years ago, the Jerry Fields advertising employment agency in New York ran an advertisement the headline of which said: 'At five o'clock, my inventory goes down the elevator.'

The point was that an agency's stock in trade is its staff. This is what you are paying for. It is very much in your interest that they care about you, and like you. Yet very, very few clients have the intelligence to get to know the agency's people.

First, make sure you meet *all* the people working on your business. Not just the principals. The man who is running the agency may be very good at running agencies; this doesn't necessarily mean he is talented creatively, for instance.

For that reason, quite apart from the people who are deputed to deal with you on a day-to-day basis – the account handlers – do make it your business to get to know the creative people. They are the ones who come up with most of the ideas which will make you rich.

Agency personnel are temperamental creatures. For a client they like, they will work nights and weekends. For one who is arrogant and uncaring they will simply do the level of job that gives them adequate professional satisfaction. Maybe less if you're a real pig.

It is a red letter day when a client takes the trouble to congratulate a creative team on their work. Few ever do it. It is not irrelevant that the only clients who have done so at our agency are the ones who get the best work from us and – as far as I know – the best results themselves.

The surprising thing is that it doesn't take a great deal of effort on your part. One of our clients won golden opinions by simply sending a note congratulating us on our efforts in helping him reach record sales, accompanied by a couple of cases of champagne. That little investment will pay off for months and months. For a couple of hundred pounds he has bought himself hundreds of thousands of pounds worth of extra commitment from people.

Joy ride?

Many people imagine that working in an agency is something of a joy ride: a life spent dreaming up wacky ideas, punctuated by an endless series of splendid lunches and dinners.

This may be one reason why advertising does not enjoy particularly great respect amongst the community. UK research I saw recently indicated that the public – leaders of industry, members of parliament, the press, consumers – all regard advertising as of less than average merit amongst a wide range of occupations.

This is sad, because we do fulfil an essential economic function. Certainly our life is not nearly as easy as you might think. In my experience people in our business tend to work far harder than most.

This is reflected in some revealing ways. For example, some years back one of my colleagues sat down with a friend and went through a list of all the directors of a well known Manchester advertising agency since the end of the Second World War. Not one of them had lived to reach the statutory age of retirement, which was 60. In fact, I well recall in 1958 reading with some alarm that the average life-span of the advertising man was 58.

Many factors conspire to make our life a stressful one. There is great instability, for although clients do not move their accounts with the frequency one might think after reading an issue of *Campaign* or *Advertising Age* they do move them more than, for example, accountants' or lawyers' clients do. What's more, they move them for the oddest of reasons very often. More to the point, most agents spend (in fact waste) far more time than they should worrying that their clients *might* depart.

In addition, our business is one of constant deadlines. You have to plan everything well in advance to meet them – yet clients rarely keep to timetables. Despite this, the creative work *has* to be prepared by a certain date. Then it has to be reviewed to make sure it's OK. Then the client has to see it and everyone worries lest he change it – which he often does, losing more precious time.

Then, of course, there is the production process. The finding of the right photographer, illustrator or director, the selection of the appropriate models: a fruitful field for discussion – and more time ticking away. Then when it's all been done the client has to approve the finished product.

Finally the work appears – a point at which you would have thought we could all relax, having mutually agreed beforehand that what we are doing is right. Not at all. Many clients feel no compunction whatsoever about unilaterally foisting the responsibility for anything going wrong after the event on to the agent. A distressingly high percentage will shamelessly lie about what they had or had not agreed to previously. In some cases they will do this despite clear documentary evidence to the contrary.

One fertile area for discussion is always the quality of reproduction in the press or print, or the calibre of the direction in the broadcast media. These are very much a matter of opinion, where any one person's view is as good as the other's.

And even then, there is the post mortem to look forward to. The results can be pored over, and the agency allocated any blame for the consequences.

You may feel from reading thus far – and indeed, when you read the rest of this chapter – that my views are partisan. Of course you are right:

'I can but speak of that which I do know', and what I know is based on over 30 years of experience; but I would add that I have acted as a client on occasion and been astonished at the all-round incompetence, shallowness and arrogance of the average agency.

Accordingly, if you are a client, if you can put your hand on your heart and honestly say you are not guilty of any of the sins I am discussing, I would be astonished. If you are an agency man or woman, I am happy to declare you guilty without even the privilege of a trial.

Two types of relationship

Are you familiar with the following two liner?

'What time is it?'

'What time would you like it to be JB?'

This old joke epitomises a common type of client-agency relationship, where the client is always right.

Years ago I acted as a consultant to a well known agency which held a very lucrative account on this basis. If the client said black was white, then the servile account director would leap to concur. The advertising was created on the basis of the client's whims; the account director was in a constant state of nervous panic, and very rarely sober after lunch.

How could he possibly handle the client's account on any logical basis when the only constant factor was his 'yes' to the client's every request? In the end, the agency lost the account and he lost his job.

The other type of relationship is well characterised in Robert Townsend's lively book *Up the Organisation*. He reports that when he ran the Avis Rent-a-Car business he had a plaque in his office on which was inscribed his advertising philosophy.

It recorded quite simply that Avis would never know as much about advertising as the agency; and the agency would never know as much about car rental as Avis – and from this deduced that except in matters of fact, the company would always take its agency's advice.

For reasons I shall now explain, although this would be a happy state of affairs I think it is really too ideal for the relationship between the direct marketer and his agent. Nonetheless it is a consummation devoutly to be wished, as Hamlet put it.

Intermingled

Many agents would be delighted if their clients accepted unquestioningly everything they proposed. And many clients would as a result go broke.

In the case of Avis the agency was simply advising on what sort of advertising to run. Direct marketing, however, generally encompasses many facets of business which are crucial to any organisation – like what sorts of prices to charge and what sorts of offers to make.

I must confess I have met clients who would be only too happy to have the agent take over the worry of finding the right product, deciding on the offer; seeking the incentive; buying it; dealing with the mailing house; finding the right company to computerise the list, setting up an adequate record system . . . in fact, almost running his business for him.

I do not think a client should simply resign so many aspects of his business to the agency (though he ought to take advice and pay attention to it). That is because he is surrendering his own function to somebody who can never be as interested in the consequences as he, and who moreover – if we're honest – has a vested interest in encouraging him to spend on promotion.

I also think it is unwise on the part of the agent. One of my friends who runs a successful direct marketing agency in London very nearly went bankrupt as a result of undertaking many of these functions for his client. This made the account rather unprofitable; the problem being compounded when the client went broke – nearly carrying the agency with it.

The truth, of course, is that agencies' and clients' functions are so intermingled, it's hard to know where to draw the line between them. Indeed, on occasion we have become involved in all the functions mentioned above for one or other of our clients (though, happily, not all at the same time.) As long as we are well remunerated and it is not seen as a permanent arrangement, we are happy to do so.

The business of direct marketing is, as you will have realised already, so fast-changing, moving into so many areas of business – and indeed society – that it's difficult to lay down any binding rules. Compare what happens when you go to consult an advertising agency. The relationship is relatively simple. The agency will plan, prepare and place advertisements for you in exchange for a commission or an agreed fee. You will find it easy to agree also on rates for additional services such as research.

The relationship you set up with your direct marketing agency could involve far more varied factors. But there are certain considerations I think you should be aware of when you are dealing with (or choosing) an agency. Accordingly, I have set out a list of the areas where I think agencies and clients should be particularly sensitive to each other.

Where things go wrong and how to get them right

Was it sod's law or Murphy's law that stated that anything that can possibly go wrong will? Either way, it is a law which applies with peculiar force to our business. I have noticed over the years, nine areas where things go wrong most. They are:

1 No agreement on the criteria whereby results will be assessed.
2 Not enough planning ahead – or time given to execute the plans.

3 Poor briefing.
4 Rotten communication of the brief.
5 Too many layers of decision-making.
6 Confusion about who gets the money – and how much.
7 Passing the buck on mistakes.
8 No clear contract between agency and client.
9 Mutual suspicion.

1 Judging the results

You are probably familiar with the old Chinese saying about a the 1,000-mile journey beginning with but a single step. One thing is certain: you had better make sure that the first step is the right one. That means you must have a clear view of the objective.

Both agency and client must know what they are trying to achieve and by when, in terms of numbers and money. How much profit are you trying to make? How much money are you prepared to spend? How much is a customer worth to you?

Frequently I have seen any or all of these shrouded in secrecy. What they add up to is the very first of my points: have we an agreed criterion? How are you going to judge the performance at the end of the year? Both of you – agency and client – must know and *agree* in advance.

2 Planning – and time.

We have calculated that you need about six months from the time you first conceive of the need for a mailing to the moment it goes out, if you wish to allow the right amount of time. And whether you are considering a mailing or a series of advertisements or commercials, time is extremely important.

At Ogilvy & Mather it is generally recognised as a principle that the agency should always delay a presentation rather than produce work we do not believe to be up to snuff. That is wonderful in theory, but I can think of a great many occasions when it has been ignored in practice for business reasons.

Nevertheless, the faster you need something to be done, the more likely it is there will be mistakes. The answer is either give more time, or pay a great deal more money. If you want to get a good job done fast, that means you will have to have the top creative people in the agency working on it. You'll need to pay double rates to studios, photographers, and process houses. Even then you will still run the risk of things going wrong.

It is difficult to think ahead in a business that is constantly demanding on-the-spot reaction to an unpredictable market place. But if everything is done in a rush, allowing little time for planning, the agency is unlikely to be able to do more than *react* to the client's request. They will not initiate ideas as often as you would like, or they would wish to.

In any case agencies are often tempted to take on more work than they can properly handle. Their little piggy eyes light up at the thought of increased revenue, when they should be thinking more about their existing clients. But if those clients are constantly inundating them with rush work, that essential thinking will never develop.

3 Vague briefs

I have already dealt with this subject when discussing the matter of choosing an agency. But of course, every job your agency does requires a brief. And I would like to emphasise here that by this I mean a *written* brief, not a verbal one. Verbal briefs are written on the wind, and invariably give rise to dispute and misunderstanding.

The type of verbal brief that is particularly infuriating is one where the agency is invited to let their imagination run freely. Some clients think that agencies regard this as a glorious opportunity. On the contrary, just to say: 'Go and have an idea – any idea – as long as it's amusing, or entertaining, or selling' is far too vague. One needs to know exactly *what* one is requested to do.

Vague briefs result in vague work.

You should be able to give a brief which covers your objective, precisely stated, the background to the job, who you think the target prospects are, and how you think the job ought to be tackled.

Bad clients play the second-guessing game. The agency sits wondering what the client wants. The client thinks he is putting the agency to the test. What he is actually doing is fooling about and wasting money and emotional energy better employed realising (or improving) whatever he has in mind.

Bad clients haven't considered what they want properly, so they keep fiddling with the brief.

Bad clients are weak. Their bosses keep changing the brief over their heads.

Bad agencies put up with all this nonsense for *money*.

What it all ends up in is work produced for no reason with no objective and altered simply for the hell of it. That results in bankruptcy.

If I had to say what *the* most vital contribution to successful work is, it is probably ensuring that agency and client have jointly agreed on the brief before the work begins.

If the brief is wrong, skimpy or misleading, this leads to the next problem: by definition, whatever was in the mind of that person conceiving the concept is unlikely to be communicated well.

4 Poor communications

Agency executives often relay your requests inaccurately. This, of course, won't happen if you have a clear, written brief. But sometimes your brief is inadequate simply because the person who actually briefs the agency does not eventually *judge* the work. That's because a junior has been sent to do the leg work whilst somebody much more important is going to judge: someone who may decide the original brief was not right.

You can well imagine how confusing and frustrating this is. And don't imagine it doesn't happen often. I can think of very few clients indeed where this is not the rule rather than the exception. In fact, in the week I wrote this it occurred twice on work I have been engaged in myself, with large sophisticated companies.

5 Hydra-headed indecision

This brings me to the fifth of the areas where problems appear, which I would categorise as hydra-headed indecision. Frequently, clients have too many people involved in making decisions. And unfortunately it is much easier to say 'No' to something than to say 'Yes' – nobody can ever criticise you for something that doesn't run. In the end, there is an endless series of meetings and proposals – and an agency which simply doesn't give a damn. They will run anything you approve.

One of the least satisfying clients I ever worked for suffered from having about 94 layers of management, each and every one of which got involved in the judging of creative work, and none of whom knew a thing about direct marketing.

The problem reached a point where one set of artwork had a dozen sets of corrections on it, all emanating from different places. The art director was about to refuse to work any more on the business. We suggested we would not work further with the client unless they paid double the fee, or ran their business sensibly. We parted company. What a relief! The client learned nothing from the exercise. They were even more indecisive with their new agency.

The agency should be able to deal with *one person* from *one department* with plenipotentiary power. Otherwise, everything dissolves in chaos.

6 It may be your money but it isn't his

One of the principal factors that bedevil agency-client relationships is – not surprisingly – money. The agency has all the responsibility, but none of the power.

The client may be spending millions of pounds a year on direct marketing. He spends it *through* the agency, and emotionally feels he is giving it *to* the agency. That kind of money one takes seriously, and expects a lot of service for.

The agency will have the responsibility for this money in almost every sense. Indeed, where the money is being placed through the media, then an agent in this business (unlike any other sort of agent in business) is a *legal principal*. That means that if there is no payment, it is to the agent that the media come for redress, not the client.

This is one of the things that give rise to not infrequent bankruptcy in the advertising agency business – in addition to exacerbating the worries of the agent himself.

Yet although all this money is floating around, the agent will only see a percentage of it. Either a commission, or his fee. This does not alter the client's feeling that he has invested the entire sum with the agent. This simple, if unjust, disparity explains why clients get so excited about their investment, whilst agencies can't really understand why.

Both parties should occasionally give thought to this.

7 Mistakes

You will have realised by now that it is not difficult to make mistakes. Every agency makes them. Every client does.

In fact, in our business mistakes sometimes seem to occur much more frequently than in, for instance, general advertising. This is partly because the technology is evolving very quickly; partly because in a fast-growing industry many of the people on either side of the client/agency divide are very inexperienced. And partly because the mistakes show up more easily: they are measurable.

Remember, only God is perfect. Don't kick your agency for mistakes. In most cases, they will be errors you acquiesced in, since you ought to OK everything that is done. Don't pass your guilt on to them. Share it!

When mistakes are made, the agency should admit to them promptly if it is responsible – and vice versa. It takes courage to say 'I was wrong'. The thing to concentrate on is making sure they don't happen again, by working together.

If you change agencies in the hope that your new agency will make fewer mistakes, don't put money on it. They will *certainly* make mistakes when learning your business.

Obviously, I am not saying you should stay with a bunch of half-wits. They won't get any better because you keep hoping they will. But if you have had a good relationship with an agency for a number of years, and they perpetrate a number of awful gaffes, you are almost certainly better off sorting them out than going elsewhere.

8 Legalities

There is a wonderful feeling that overcomes the agency when it realises it has won a new account. Often the effect is so overpowering that mere details like getting a proper *contract* agreed are forgotten.

We have lost a lot of money through not having proper contracts with some clients.

Particular areas where things can go wrong include how much the artwork and the production should cost as a percentage of the expenditure; precisely when payments are due; how much work has been agreed to at the beginning of the contract (often a client gets carried away, commissions more work, then decides he didn't really want it and won't pay for it); and finally, no clear indication of what is and is not going to be done by the agency for nothing. One tiny instance is the cost of travelling to and from the client's establishment.

9 Mutual suspicion

I have worked in agencies where people sincerely believed the client started every morning determined to give the agency a hard time. I know this isn't so. I have very rarely met a client who did not want good advertising just as much as the agency does. But the factors I have mentioned tend to create this air of confusion. This feeling of mistrust is where the relationship between agency and client finally breaks down.

How do you create an atmosphere of trust? First of all, you're *honest*. You say what you think and you ask the agency to say what they think. This includes being honest with the agency when you're fed up. Tell them so. Tell them why.

Next, you *listen* to what they say. Make it clear to them that you value their opinion. If you treat your agency as an equal and confide in them – tell them what your goals are and what your problems are – the agency will become involved, and identify with you and feel obliged to perform well.

It is also important to tell them the *results*. Every client judges his agency by results. Every agency likes to know how well the work is doing. If not in actual figures, then by comparison. It spurs people on, and gives them something to aim for. Human beings like goals.

One of our best account handlers left us because the client would never give him any details of his results. He found it too frustrating. When we saw the figures he wanted, we realised how right our account man was. They were dreadful. The client had no idea how much money he was losing.

Without knowledge of the results, your agency is struggling in the dark, and cannot help you.

If you pay attention to all these nine points I've mentioned, you can build a kind of partnership in our business which is so rare, yet so valuable.

If you look at the truly successful marketers – the Proctor & Gambles, the General Foods, the Unilevers, – you will find they rarely tend to switch agencies. They build *relationships* with agencies.

They realise that constantly switching is an uneconomic way of operating. A great deal of the money you are investing is really being spent to teach a fresh set of people about your business. Far better to have an agency which already has the knowledge, and can spend its time (and your money) seeking better solutions.

That, after all, is what we are all in business for, isn't it?

Other trouble spots

Bitching sessions

Sometimes, the relationship between a client and an agency can become so fraught that it is decided to clear the air. Somebody (usually an enlightened person on the client side) says 'Let's put your chaps and ours together and speak frankly about where we are not doing as well as we might – and see what happens'.

This type of meeting rarely works very well. This is because of the nature of the relationship.

Frequently the people on the agency side – all too conscious of where their money is coming from – are far less inclined to be frank than the people on the client side. Some agency people, cynically regard the whole exercise as an opportunity for the client to vent his frustrations and use the agency as a scapegoat, after which he will hopefully go away happy.

Sometimes, on the other hand, the agency people are unwise enough to be extremely frank and tell the client what they think. It can often be traumatic. Client personnel who are used to having the agency jump very high every time they say 'frog' are alarmed to discover that the forelock-tugging people they have been dealing with for so long dislike them intensely, and find them an utter pain.

In my experience sorting out differences is best accomplished by people above the level of the battle. Senior client and agency people speaking frankly about what's going on are able to unite happily as elders in condemning the follies of their juniors – and they actually have the power to do something about it.

Of course, the truth is that the only real solution is a relationship based on mutual respect: a respect which grows from an understanding on both sides of what they are trying to achieve, and what their respective difficulties are. This requires hard work, commitment and decent people.

Fearless advice

'To ask advice is in nine cases out of ten to tout for flattery', someone once said, and it often applies in our kind of business. If your agency always gives you advice which you agree with, then either you are a genius and need no agency, or they are sycophants.

Agencies do a better job and clients benefit more if honest advice is given fearlessly, and accepted gratefully. In fact, I believe, the *major* service an agency should render to a client – apart from creating effective communications – is that of giving sound advice.

Often in general advertising, bad advice is less overtly damaging. The client may never discover that the puns he loves in his ads are a waste of money. But if the client is doing something stupid and you don't tell him in our business, then the public soon will – by not buying

You and your big mouth

I have been at some pains throughout this book to try and avoid any accusation of infallibility. However, I confess that I have – believe it or not – still a few more faults to confess to which fit neatly under the category of 'How not to handle clients'.

Tact is one quality I must own up about. Even my best friend would never describe me as tactful. So to do at all well in this business I had to try and alter my personality for the better. I have not always been as successful as I would wish. My enormous mouth has got me into dreadful trouble, especially when combined with my matching ego.

Early on in my career I managed not once, but twice to get involved in *client politics* with disastrous results barely averted.

First, I took pity on a travel courier working for one of my clients. What a dreadful job he had, I thought. And suggested to him that he bring his literary talents into the agency business. All with the best of intentions.

When he told his boss, that gentleman was not at all amused at my thoughtlessness – trying to seduce one of his best, most underpaid (and therefore profitable) people.

I should have learned from this. But a few short years later I suggested to the advertising manager of one client that his mendacity and incompetence were such that he ought to find another job.

His boss forgave me eventually, and became a valued client at our agency. But it was still a silly thing to do.

Never get entangled in the client's internal business. Be everyone's friend and keep your mouth shut.

Indiscretion

Shortly after we started Trenear-Harvey, Bird & Watson, John Watson and I nearly lost us our biggest account through not being discreet enough.

At a major international conference we quoted figures given to us by a third party about a separate division of our client's business which we did not handle. Confidentiality hardly occurred to us.

After all, the client had not given us the figures. In any case the account in question was not actually ours. The client did not see it that way at all. He was observed to turn puce with rage. He approached us afterwards at the top of his voice.

My partner got excited, and threatened *sotto voce* to thump him (thank God he never heard; we kept the account).

Direct marketing companies are very nervous about their figures. Be careful.

Ego

Arrogance is a major failing with people in our business. After I have three successful mailings in a row, I begin to think I am God.

Fortunately, two things prevent this problem becoming too chronic. First, my competitors keep producing work I admire and envy. I realise there are a great many people out there – and they're getting better every day. Second, it's never too long before I write a flop and am recalled to reality.

The characteristic that gives me most problems is one I have never been able to resolve. Some people cannot put names to faces. Some cannot put faces to names. I can do neither. This makes it hard for me to avoid constantly offending clients.

15

The Future: Full Circle

'Another damned, thick, square book!
Always scribble, scribble, scribble!
Eh, Mr. Gibbon.'

The Duke of Gloucester, upon being
shown by the historian Gibbon the second volume
of his *Decline and Fall of the Roman Empire*.
The work was dedicated to this princely
bibliophobe.

When I entered advertising with such high hopes in the 1950s, I little realised I would end up in an advertising ghetto located 'below-the-line'.

We didn't draw any lines then. My first job was to write an ad selling a chain of restaurants. My second, a salesman's brochure for somebody's sausages. My third, a mailing to sell seed-cleaning machinery.

But if I could not foresee the mysterious line below which I was destined to sink, still less was I able to predict the remarkable way the mail order business I knew would become today's direct marketing. If anybody had told me it would be expected to overtake general advertising by the end of the century, I would have been astounded. As a matter of fact, I will *still* be astounded – for reasons I shall give below.

A measure of the interest in any new discipline is, of course, how much discussion, writing and teaching there is on the subject. On that basis, direct marketing looks as though it's going to take over the world. There is an outpouring of books and articles; a never-ending stream of conferences, courses and seminars. Indeed, I often wonder who reads all this verbiage, or attends all these events – which is what reminded me of the quotation at the head of this chapter.

I *do not* believe direct marketing is going to conquer the world. Indeed, I would be extremely surprised if expenditure upon it exceeded that on general advertising by the end of the century.

I have two reasons for this belief. First, I do not think there will be a sufficient number of direct marketers competent to handle such a volume of expenditure by the end of the century; second, I am not at all sure that the advertising and marketing business will be organised as it is now in the year 2000. I certainly hope not.

To take these two reasons in turn, one of the great current problems in our industry, quite simply, is the poor calibre of much of our work. Just about anywhere I go in the world, if I am interviewed by a trade paper or newspaper, the question always arises in one form or another – what do you think about junk mail?

Direct marketers loathe the idea of being seen as producers of junk mail. So much so that a while ago a British magazine – *Direct Response* – inaugurated a competition amongst its readers to find a more agreeable phrase for what they produced. Of course, the truth is if people think the mail we send out is junk, then there is not much we can do to alter that view or that expression, apart from improving the quality of that mail.

Honesty

Another thing we could do is to start being a little bit more honest with people. All over the world, customers dislike a lot of the ploys we make use of. They may not lose sleep over them, but they do get irritated.

For instance, in a recent survey by the American Speciality Advertising Association International, it was revealed that 85 per cent of business managers had recently been contacted by somebody who told them they had won a valuable prize – as long as they agreed to buy something.

These shrewd, perceptive business folk, it would seem, fell for this one. Twenty-two per cent did buy something. Of these 64 per cent later decided their decision was not necessarily all that smart. They thought the products they'd bought were of inferior quality. Sixty-two per cent thought they were overpriced. And 7 per cent of the poor souls never received a product at all.

Until our business outlaws this sort of thing, direct marketing is unlikely to attain respectability. It will still seem to some extent the province of a bunch of fast-talking rogues. Until we recruit better people – first-class people – train them better and improve our behaviour, I do not see how serious marketers are going to pour the vast sums of money into direct marketing which are predicted.

Happily, we are trying to encourage virtue amongst the industry as a more palatable alternative to being legislated into honesty. Typical are the various mail preference schemes around the world whereby customers can have their names removed from mailing lists. And the good news is, according to the only figures I have seen, that only a very small percentage of people at the moment don't like receiving direct mail. Most are prepared to put up with the occasional irritant in exchange for the valuable information they often receive.

But, as I say, until we have an industry with the kind of reputation which encourages really talented people in large numbers, and has the intelligence to invest in properly educating those people, we will never meet the challenge posed by the future.

That's one reason why I'm sceptical about the degree to which direct marketing is likely to take over. The other is that marketing itself is changing. The marketing of the future will not be broken down into different specialities working independently of each other. Tomorrow's world will be a world of integrated marketing: 'maxi-marketing', as it is tagged in an excellent book with that title by Stan Rapp and Tom Collins. Orchestrated marketing, as we call it at Ogilvy & Mather.

Because ours is, above all, an age of specialisation, direct marketing has come to be regarded as a discipline unto itself. It has been seen, particularly by advertising agencies, as an adjunct to their other activities. They have felt they should be able to supply this particular facility to their clients. This, of course, is quite correct.

But because many of the new direct marketers on both agency and client side come from a background of advertising or conventional marketing, they are beginning to see direct marketing and its relationship to the other disciplines in a different way. This illustrates what I mean:

What agencies are doing is not new, but now they are really moving into it [non-advertising developments]. The advertising agency is still the centre of the group – that is the flashy part; and then they are putting out a net to try to find ways of catching up all of that spending.

So it ends up that the direct marketing unit is saying 'Why not put more money into direct marketing?' whereas the advertising people say: 'You need to spend more on advertising.' That is not the consultancy we need.

This comes from an article which appeared in *Advertising Age* early in 1988. The speaker: Michael Reinarz, director of visual communications for Nestlé.

He went on to say:

What could be the agency 10 or 15 years from now? I would not see the agency being the centre part. They may not even be called advertising agencies. A core business, a communication consultancy, does that coordination. It gets involved in understanding what your long-term and medium-term objectives are on brands and products.

They understand what profitability you are after, and within that they will recommend how you should split your money. Then once they have done that, they use those specialist units.

Tomorrow's marketing is going to call for people who understand the *totality* of business. People who have allegiance not to general advertising, or direct marketing or any of the other disciplines. People who are solely concerned (as they should be) with doing a better total marketing job.

These people will be interested in everything – right down to the role of packaging (a role which in my view is frequently neglected: for if ever there were a perfect place to sell effectively, it is on your pack. It's the one medium whereby you are *absolutely* guaranteed to reach your most important target audience: your existing customer.)

In any case, try as you will to draw rigid demarcation lines between one discipline and another, it's impossible. There is no reason why your packaging cannot – as I suggested above – initiate a direct marketing activity. Most sales promotions can generate a database. And I can't see why your general advertising should not carry some device like a coupon or telephone number to record and collect names – even though its principal purpose may be building image or awareness.

For that matter, new technology is enabling retailers to make their marketing precisely accountable. It's already possible for people reaching supermarket checkouts to be offered incentives as they leave which relate to what they have purchased. So the idea of reaching people as individuals and dealing with them in a way based upon what you know about them is not restricted to the world of direct marketing. It's happening everywhere.

Full circle

I believe – and I hope – that in the future, people will be expected to do exactly what I was expected to do back in 1957 in my first job. They'll be expected to work within every marketing discipline. They will be expected to understand the role of all communications tools. Some people seem to think the intellectual challenge of doing this is too great; that specialisation will always rule. I do not.

Of course there will always be those who are better at one thing than another. But those who succeed will be those who *understand* everything. And this is true of those planning marketing, as well as those executing it. People will be increasingly concerned when preparing direct marketing communications to project an appropriate image: not merely to reflect that created by the general advertising, but help build it. Those preparing general advertising will see it as part of their natural role to try and help enrich the database.

In short, I believe that tomorrow's marketing world will look surprising similar to yesterday's. That the approach of pioneers like Claude Hopkins, who saw no boundaries between one discipline and another, will return. I believe that the present era of specialisation is little more than a blind alley. I think it's time we all got back on the right track.

Index